I0824979

IMAGES
of America

Tampa's Gasparilla Pirate Festival

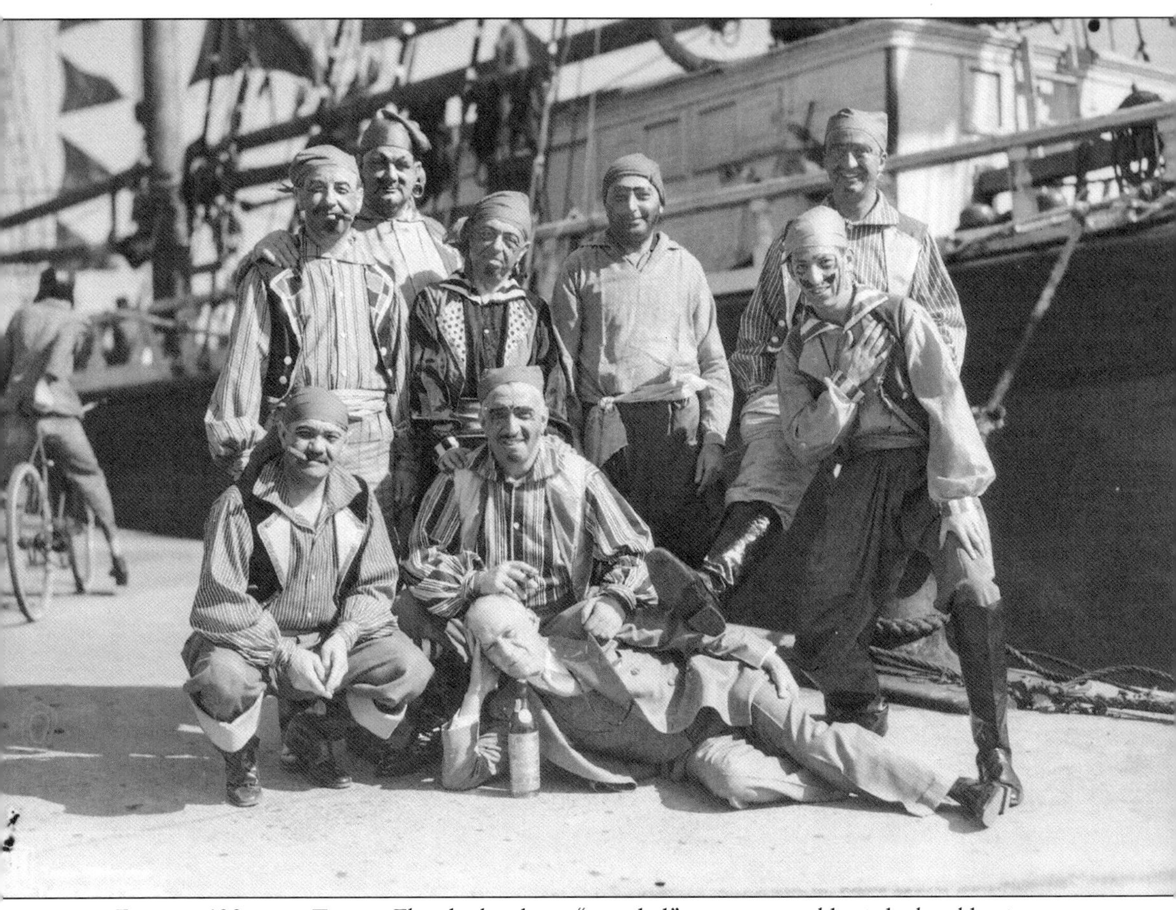

For over 100 years, Tampa, Florida, has been "invaded" on an annual basis by local businessmen, professionals, and civic leaders posing as cutthroat and mischievous pirates, a tradition that has become known as Gasparilla. The parade that follows the invasion is the third-largest one-day parade in the Unites States. Seen here, Ye Mystic Krewe of Gasparilla pirates pose for a photograph on February 2, 1935. (Tampa–Hillsborough County Public Library System.)

ON THE COVER: Gasparilla begins each year with a mock "invasion" of Tampa, Florida, led by Ye Mystic Krewe of Gasparilla. In 1949, large crowds on Bayshore Boulevard and the Lafayette Street Bridge, now Kennedy Boulevard, watch the ship as it clears the bridge on its way up the Hillsborough River into downtown Tampa. (Tampa–Hillsborough County Public Library System.)

IMAGES
of America

Tampa's Gasparilla Pirate Festival

Ye Mystic Krewe of Gasparilla

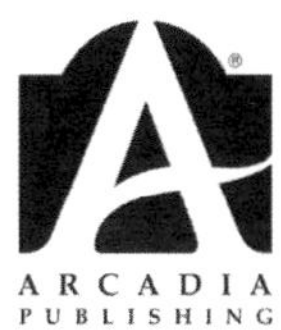

ISBN 978-1-4671-6297-5
Hardcover ISBN 978-1-5402-9961-1

Published by Arcadia Publishing
Charleston, South Carolina

Printed in the United States of America

Library of Congress Control Number applied for

For all general information, please contact Arcadia Publishing:
Telephone 843-853-2070
Fax 843-853-0044
E-mail sales@arcadiapublishing.com

Visit us on the Internet at www.arcadiapublishing.com

This book is dedicated to the city of Tampa and to all the organizations and individuals whose hard work and cooperation have ensured the continued remarkable success of Gasparilla.

One hundred percent of Ye Mystic Krewe of Gasparilla proceeds from the sale of Tampa's Gasparilla Pirate Festival will be used to continue support for the Ye Mystic Krewe of Gasparilla Community Fund Corporation, a qualified 501(c)(3) not-for-profit organization that provides college scholarships to graduating high school students who need financial help attending a college or university.

Contents

Acknowledgments

Ye Mystic Krewe of Gasparilla acknowledges the work of its history committee for its research and preparation of this book:

William G. Carson Jr., MD—Krewe Historian I
William P. Curtis—King Gasparilla CIX
O. Fred Dobbins—King Gasparilla XCII
George F. Gramling III
George B. Howell III
Judson B. Parker
Richard H. Sessums
Clay O. Thomas—Krewe Historian II
David M. Williams

The majority of images in *Tampa's Gasparilla Pirate Festival* appear courtesy of the following:

Tampa-Hillsborough County Public Library System (THCPL)
State Archives of Florida (SAF)
University of South Florida Library Special Collections (USF)
Ye Mystic Krewe of Gasparilla (YMKG)

Photographs were also obtained from private collections, professional photographers, and other krewes.

INTRODUCTION

For over 100 years, the city of Tampa, Florida, has been invaded on an annual basis by local businessmen, professionals, and civic leaders posing as cutthroat and mischievous pirates, a tradition that has become known as Gasparilla. The event is based on stories of José Gaspar, a legendary pirate who reportedly roamed the waters of the Gulf of Mexico on Florida's west coast in the early 1800s.

With the exception of several years when Gasparilla was not held, Tampa has witnessed an extraordinary yearly event. The mock invasion begins with the arrival of the massive ship *José Gasparilla*, carrying pirates of Ye Mystic Krewe of Gasparilla wearing elaborate costumes and pirate makeup. The sound of gun and cannon fire can be heard for miles across the Tampa Bay area as thousands of spectators line the waterways to watch the ship and the accompanying flotilla of hundreds of boats that make their way up Seddon Channel to dock at the Tampa Convention Center. A parade is then held with thousands of participants and attended by several hundred thousand spectators. Gasparilla has become the third-largest one-day parade in the country, behind Macy's Thanksgiving Day Parade and the Rose Bowl Parade.

As part of a long-standing tradition, Ye Mystic Krewe of Gasparilla sends an advance group of pirates prior to the actual invasion to confront the mayor and demand the key to the city. If the mayor refuses to surrender the city, the pirates vow to return with their full armada, ready to invade by land and sea. On the day of the invasion, if the mayor hands over the key to the city, as is always the case, the attack on the city is cancelled and a celebratory parade is staged. For the city of Tampa, Gasparilla is another holiday, and for some of its residents, this is their favorite one.

A look back at the late 19th century illustrates the events that foreshadowed a wave of economic success in Tampa that includes the birth and ensuing success of Gasparilla.

Florida was one of the least populated of the southern states in 1880. On Florida's west coast, Tampa was still a small and mostly undeveloped town with a population of just 720. There were a few paved roads, and the others were either unpaved or covered with cypress wood planks. The economy for Tampa was about to dramatically change when railroad, steamship, and hotel magnate Henry B. Plant proposed extending his railroad to Tampa. The arrival of the railroad was undoubtedly one of the most significant events in the history of the city. Another of Plant's major achievements was the construction of the Tampa Bay Hotel, an architectural wonder that is still operational today as Plant Hall at the University of Tampa. Completed in 1891, the hotel played an integral role in the early years of Ye Mystic Krewe of Gasparilla, which held its first coronation ball in the main dining room of the hotel in 1904. Additionally, for many years, *José Gaspar*, later succeeded by *José Gasparilla*, docked at the hotel following the mock invasion of Tampa. Today, Ye Mystic Krewe of Gasparilla continues its close relation with Plant Hall through the Henry B. Plant Museum, which hosts Gasparilla exhibits and events throughout the year. The iconic minarets of this historic building are easily recognizable in many of the photographs in this book.

With the tremendous economic impact of the railroad and the opening of his magnificent hotel, Henry Plant energized Tampa residents, who wanted to keep the momentum going. This new sense of prosperity also included the premier of Gasparilla, which would begin in a rather serendipitous manner. Louise Francis Dodge, the society editor of the *Tampa Morning Tribune*, was working on plans to make Tampa's May Festival much more interesting and wanted to make this a three- or four-day event. To accomplish this, a unique and exciting theme was needed. Coincidentally, at about the same time, close friend George Hardee stopped by to see how Dodge was doing with the plans for the festival. He immediately suggested a more exotic pirate theme based on the legend of José Gaspar, who later changed his name simply to "Gasparilla." Hardee had just returned from a trip to Charlotte Harbor, where he had become fascinated with the pirate's legends and tales. A native of New Orleans, Hardee was very familiar with the Mardi Gras celebration and felt that this more exciting pirate theme, to include an invasion of the city, would energize the May Festival parade. Hardee immediately began recruiting members for a "Mystic Krewe" of pirates. With all the planning in place, on May 4 ,1904, fifty men wearing pirate costumes and masks briefly invaded the May Festival parade. They took part in the procession for several blocks and then vanished just as quickly as they had arrived. Following this brief appearance of pirates, the Gasparilla festival was born.

The charismatic pirate originally known as José Gaspar was allegedly born into an aristocratic family in Spain and was an officer in the Spanish navy. Disillusioned with military life, legend has it that he and his crew, all expert sailors who were well trained in warfare and military tactics, successfully mutinied and commandeered the sloop of war *Florida Blanca*. The first order of business was to sail across the Atlantic Ocean to Florida to find fame and fortune as pirates. On the long journey across the sea, José Gaspar changed both his name and the name of the ship to Gasparilla.

Much has been written about Gasparilla through the years, with many sources adding to or changing the original storyline about the legendary pirate. Most of the generally accepted stories about Gasparilla that have been popularized have come from only two primary sources.

The first source was a tourist publication created by the Charlotte Harbor & Northern Railway, which had a regular route that included Boca Grande, where Gasparilla reportedly made his headquarters. The brochure, entitled *The Story of Gasparilla*, was written by Pat LeMoyne, the press agent for the railroad. In this booklet, he detailed the stories told by an elderly man in his hundreds named Juan Gomez, who claimed to have been a cabin boy on Gasparilla's ship. It was the hope of LeMoyne that the story of Gasparilla would encourage people to ride the railroad down to Boca Grande, buy property, and visit the Gasparilla Inn, also owned by the railroad. The tourist pamphlets were so popular they were quickly all consumed. The railroad patrons took them home, and the story of Gasparilla's legend spread throughout the country.

At the time the stories about Gasparilla were popularized, Juan Gomez was already well known in southwest Florida because of his age of over 100 years old. On one occasion, he was even interviewed by *Forest and Stream* magazine in the late 1890s because he was thought to be the oldest person in America. Gomez, known as "Panther Key John," lived with his wife in the Ten Thousand Islands area, a mostly uninhabited remote archipelago of barrier islands located along southwest Florida's Gulf Coast south of Marco Island. He spread stories about maps and buried treasure as well as stories about the day he and the remaining pirates of Gasparilla's crew were captured and arrested on December 21, 1821. His stories in turn were shared by word of mouth by individuals, including George Hardee. Gomez would later drown while fishing off Panther Key on July 12, 1900, at the reported age of 122, although census records could not substantiate that age. The fact that he was even still actively fishing at an age well over 100 is quite remarkable. A 1900 obituary in the Fort Myers *Weekly Press* states that Gomez drowned after he became tangled in a rope as he was leaning over the side of a fishing boat. Another account has him drowning while attempting to climb aboard a Cuban schooner in search of some rum.

The accuracy of Juan Gomez's stories and exact age have always been doubtful. The man who continued spinning stories about his time as a pirate was unquestionably a primary source for the tales about Gasparilla.

In addition to Juan Gomez, the second person primarily responsible for the legend and considerable expansion of Gasparilla was Edwin Lambright, a respected former editor of the *Tampa Morning*

Tribune. He provided additional detailed stories of Gasparilla in his 1936 book, entitled *Life and Exploits of Gasparilla, Last of the Buccaneers, with the History of Ye Mystic Krewe of Gasparilla*. Lambright claimed to have corresponded with an anonymous "American" who had access to Gasparilla's diary and Spanish naval records. He claimed that the diary was the primary source of additional information about Gasparilla up until 1800. After that date, the history was traced through victims' reports. In his book, Lambright provides the details of the demise of Gasparilla on December 21, 1821, when, on the verge of retirement, Gasparilla and his crew decided to attack one last ship. What they thought was a harmless merchant ship turned out to be a US war vessel in disguise. Completely outnumbered and unwilling to surrender, Gasparilla wrapped a heavy chain around his waist and jumped into the Gulf of Mexico, saying "Gasparilla dies by his own hand, not the enemy's." Through the years during the Gasparilla Festival, Lambright would reprint portions of his Gasparilla story in the *Tampa Morning Tribune*, adding further authenticity to the existence of the legendary pirate. Several researchers and scholars have since refuted the account given by Lambright and the authenticity of the sources for the stories, and the stories themselves are disputable. Although there have been other books written that have expanded and even changed the story of Gasparilla, the Lambright book is considered the bible of Gasparilla legend. This 223-page book has an embroidered black cover, begins with a 34-page history of José Gaspar (Gasparilla), and provides a history of the origins of Ye Mystic Krewe of Gasparilla. This rare book is the most comprehensive account of Gasparilla and the beginnings of Ye Mystic Krewe of Gasparilla and the Gasparilla festival.

Over its 121-year history, Ye Mystic Krewe of Gasparilla has maintained the legend of the pirate Gasparilla and the beloved traditional invasion of Tampa while adding more events, such as a family-friendly Gasparilla Children's Parade and Piratechnics fireworks show. Other Gasparilla-inspired activities include the Gasparilla Music Festival, the Gasparilla Arts Festival, and the Gasparilla Distance Classic Association.

Most communities in America have a variety of iconic places, people, or events—the iconic event for Tampa is Gasparilla. Whether there was ever a pirate named Gasparilla is unimportant. What is important is that the legend of this mysterious pirate has been alive and well for over a century and inspires a celebration enjoyed by hundreds of thousands of residents and visitors each year in Tampa. This inspiration can be felt in many places throughout the Tampa Bay area, even to the name of the National Football League's Tampa Bay Buccaneers.

Through historically accurate and rare photographs from leading educational and historical institutions, professional photographers, private collections, and Ye Mystic Krewe of Gasparilla, *Tampa's Gasparilla Pirate Festival* provides a comprehensive pictorial story of Gasparilla.

One

The Myth of the Pirate Gasparilla

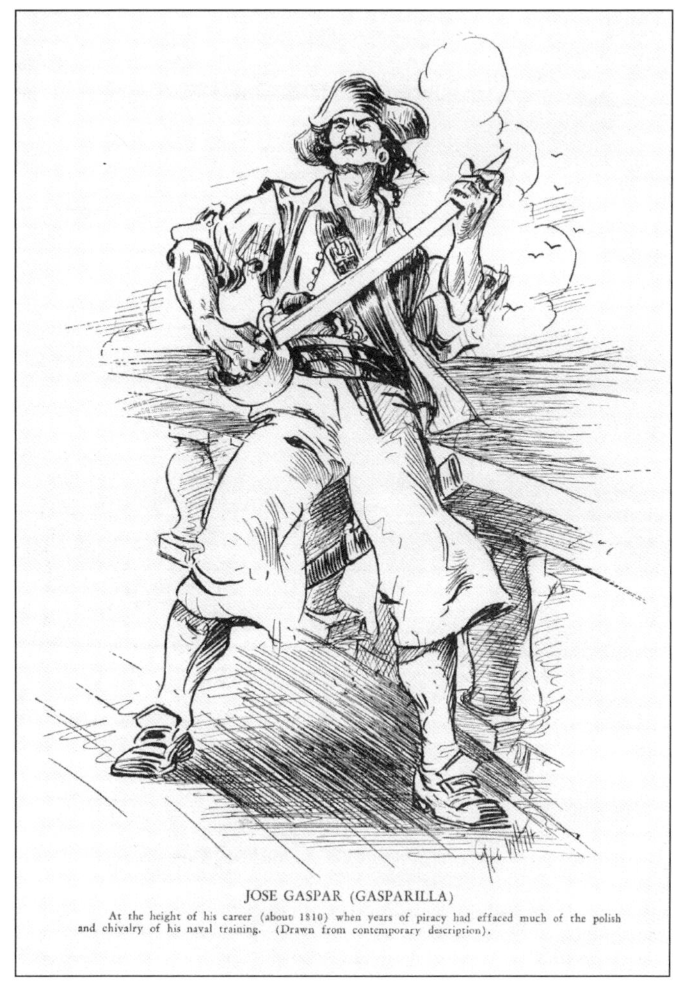

Tampa's Gasparilla Pirate Festival is based on the life of Gasparilla, a legendary Spanish pirate who reportedly roamed the waters of the Gulf of Mexico in the early 1800s. Pictured here is one of the rare drawings of Gasparilla from Edwin Lambright's 1936 book, *The Life and Exploits of Gasparilla, Last of the Buccaneers, with the History of Ye Mystic Krewe of Gasparilla*. (YMKG.)

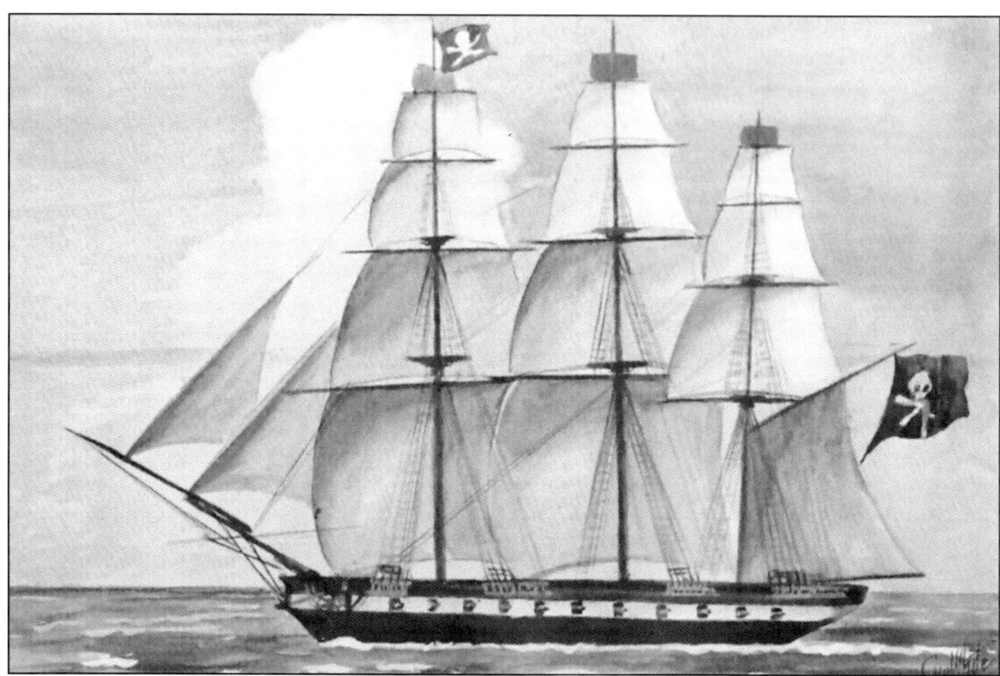

According to legend, José Gaspar (Gasparilla) was born into an aristocratic family and was an officer in the Spanish navy. Disillusioned with military life, he and his crew mutinied from the navy on the sloop of war *Florida Blanca* (above), sailed to the Gulf of Mexico waters off the coast of Florida, and began a long career of piracy. On the journey across the Atlantic Ocean, Gaspar changed his name as well as the name of the ship to simply Gasparilla. After arriving in Florida, Gasparilla then began using another ship that he captured around 1795. This ship was originally a Spanish merchantman that was converted into a pirate ship and renamed *Gasparilla II* (below). Both drawings are from Edwin Lambright's 1936 book, *The Life and Exploits of Gasparilla, Last of the Buccaneers, with the History of Ye Mystic Krewe of Gasparilla*. (Both, YMKG.)

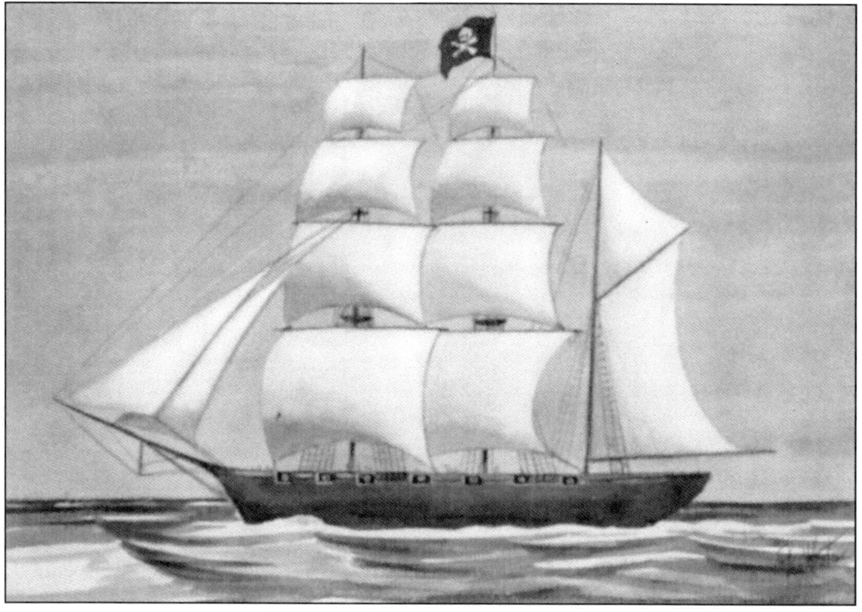

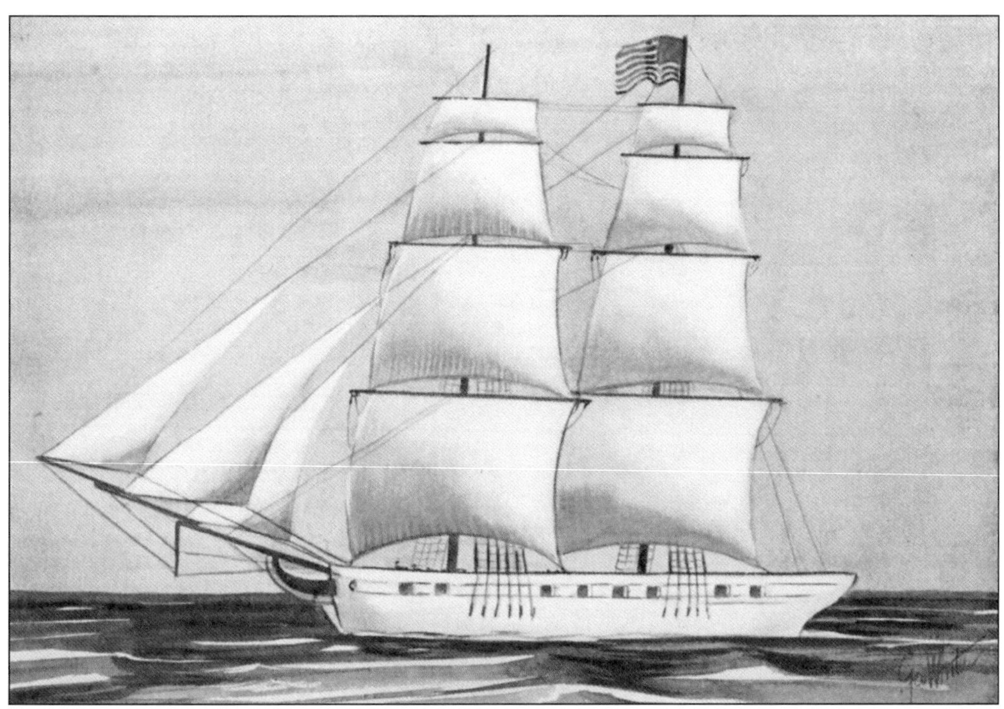

On December 21, 1821, and on the verge of retirement, legend has it that Gasparilla decided to attack one last ship. His crew attacked a naval war vessel, USS *Enterprise*, disguised as a merchant ship. Rather than being captured, Gasparilla wrapped a heavy chain around his waist and dove into the Gulf of Mexico, saying "Gasparilla dies by his own hand, not the enemy's!" (YMKG.)

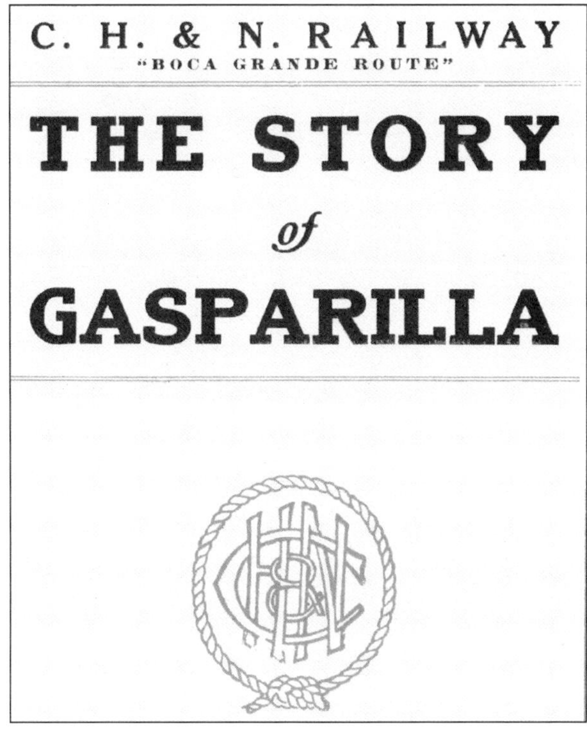

C. H. & N. RAILWAY
"BOCA GRANDE ROUTE"

THE STORY
of
GASPARILLA

In the early years of Gasparilla, Pat LeMoyne, a press agent for the Charlotte Harbor & Northern Railway, published a tourist brochure, *The Story of Gasparilla*. It was his hope that people would be interested in visiting the Charlotte Harbor and Boca Grande area, home of the infamous Gasparilla. The primary source of the story came from an elderly man named Juan Gomez, who claimed to be a cabin boy on Gasparilla's ship. (YMKG.)

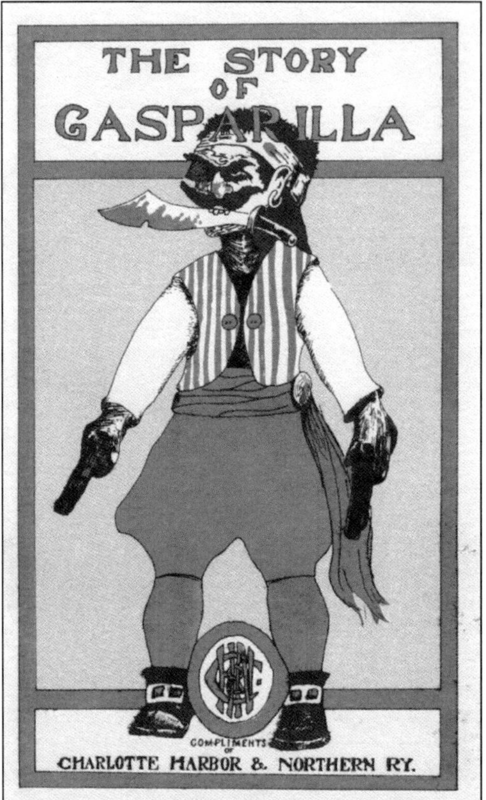

The tales and legends about the pirate Gasparilla have come from several sources, one of which was in the form of a short story about him from a railroad company souvenir pamphlet. The Gasparilla stories in the Charlotte Harbor & Northern Railway tourist brochure primarily came from Juan or John Gomez, also known as Panther Key John, who claimed to be a survivor of Gasparilla's former crew. It was the hope of the railroad's press agent that the story of Gasparilla would encourage people to ride the railroad down to Boca Grande, buy property, and visit the Gasparilla Inn, also owned by the railroad. The pamphlets were so popular they quickly sold out. The railroad patrons took them home, and the story of Gasparilla's legend spread throughout the country. Many of Juan Gomez's stories included tales of millions of dollars in buried treasure, including maps describing hidden locations. (Nancy Turner and YMKG.)

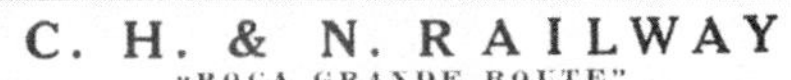

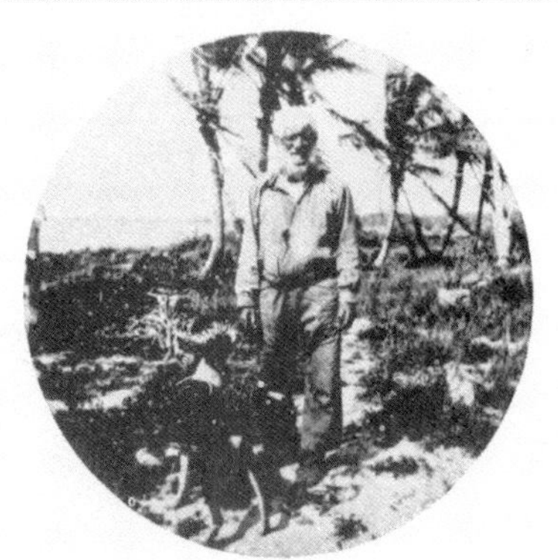

JOHN GOMEZ,

Generally known as Panther Key John, a brother-in-law of the Pirate Chief Gasparilla and a member of his crew, who died at the age of one hundred and twenty years, at Panther Key, Florida, 12 miles below Marco, in the year 1900.

The above photograph was taken with one of the old-style "Pull-the-String Press-the-Button" Kodaks during the winter of 1895, when he was one hundred and sixteen years old, by one of our winter tourists, who kindly loaned us the negative.

WICKMAN'S PHOTO SHOP
Boca Grande. Florida
Nineteen-Eighteen

Juan Gomez, or Panther Key John, was the source of many tales regarding the pirate Gasparilla. Gomez's story would often change. At times, he claimed to be a cabin boy on Gasparilla's ship, and at other times, he claimed to be a regular member of the crew or Gasparilla's brother-in-law. Sometimes, Gomez would even say he was Gasparilla himself. In *The Life and Exploits of Gasparilla*, Gomez was reportedly captured and arrested on December 21, 1821, along with the remaining pirates of Gasparilla's crew. As reported in several South Florida newspaper obituaries, Gomez drowned while fishing on July 12, 1900, at a reported age of 122. His stories continued in *The Story of Gasparilla*, the tourist brochure published by the Charlotte Harbor & Northern Railway. The original brochure is difficult to find, but reprints were published in 1980. (Nancy Turner and YMKG.)

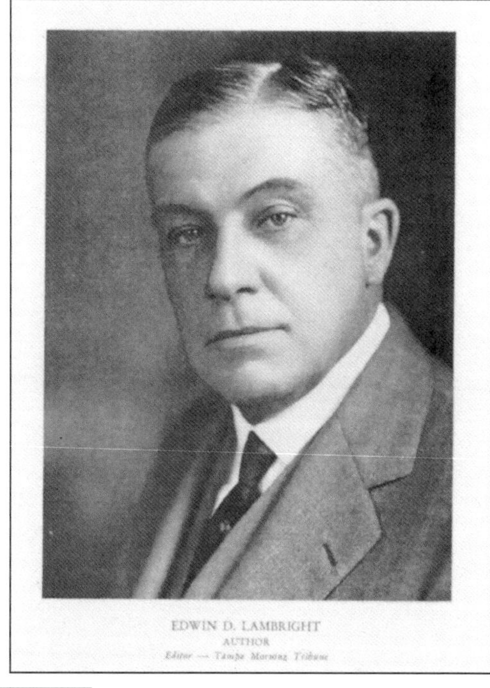

In addition to Juan Gomez, the other person most responsible for the perpetuation of the legend of Gasparilla is Edwin D. Lambright, respected former editor of the *Tampa Morning Tribune*. Lambright was an active member of Ye Mystic Krewe of Gasparilla and added a bit of authenticity to the story of Gasparilla in his 1936 book, *The Life and Exploits of Gasparilla, Last of the Buccaneers, with the History of Ye Mystic Krewe of Gasparilla*. Lambright claimed to have corresponded with an anonymous "American" who had access to Gasparilla's diary and Spanish naval records. He claimed that the diary was the primary source of additional information about Gasparilla up until 1800. After that date, the history was traced through victims' reports. Through the years at Gasparilla time, Lambright would reprint portions of his Gasparilla story in the *Tampa Morning Tribune*. Several researchers and scholars have since refuted the account given by Lambright. (Nancy Turner and YMKG.)

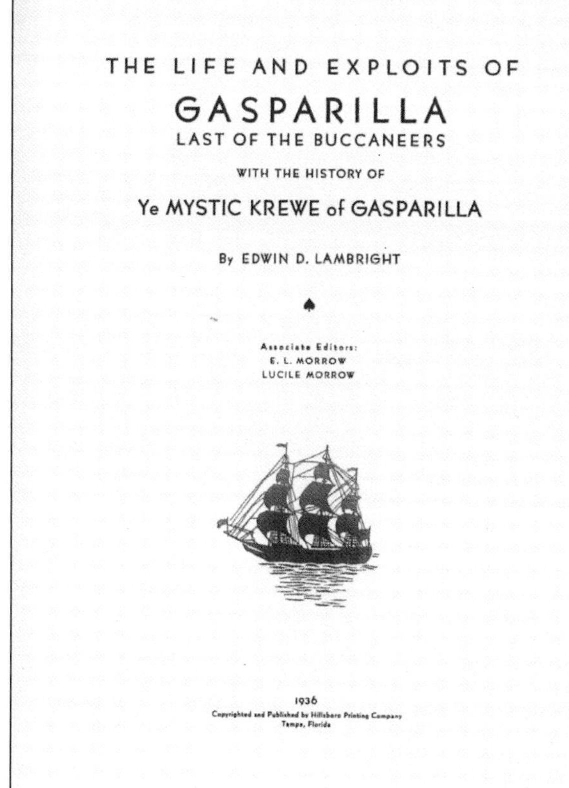

THE LIFE AND EXPLOITS OF

GASPARILLA

LAST OF THE BUCCANEERS

WITH THE HISTORY OF

Ye MYSTIC KREWE of GASPARILLA

By EDWIN D. LAMBRIGHT

Associate Editors:
E. L. MORROW
LUCILE MORROW

1936
Copyrighted and Published by Hillsboro Printing Company
Tampa, Florida

In *The Life and Exploits of Gasparilla, Last of the Buccaneers, with the History of Ye Mystic Krewe of Gasparilla*, Edwin D. Lambright provided a comprehensive story of the pirate Gasparilla. The book is extremely rare and difficult to find, with few remaining copies available. Although the authenticity of the source of the stories about the pirate Gasparilla and the stories themselves are disputable, the book is considered the bible of Gasparilla legends. Although many other books have expanded and even changed the story of Gasparilla, the Lambright book is considered the authoritative text. This 223-page book has an embroidered black cover, begins with a 34-page history of José Gaspar (Gasparilla), and provides a history of the origins of Ye Mystic Krewe of Gasparilla. On the second page of the book is a certificate of authenticity document stating "Limited Member's Edition," complete with the book number and member's handwritten name. (YMKG.)

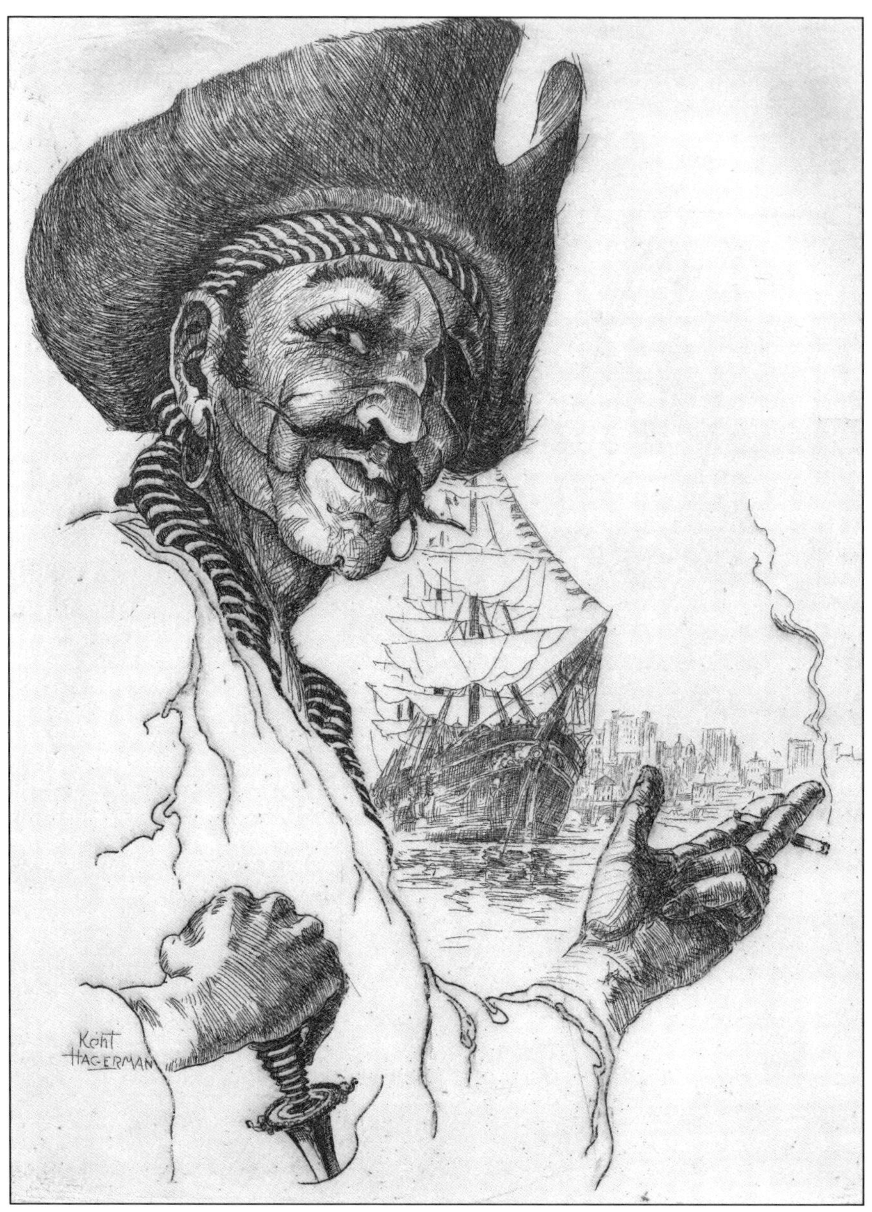

Talented artists have depicted the pirate José Gaspar (Gasparilla) in various ways throughout the years. At times, he is depicted as jovial and mischievous, but at other times, he is seen as a maniacal, cutthroat pirate. Some of the most famous Gasparilla drawings are by Kent Hagerman (1893–1978), an influential commercial and fine art printmaker who moved to Lakeland, Florida, in 1933 and began producing a line of fine etchings of Florida scenes. Hagerman frequently produced images for Maas Brothers department store in Tampa and for other friends and businesses in the region. Maas Brothers would use Hagerman's scenes of Gasparilla for advertisements around invasion time. The image displayed above showing a pirate and his ship in the background, titled *Spirit of Old José Gaspar,* is one of his most popular pieces. Hagerman's drawings have been reproduced in countless publications and brochures as well as on invitations to Ye Mystic Krewe of Gasparilla events. These years of artwork have added to the lore associated with the annual Gasparilla festival. (Tampa Bay History Center Collection, gift of J. Thomas Touchton.)

Two

The Early Years of the Gasparilla Festival

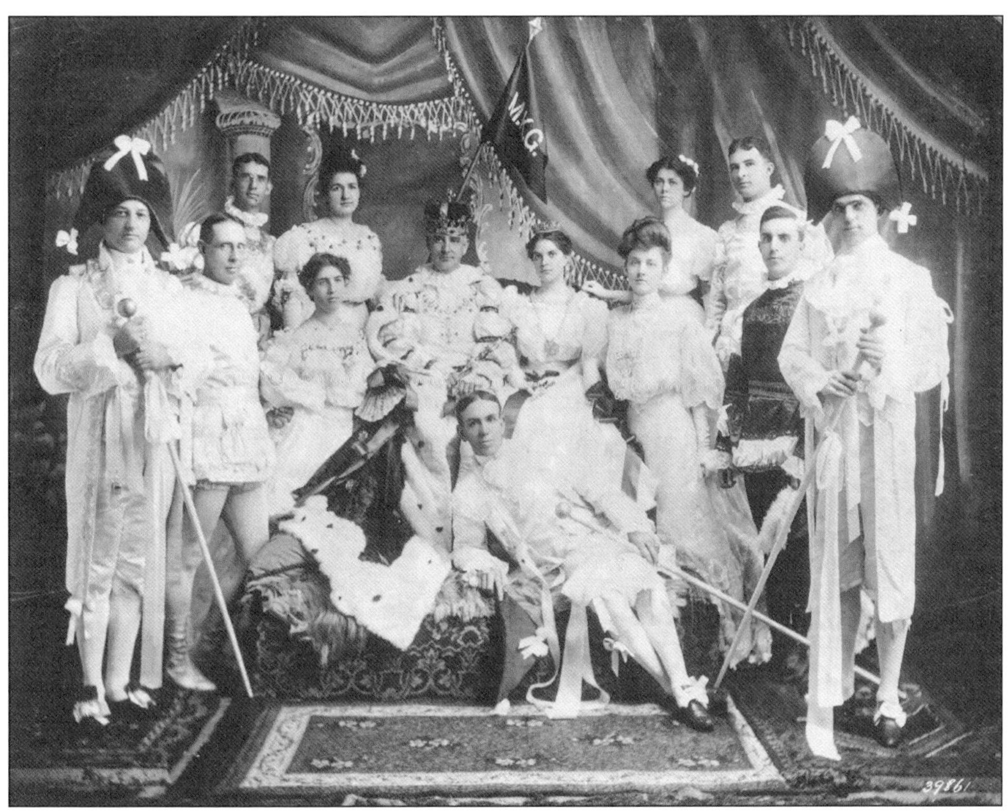

Since 1904, Ye Mystic Krewe of Gasparilla has staged a mock pirate invasion of Tampa, Florida. In addition to the arrival of *José Gasparilla* and the parade, other Gasparilla-related activities occur throughout the year, including a coronation ball that crowns the King and Queen of Gasparilla for the year. The 1905 Ye Mystic Krewe of Gasparilla Coronation Ball was held at the old Tampa Bay Casino on the grounds of the Tampa Bay Hotel, now Plant Hall at the University of Tampa. (THCPL.)

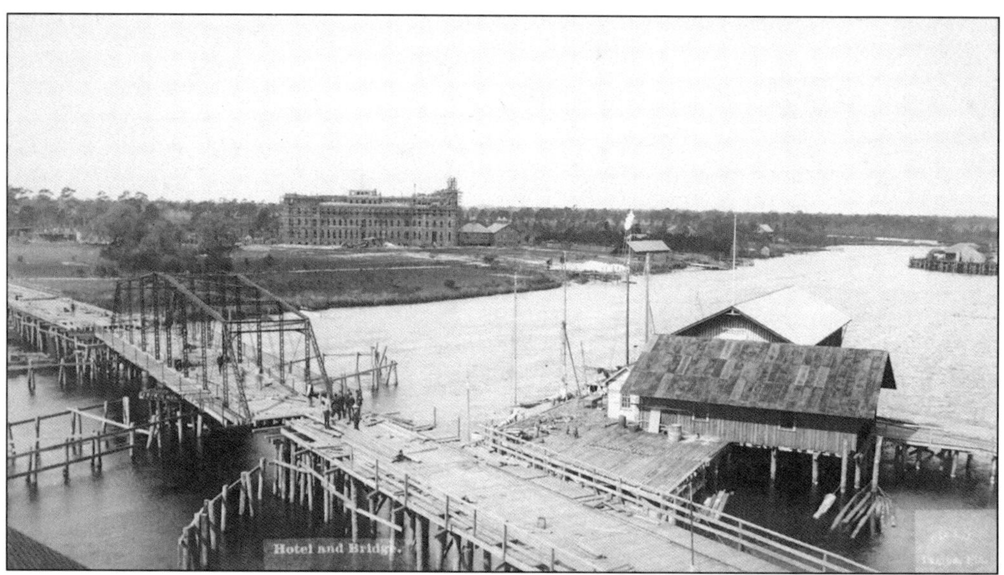

Tampa had few paved roads when Ye Mystic Krewe of Gasparilla was organized. The first local road was paved in 1896, but most were either compacted sand or covered with wood cypress planks. The c. 1889 photograph above shows construction of the first Lafayette Street Bridge, now Kennedy Boulevard, with the nearly completed Tampa Bay Hotel, now Plant Hall at the University of Tampa, in the background. The 1900 photograph below is a view of downtown Tampa looking west. The intersection of Franklin and Lafayette Streets shows sandy streets and horse-drawn carriages. The iconic minarets of the Tampa Bay Hotel, completed in 1891, can be seen on the other side of the Hillsborough River. At the time, Tampa's population was only 15,839. (Above, Henry B. Plant Museum Collection; below, SAF.)

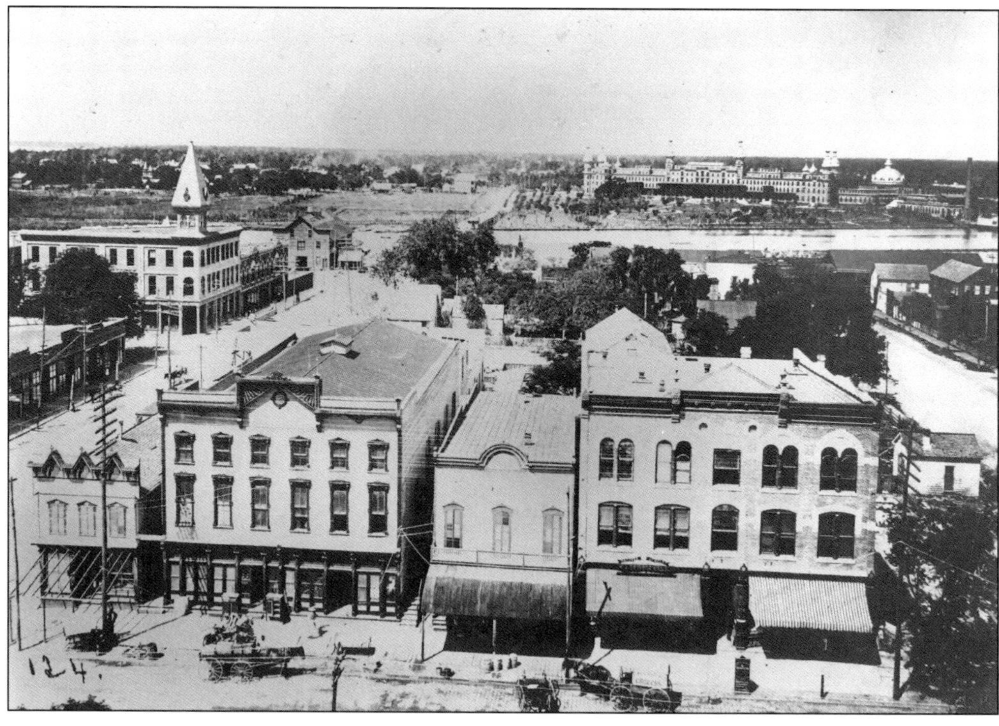

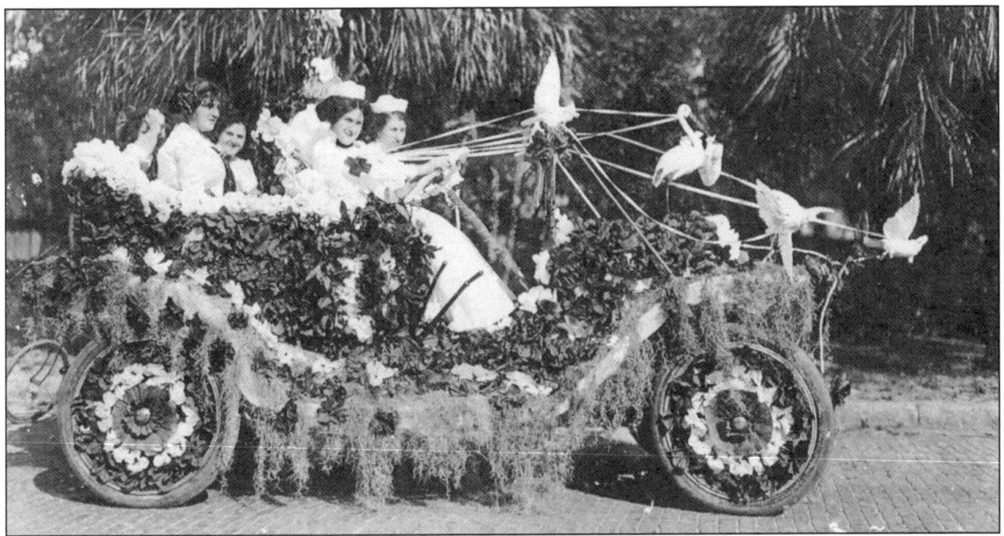

The first Gasparilla celebration and parade took place on May 4, 1904, at which time automobiles were still a novelty, with few participating in the event. Over the next few years, cars were decorated to participate in the parade. This 1910 photograph shows a group of Red Cross nurses in their car, adorned with flowers and Spanish moss. (SAF.)

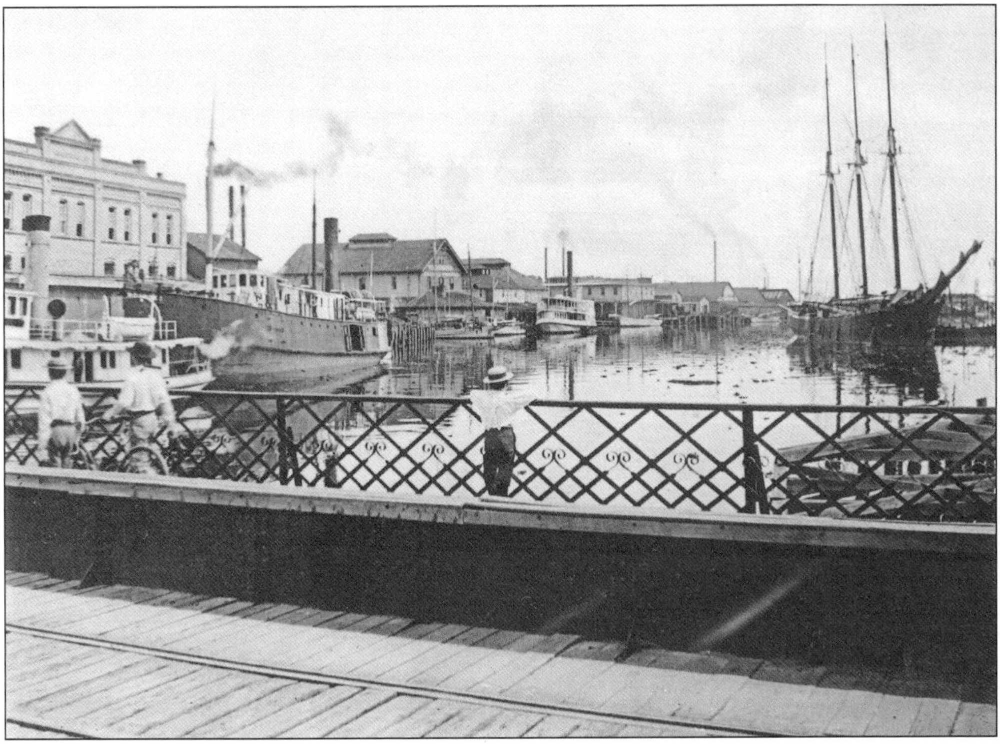

Tampa was still mostly undeveloped when the second Gasparilla was held on November 15, 1905. Many cities first grew along waterways because of their easy access for transportation and recreation. This is a photograph looking south from the first bridge on Lafayette Street, now Kennedy Boulevard. Due to heavy usage, two more bridges had to be rebuilt, with the third one opening in 1914. This last bridge is still in use today. (SAF.)

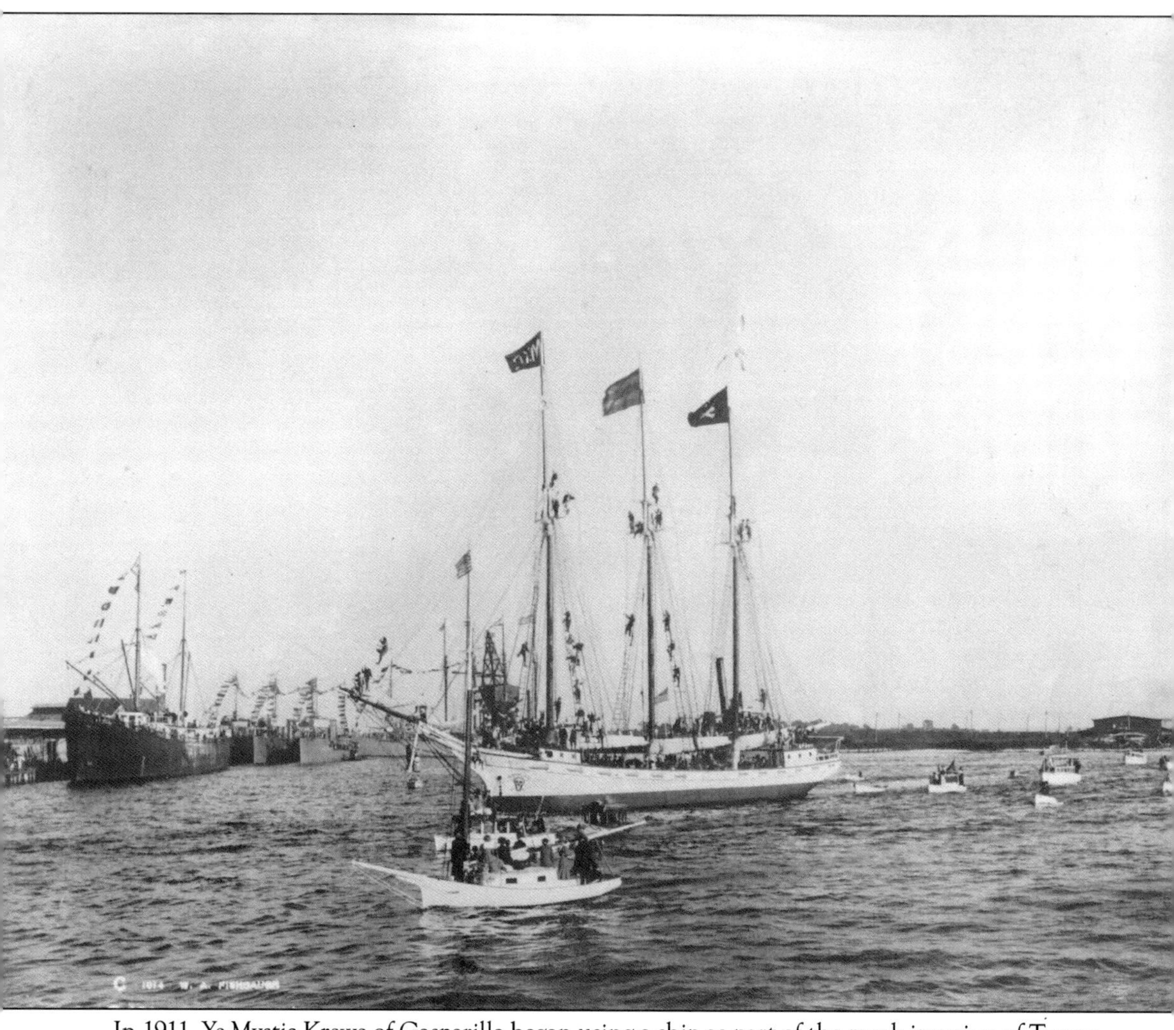

In 1911, Ye Mystic Krewe of Gasparilla began using a ship as part of the mock invasion of Tampa. Until 1938, the ships used for the invasion were borrowed vessels that were transformed into a pirate ship for the day, complete with skull-and-crossbones flags and fake cannons. On occasion, the krewe did not know if a ship was available until the day before the invasion. In 1938, Ye Mystic Krewe of Gasparilla bought its own ship, which it used until 1952, when the ship was declared unseaworthy. This 1914 photograph shows one of the borrowed ships making its way up Hillsborough Bay to the Hillsborough River. Also pictured are several pirates who are climbing up the rigging of the ship's masts, a tradition that continues to the present day. Also pictured is the flag flown on the ship's main mast, displaying "MKG" for Mystic Krewe of Gasparilla. This name was commonly used in the early years of Ye Mystic Krewe of Gasparilla instead of the more familiar "YMKG." (USF.)

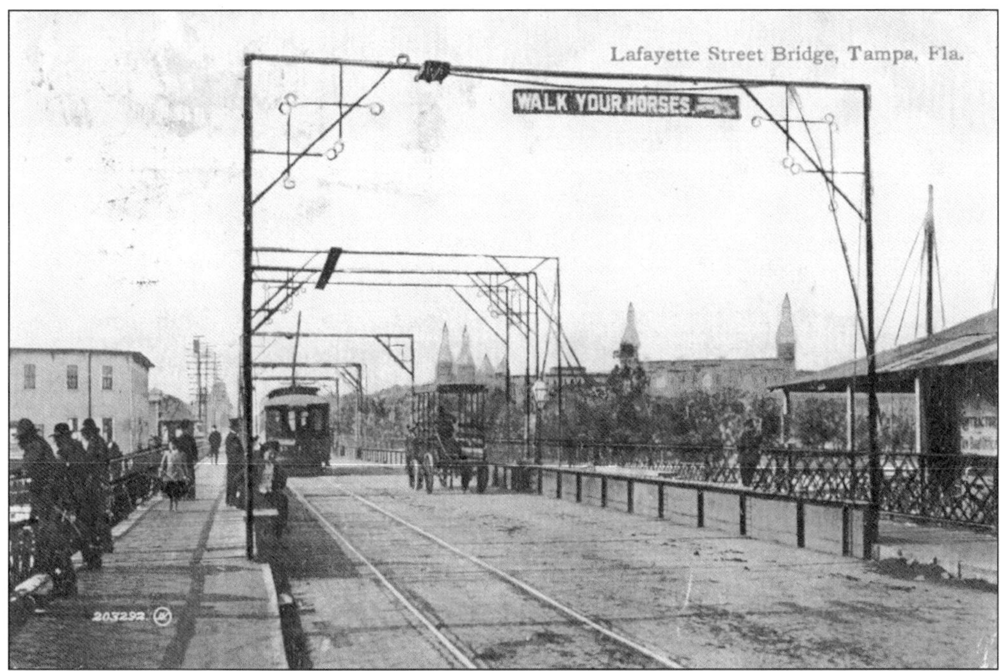

The first Lafayette Street Bridge, now Kennedy Boulevard, was built at the request of Henry B. Plant, who wanted it to benefit his Tampa Bay Hotel, located on the opposite side of the Hillsborough River from downtown Tampa. The bridge opened in 1889, but heavy usage required the bridge to be rebuilt in 1896. The 1913 photograph above shows the second bridge with the signage "Walk Your Horses." A third bridge was then required and was opened with a dedication ceremony on February 23, 1914, presided over by Mayor D.B. McKay. Still in use today, this third bridge was well built and could now accommodate Tampa's growing population. The Lafayette Street Bridge, pictured below in 1922, was only one of the five Hillsborough River bridges that Ye Mystic Krewe of Gasparilla ships would eventually have to pass under on their way into downtown Tampa. (Above, SAF; below, THCPL.)

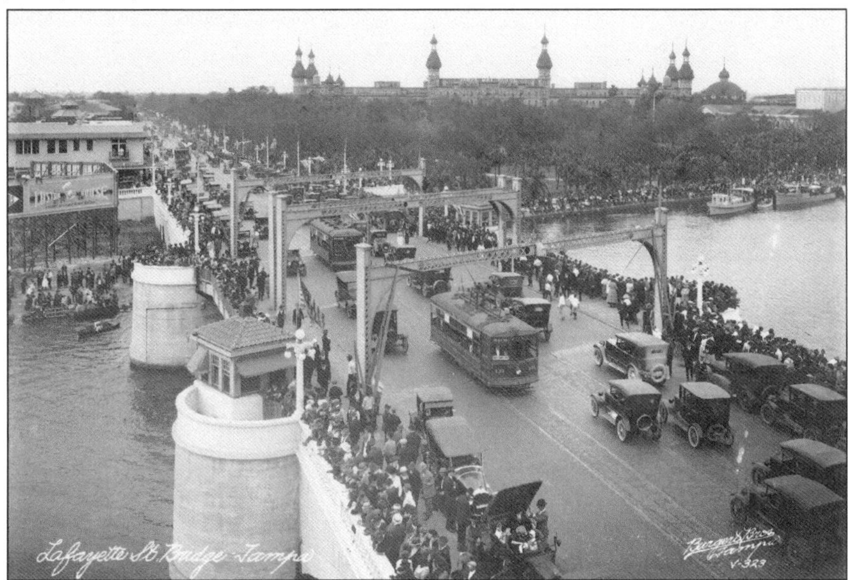

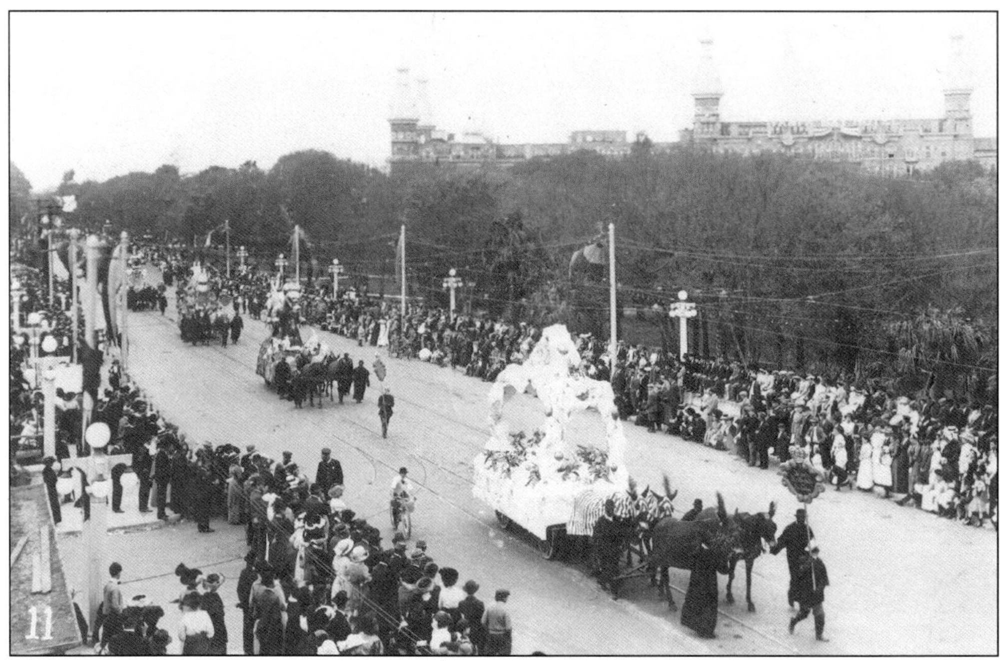

Trucks, jeeps, and tractors were not always used to pull the floats in the Gasparilla parade. Horses were used for many years when the event first began, as seen in the 1914 photograph above, which shows spectators watching the parade move east toward downtown Tampa on Lafayette Street, now Kennedy Boulevard. The Tampa Bay Hotel can be seen in the background on the right. The photograph below, from February 12, 1914, shows a large, self-propelled duck float moving through the streets of downtown Tampa. In the early years, some floats were built around motorized vehicles, but because of frequent breakdowns that caused long delays in the parade, nearly all floats in today's Gasparilla parade are pulled by trucks. (Above, THCPL; below, SAF.)

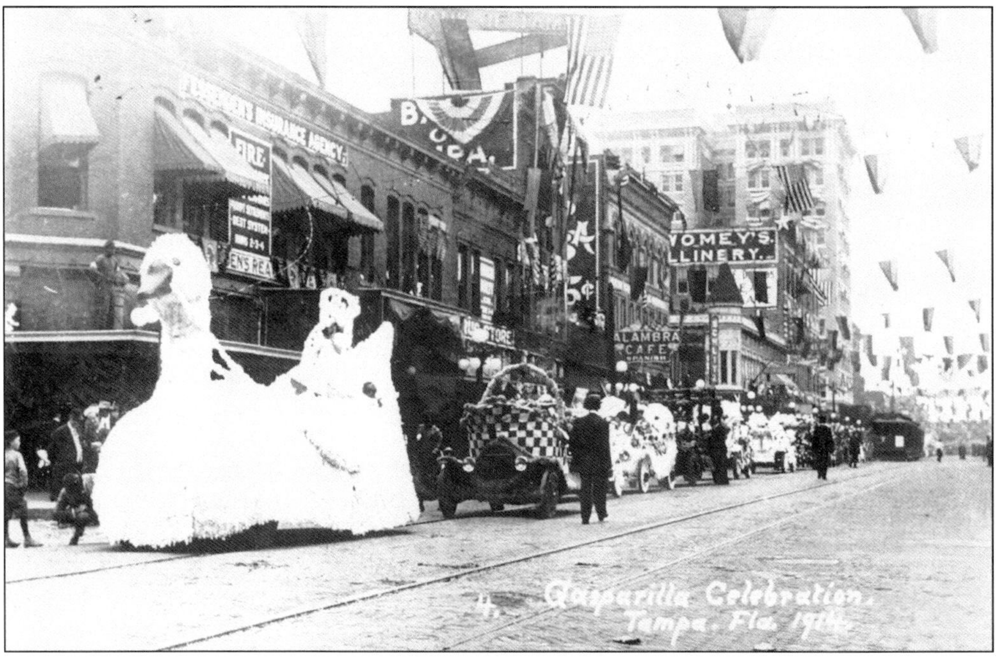

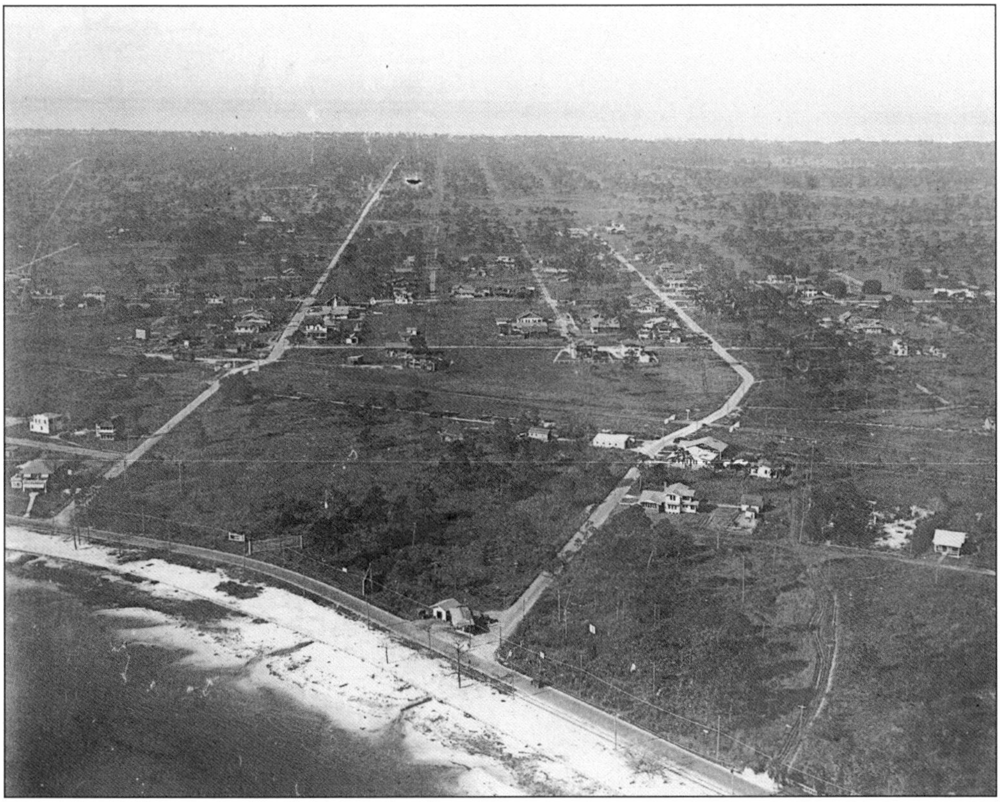

For many years, the Gasparilla parade route included mostly downtown Tampa. In 1976, the route was changed to include Bayshore Boulevard, which is still the primary route today. This 1916 photograph looking west toward Hyde Park shows the mostly undeveloped area along Bayshore Boulevard. Gasparilla is now the third-largest single-day parade in the country, following Macy's Thanksgiving Day Parade and the Rose Bowl Parade. (USF.)

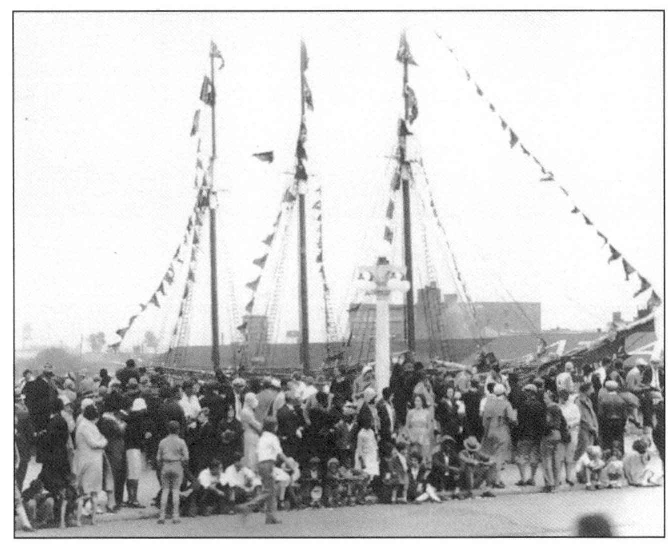

Following each Gasparilla invasion, the pirate ship docks along the water for several weeks for spectators to have an up-close view. In this 1931 photograph, the ship is docked along Bayshore Boulevard near the Lafayette Street Bridge. Other docking locations included the Tampa Bay Hotel (Plant Hall at the University of Tampa), the foot of Seventh Avenue (Armature Works), the Curtis Hixon Convention Center, Harbour Island, and the Tampa Convention Center. (USF.)

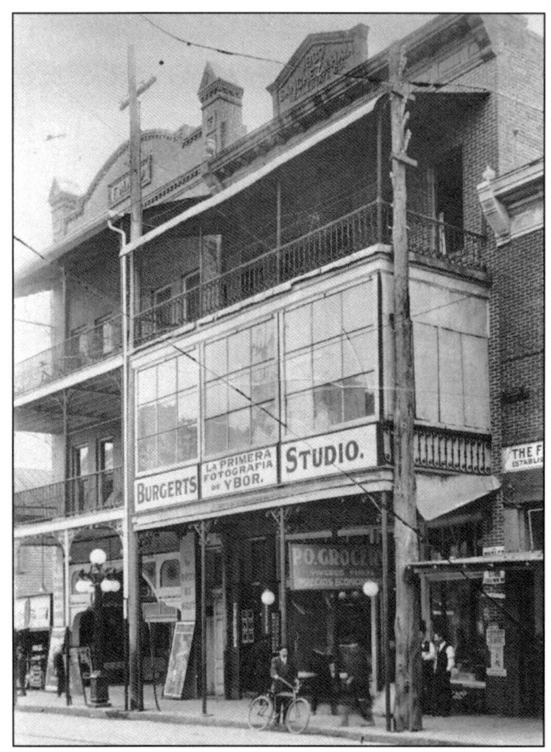

Many of the photographs in *Tampa's Gasparilla Pirate Festival* were taken by the well-known Burgert Brothers photographers. Their collection includes over 20,000 images that created a pictorial record of the residential, commercial, and social growth of Tampa and Florida's west coast from the late 1800s to the early 1960s. They used several photography techniques, including panoramic and aerial photography. The 1917 photograph at left shows Burgert Brothers' first photography studio, at 608 Madison Street, now 1515 Seventh Avenue, in Ybor City. The 1922 photograph below shows their second studio, at 407 Lafayette Street, now Kennedy Boulevard, in downtown Tampa. (Left, SAF; below, USF.)

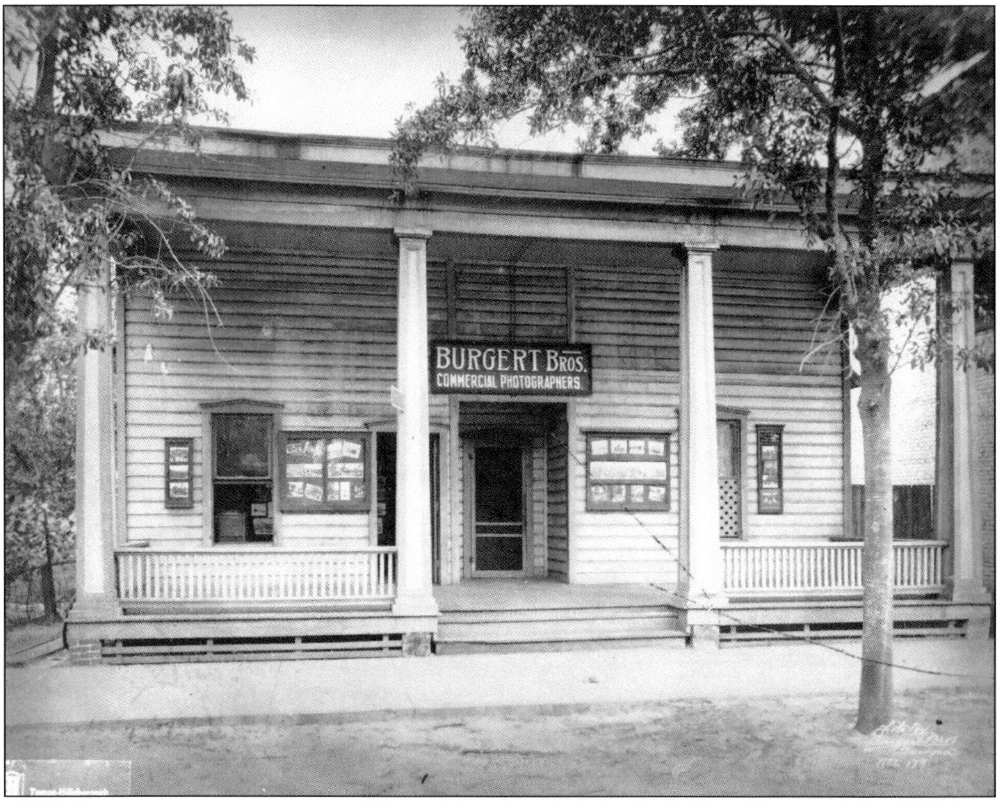

Three

The *José Gaspar* and *José Gasparilla* Pirate Ships

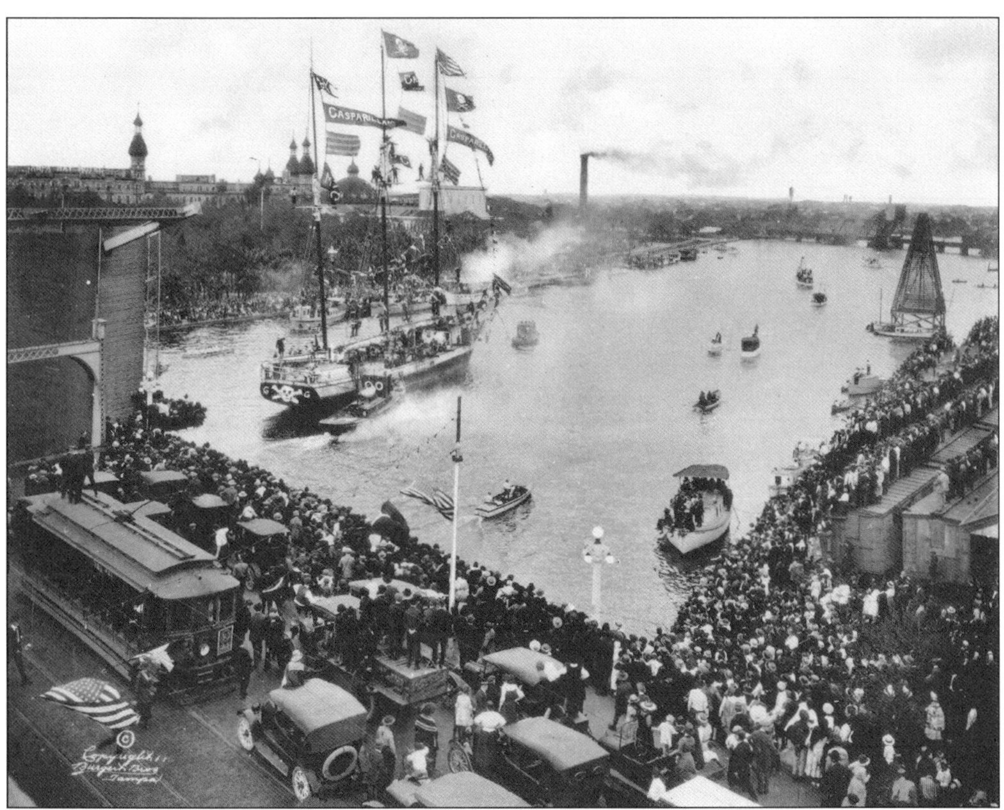

In 1922, spectators lined the Lafayette Street Bridge as the ship made its way into Tampa. Many of the earlier invasions were staged on borrowed ships that were transformed into pirate ships, such as the schooner *C.H. Hackney*, pictured here. Most of the borrowed ships as well as the first ship owned by Ye Mystic Krewe of Gasparilla were named *José Gaspar*. In 1954, the new ship was named *José Gasparilla*. (USF.)

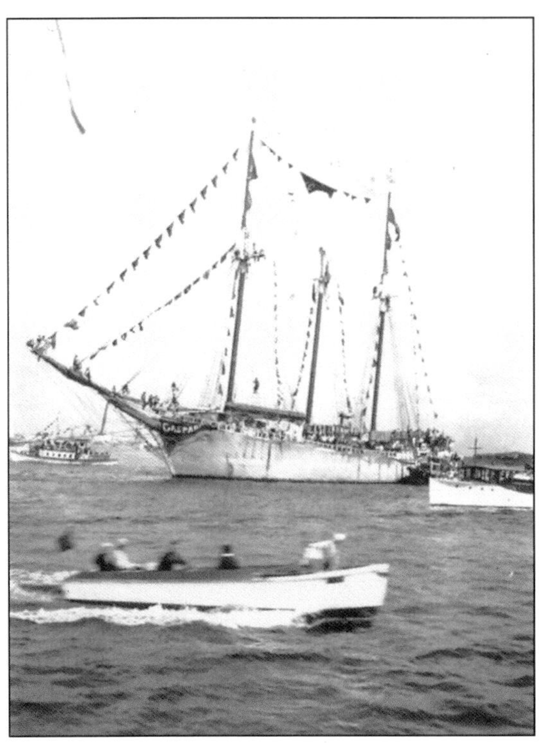

In 1911, Ye Mystic Krewe of Gasparilla borrowed the 185-ton three-masted schooner *Samuel T. Beacham* for the invasion. The ship was renamed *Gaspar V*, representing the fifth year of Gasparilla (there was no Gasparilla from 1907 to 1909). This same ship was also used for the 1912 invasion before it sank in the Florida Straits after a collision on March 30, 1913. Pictured here is likely *Samuel T. Beacham*. (YMKG.)

The first Gasparilla festival following World War I was held in 1920. Ye Mystic Krewe of Gasparilla transformed another borrowed ship, *Leonnie O. Louise*, into a pirate ship for the invasion. In this photograph, the ship has just passed through the Lafayette Street Bridge, now Kennedy Boulevard, on its way to the docks at the Tampa Bay Hotel, now Plant Hall at the University of Tampa. (THCPL.)

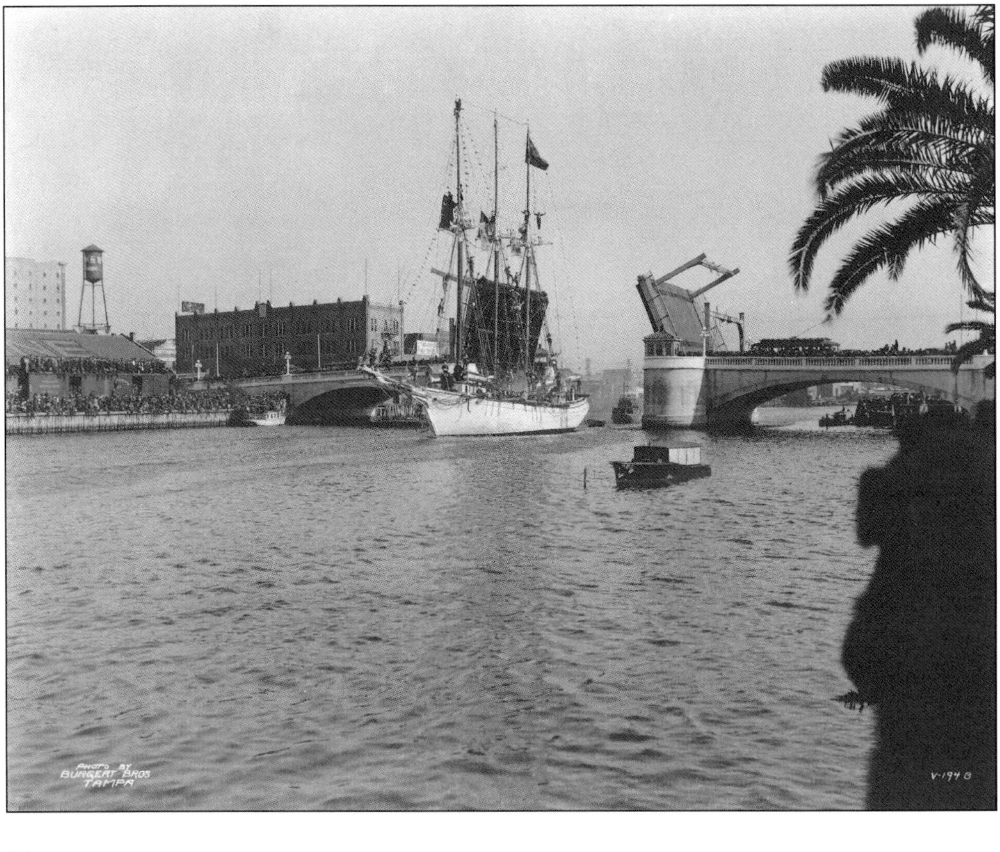

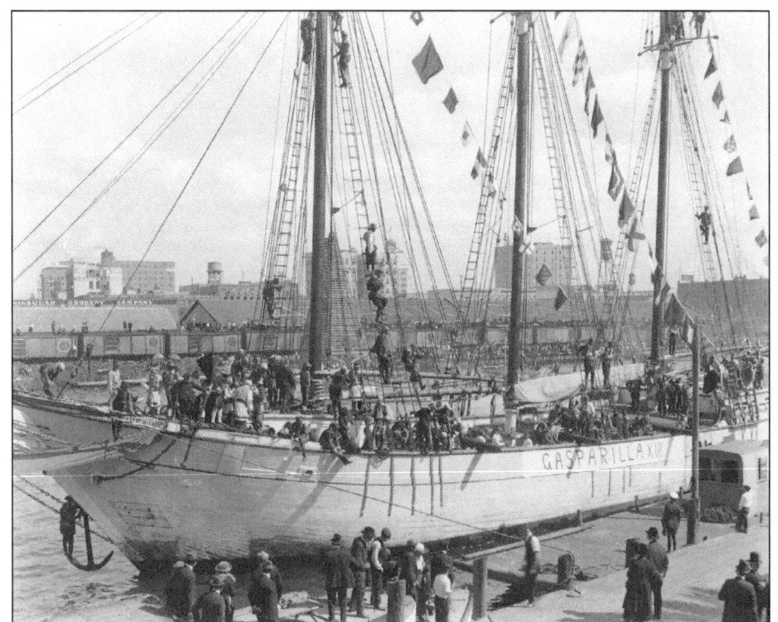

Many earlier ships borrowed for Gasparilla displayed roman numerals on their hull or flag to signify the number of Gasparilla invasions previously held. Although Gasparilla began in 1904, there were no invasions from 1907 to 1909 or 1918 to 1919. The 1921 ship displayed *Gasparilla XIII*, the 13th year of the event. (THCPL.)

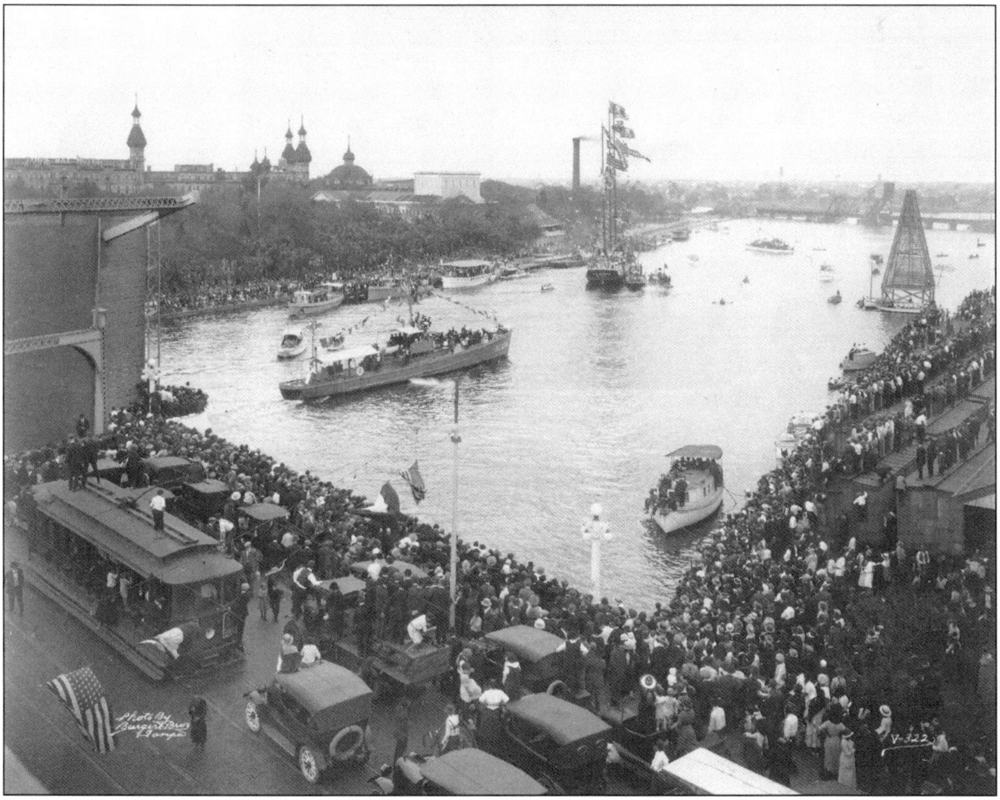

This 1922 photograph shows the borrowed *C.H. Hackney* pirate ship followed closely by a naval destroyer. In the early years of Gasparilla, naval vessels were often part of the mock invasion. Spectators fill the Lafayette Street Bridge and sit on top of railroad cars to watch the spectacle. In the background are the minarets of the Tampa Bay Hotel. (THCPL.)

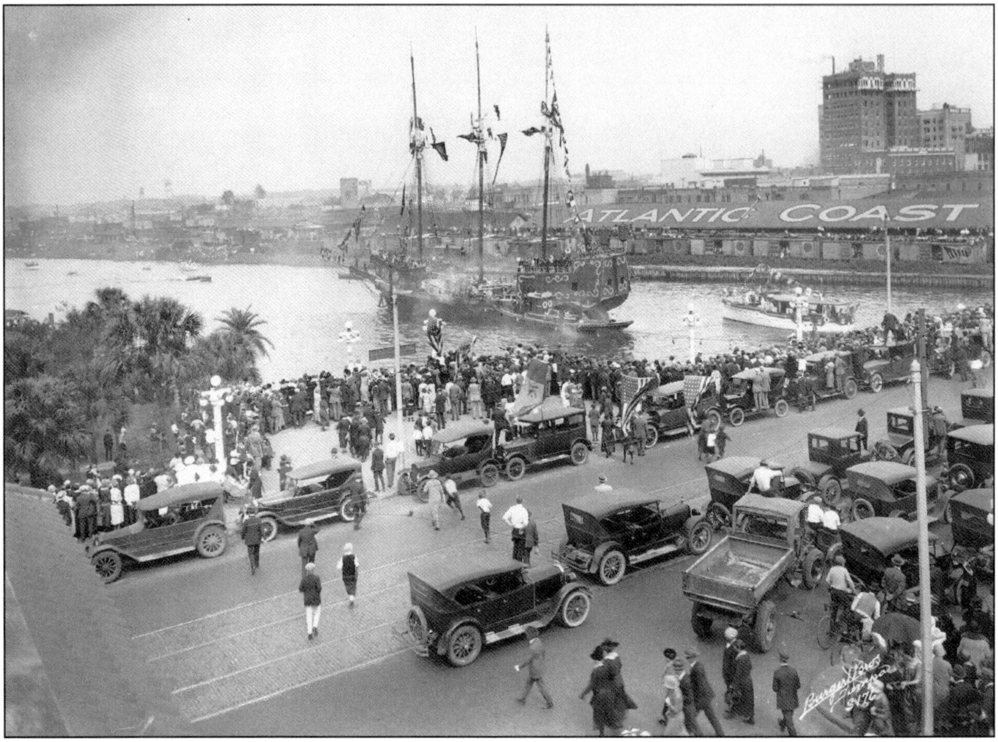

Gasparilla had become very popular by 1925, highlighted as usual by the pirate ship's arrival. In this photograph, cars are lined up and well-dressed parade-goers are positioned to get an up-close view of the ship from Lafayette Street Bridge. The Atlantic Coast Line freight terminal is visible on the east side of the Hillsborough River in downtown Tampa. (SAF.)

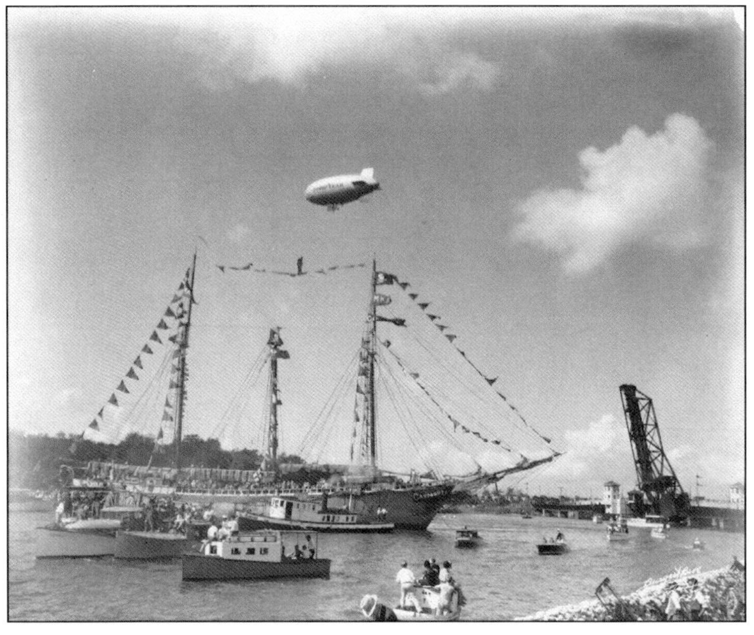

The year 2025 marked the 100th anniversary of the presence of the Goodyear blimp, which also made an appearance at the 1932 Gasparilla invasion. On the mainmast of the ship in this picture, a flag shows "MKG" for Mystic Krewe of Gasparilla, rather than the more modern "YMKG" for Ye Mystic Krewe of Gasparilla. The Cass Street Bridge railroad trestle is on the right. (THCPL.)

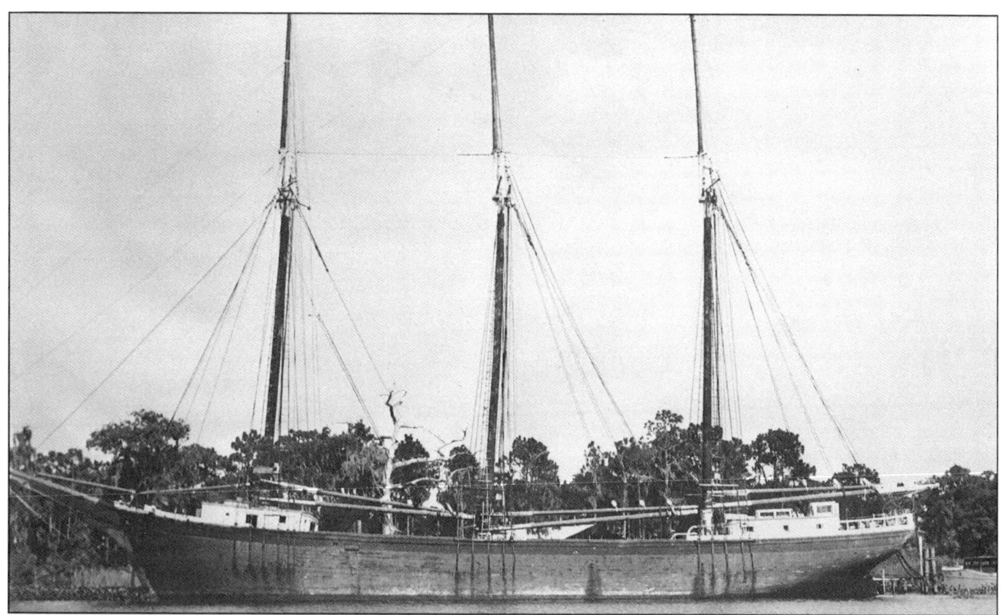

The first year Ye Mystic Krewe of Gasparilla used its own ship for the invasion was 1938. Built in 1902, *William Bisbee* was a sturdy three-masted, oak-beamed schooner with a 33-foot beam and overall length of 143 feet. Ye Mystic Krewe of Gasparilla purchased the ship in 1936 before repurposing and renaming it *José Gaspar*. Prior borrowed ships were also referred to as *José Gaspa*r, but in 1954, a new ship built specifically for the invasion was named *José Gasparilla*. Some of the previously borrowed ships would occasionally run aground on sections of the river, but *José Gaspar* had a shallower draft of only 6.8 feet, enabling clearer passage up the shallow Hillsborough River. *William Bisbee* is pictured above prior to its conversion into *José Gaspar* (below). (Above, SAF; below, USF.)

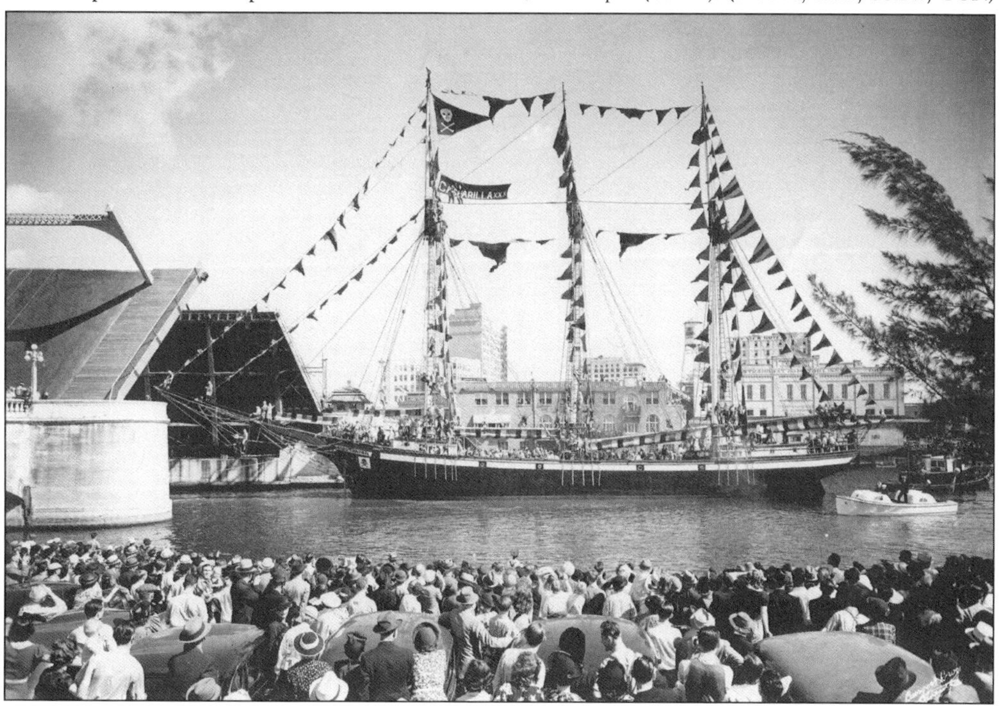

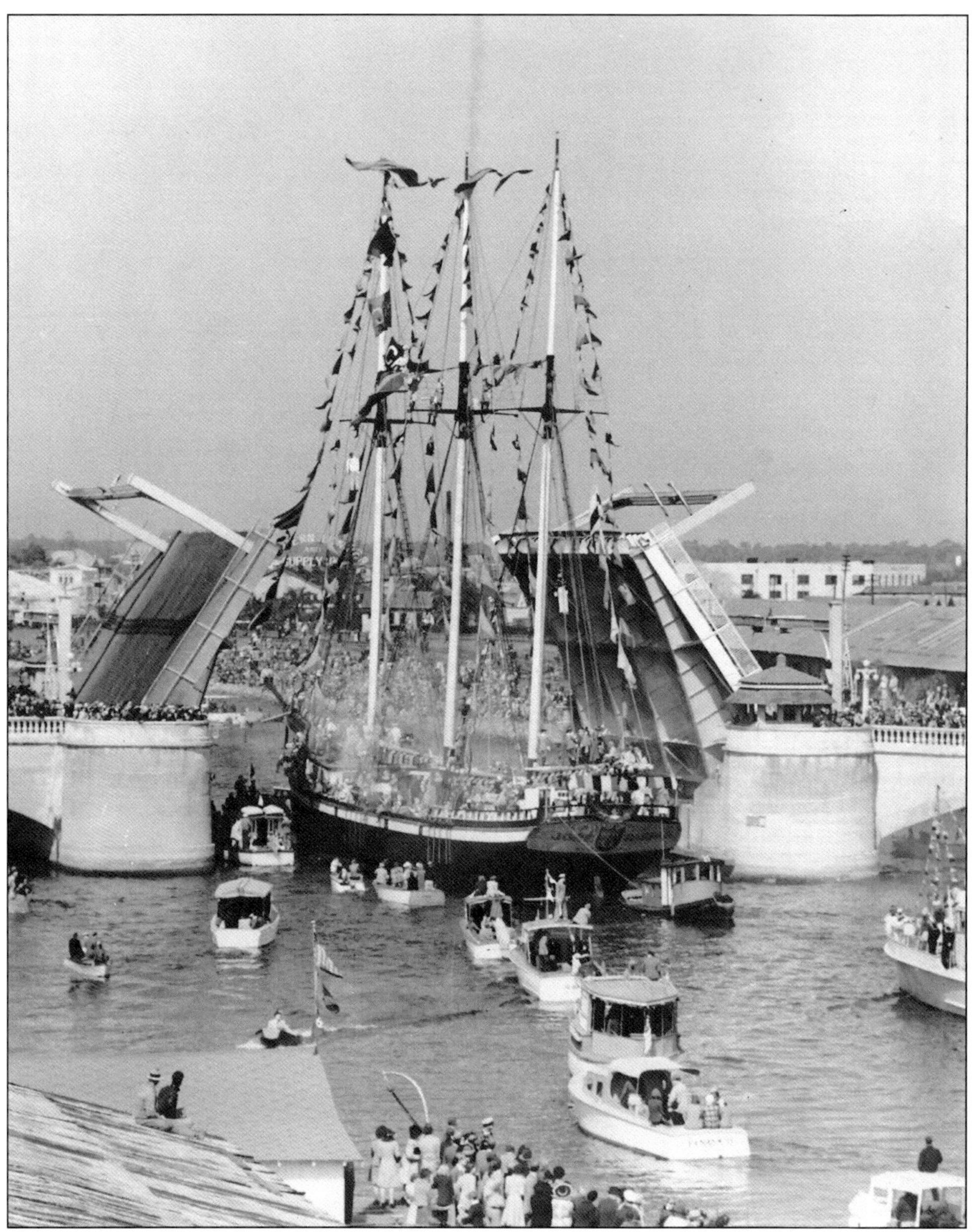

Ye Mystic Krewe of Gasparilla's ships have traditionally left from the Ballast Point Pier, adjacent to the Tampa Yacht and Country Club, and then traveled across Hillsborough Bay toward downtown Tampa. Until 1976, when the Crosstown Expressway, now the Lee Roy Selmon Expressway, was constructed, the ship would pass beneath several bridges on its way to its landing destination up the Hillsborough River. As seen in this 1941 photograph, the tall masts of *William Bisbee* (*José Gaspar*) and the narrow angle of the open Lafayette Street Bridge afforded the ship little room for error going through the passage. Also notice the tugboat attached to the ship's stern and facing the opposite direction to reverse course should this be required. In some years, the ships used for the invasion had to clear up to five bridges: the Platt Street, Lafayette Street, Brorein Street, Cass Street, and Laurel Street Bridges. (THCPL.)

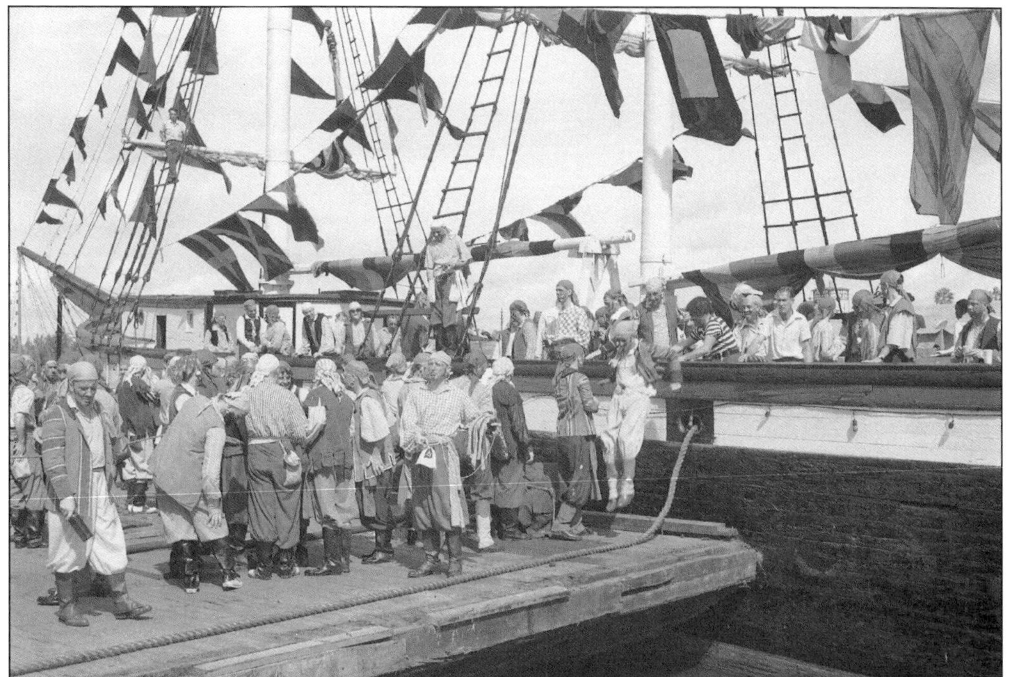

The Gasparilla ship has used several different landing locations throughout the years, including the Tampa Bay Hotel, the foot of Seventh Avenue, the Curtis Hixon Convention Center, Bayshore Boulevard (the old tarpon weigh station), Harbour Island, and the Tampa Convention Center. This February 7, 1948, photograph shows Ye Mystic Krewe of Gasparilla pirates leaving the ship following the voyage across Hillsborough Bay. (SAF.)

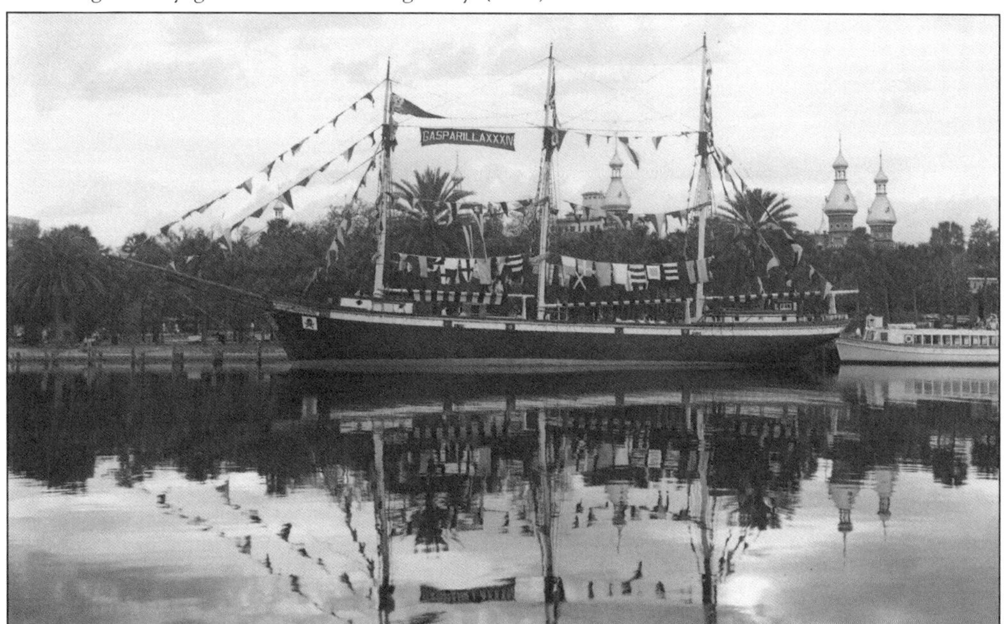

This 1949 photograph shows *José Gaspar* docked at the Tampa Bay Hotel. Built in 1902, the ship was originally the *William Bisbee* and was purchased by Ye Mystic Krewe of Gasparilla in October 1936. This is the same ship displayed on the book's cover. (THCPL.)

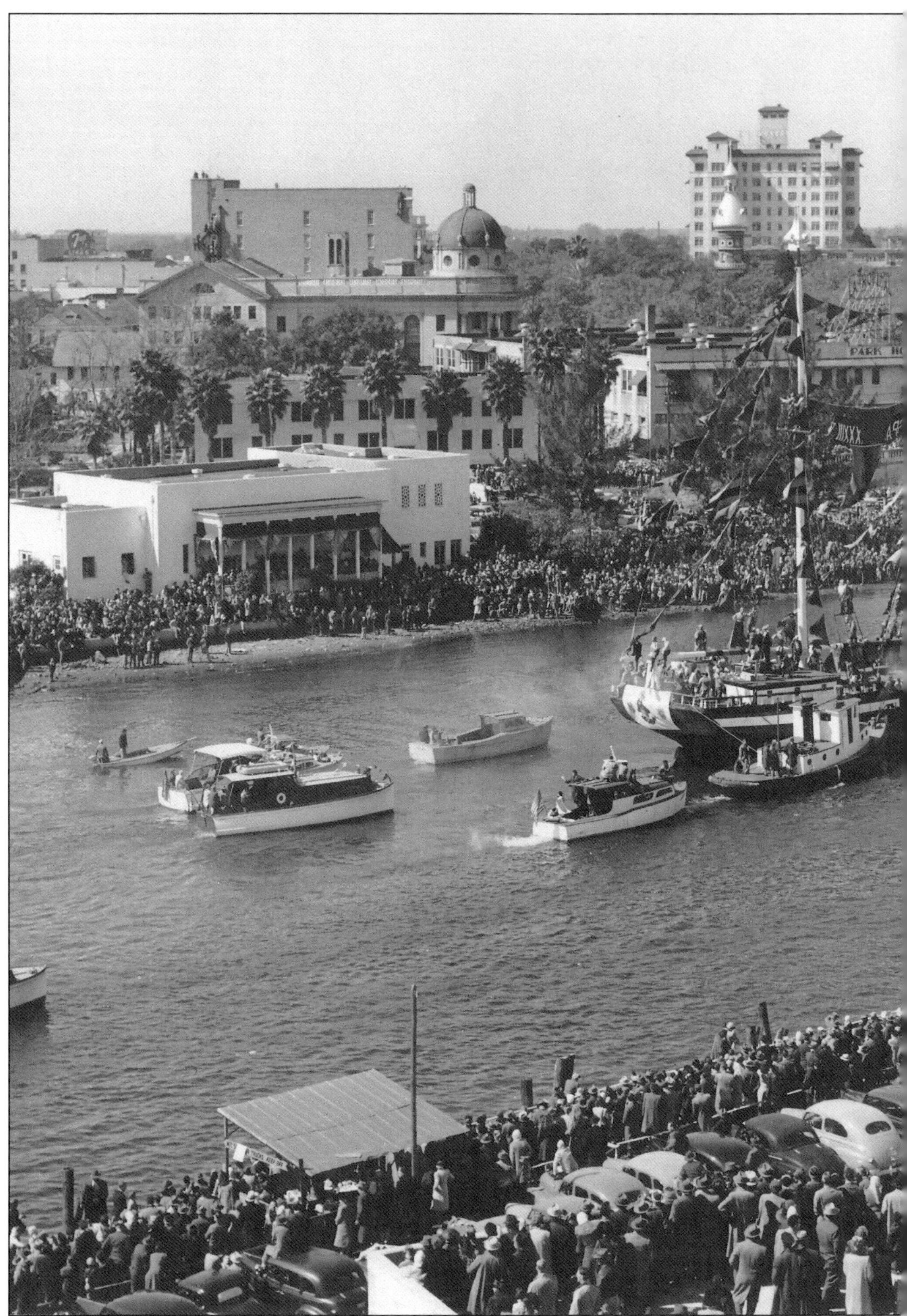

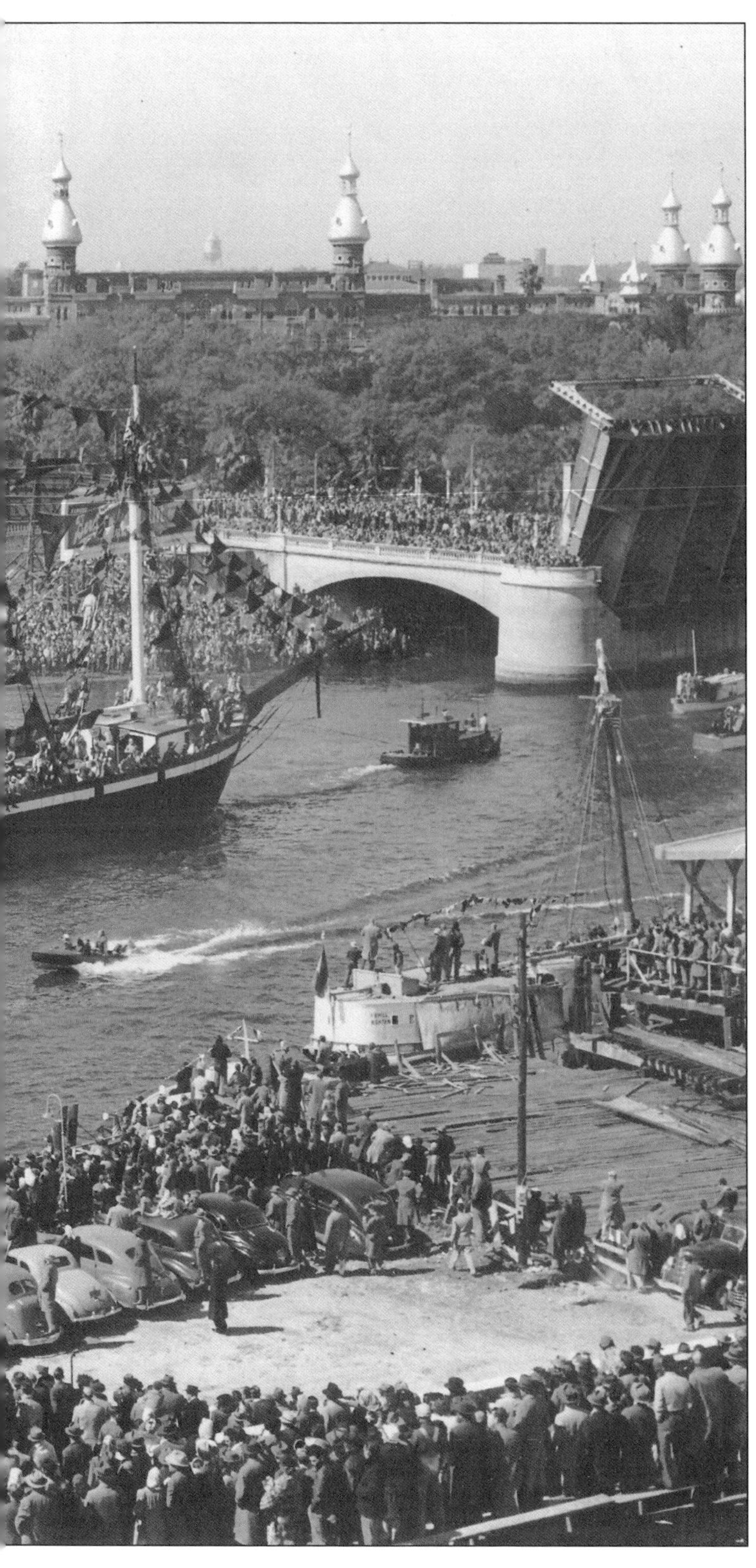

In 1947, large crowds attended the first Gasparilla invasion following World War II. As the ship sailed up the harbor, the US Navy's new Bearcat fighter flew overhead in a mock battle with a Japanese Zero. Spectators and cars lined the waterways to get an up-close view of *José Gaspar* as it approached downtown. The iconic minarets of the Tampa Bay Hotel, now Plant Hall at the University of Tampa, are visible in the background beyond the Lafayette Street Bridge, now Kennedy Boulevard. It was also in 1947 that Ye Mystic Krewe of Gasparilla began lending its name to the Gasparilla Children's Festival. (THCPL.)

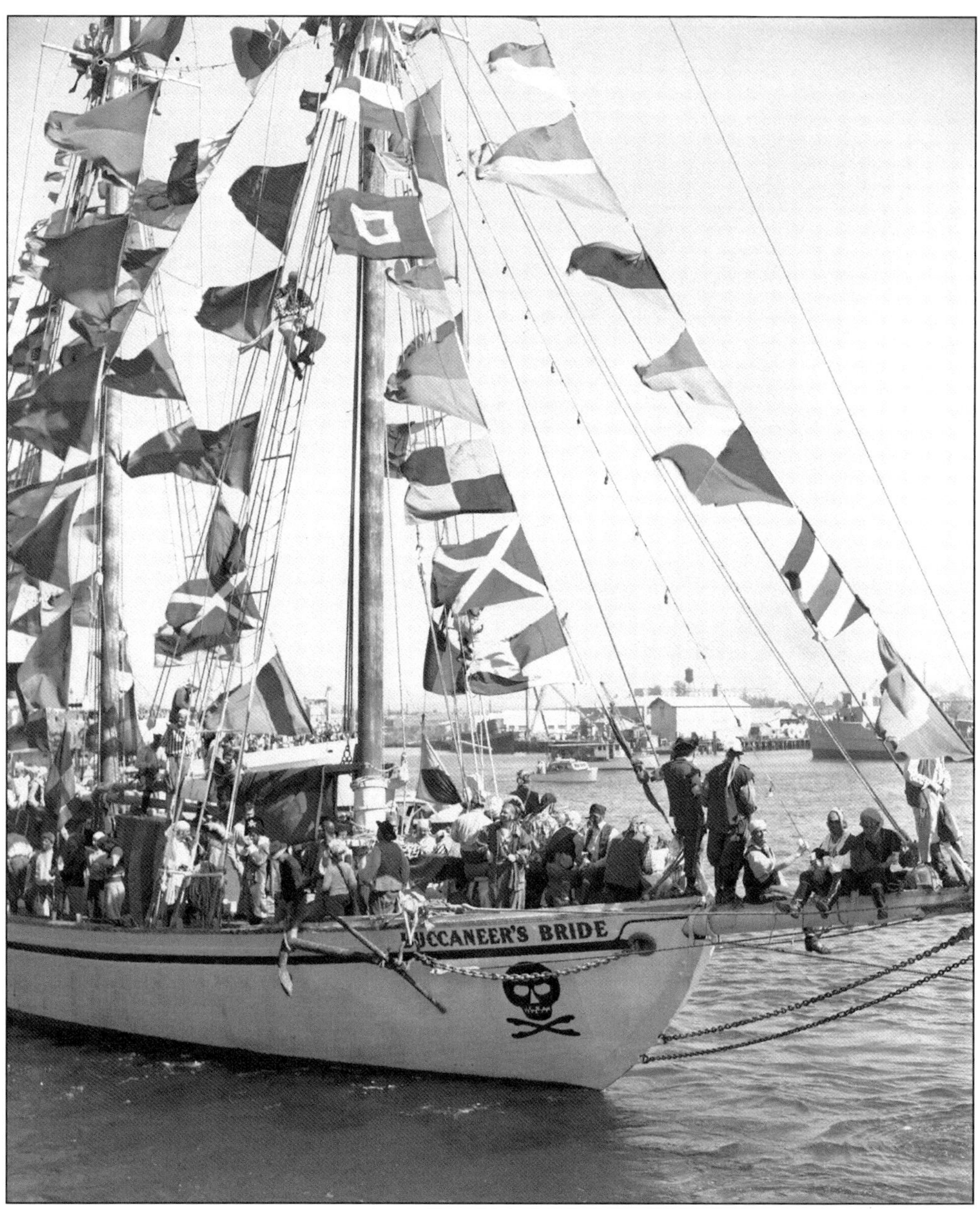

From 1911 until 1937, Ye Mystic Krewe of Gasparilla used borrowed ships for the mock invasion of Tampa. On occasion, the krewe did not know it had a ship until the day before the invasion. With the uncertainties of finding an individual or company willing to have their vessel transformed into a pirate ship for the day, a ship was finally purchased. *José Gaspar* was the first ship owned by the krewe and was used for the Gasparilla invasion from 1938 until 1951. The ship was then declared unseaworthy and would later catch fire and sink at its mooring on the Hillsborough River. Ye Mystic Krewe of Gasparilla used borrowed ships for the 1952 and 1953 invasions. Since a single ship large enough to carry all of Ye Mystic Krewe of Gasparilla's pirates was unavailable in 1953, four smaller schooners were required. These vessels were *Buccaneer's Bride*, seen here on February 9, 1953; *Joseito*; *Shark*; and *Seawolf*. Pictures of these ships appeared in the September 1954 edition of *National Geographic* in an article entitled "America Goes to the Fair." (SAF.)

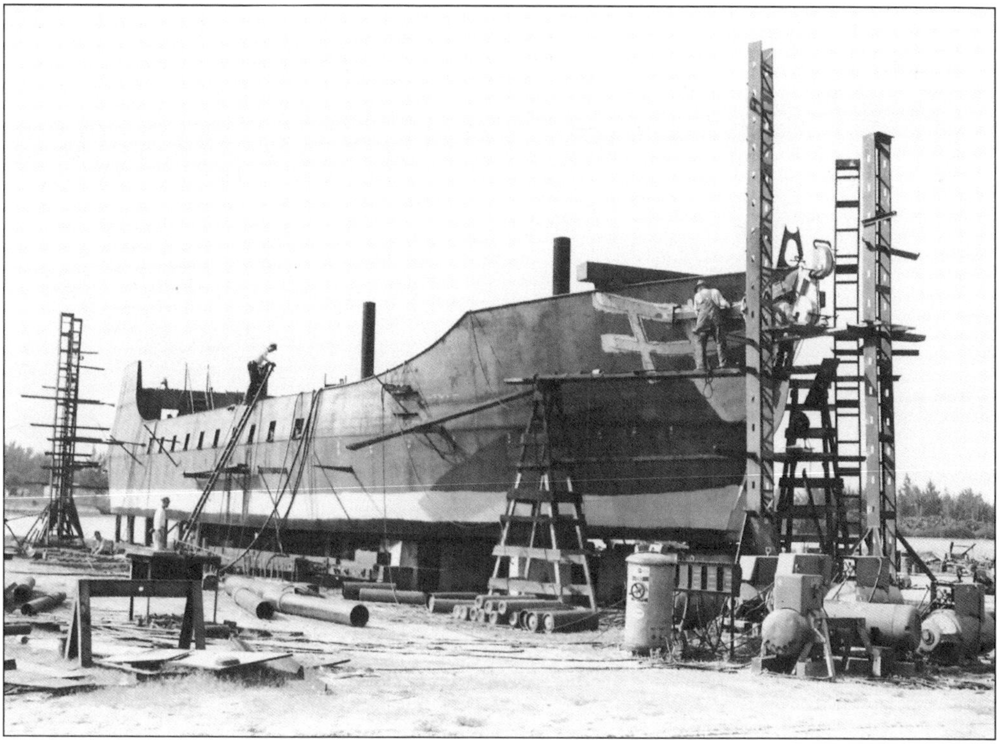

In 1953, Ye Mystic Krewe of Gasparilla began construction of its own ship, the only one built in the last 200 years to be used solely for "piratical" purposes. Tampa Ship Repair and Dry Dock Company built the ship over a seven-month period at a cost of $100,000. With prior experiences with ships running aground in Hillsborough Bay and the Hillsborough River, *José Gasparilla* was designed as a steel flat-bottomed barge. The ship is 137 feet in length with a beam of 36 feet and has much more room than previous vessels. The ship has no motor; instead, powerful tugboats maneuver *José Gasparilla* through the sometimes rough and windy waters of Tampa Bay. (Both, YMKG.)

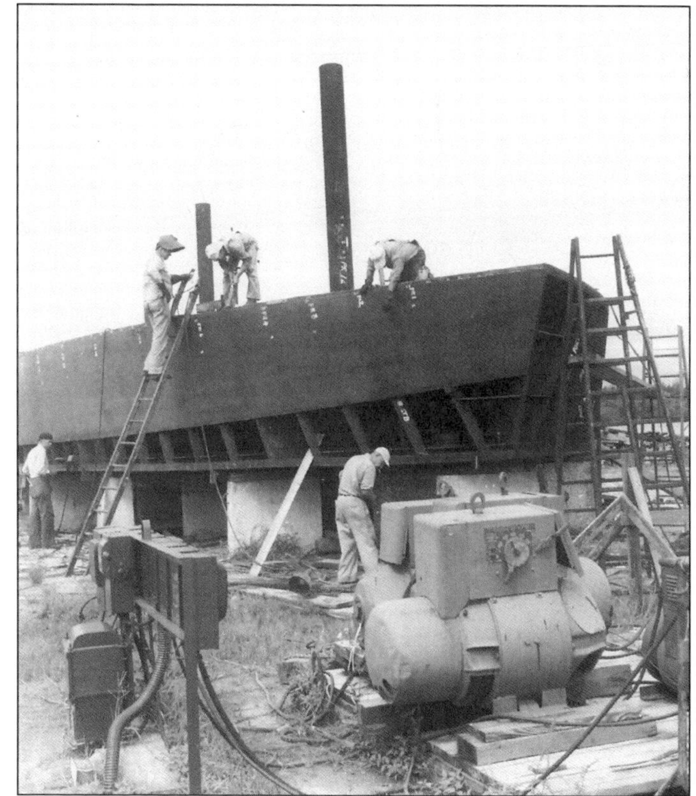

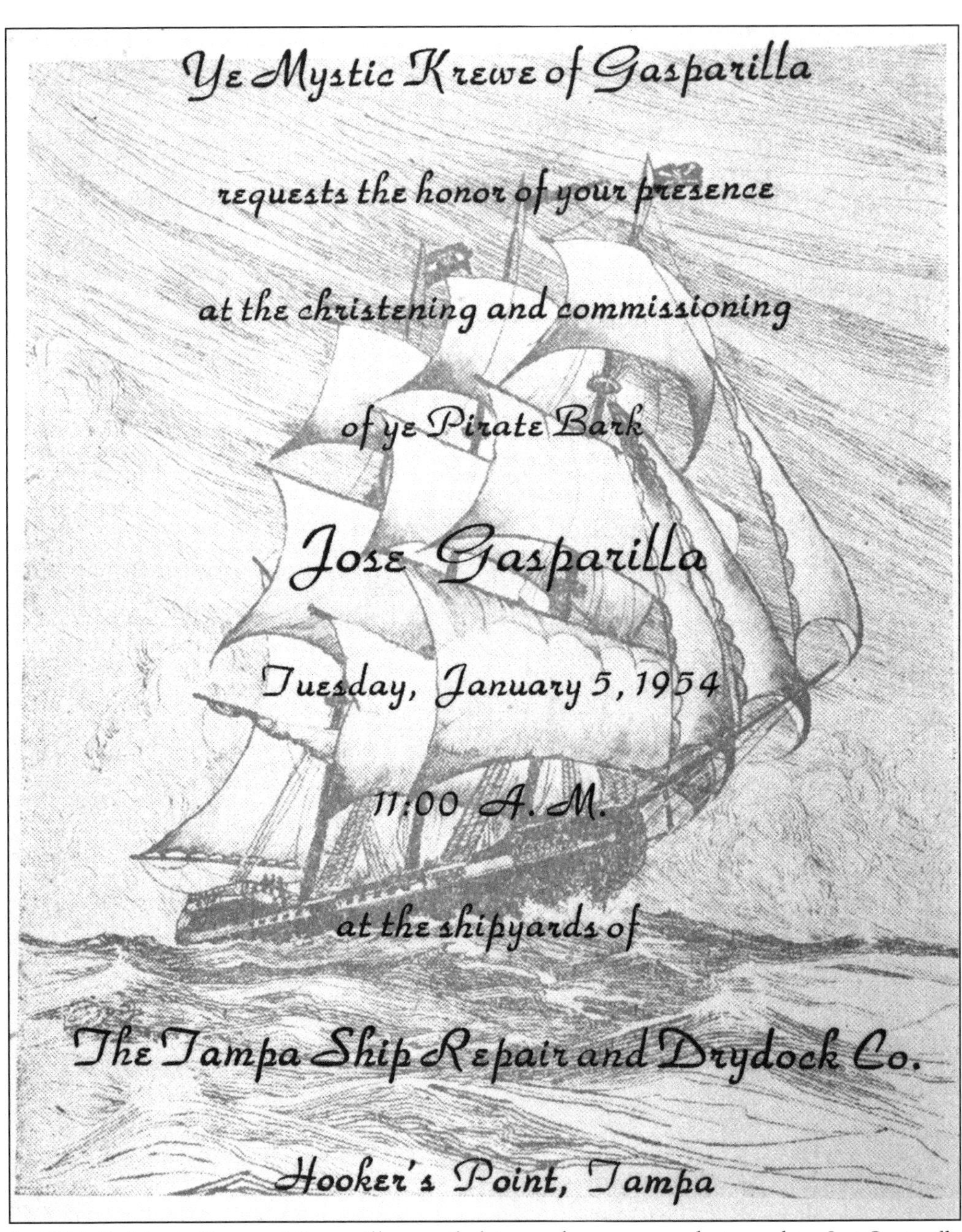
Ye Mystic Krewe of Gasparilla
requests the honor of your presence
at the christening and commissioning
of ye Pirate Bark
Jose Gasparilla
Tuesday, January 5, 1954
11:00 A. M.
at the shipyards of
The Tampa Ship Repair and Drydock Co.
Hooker's Point, Tampa

In 1954, Ye Mystic Krewe of Gasparilla unveiled its newly constructed pirate ship. *José Gasparilla* was christened with a bottle of Jamaican rum at Tampa Ship Repair and Drydock Company just in time for the 50th anniversary of Gasparilla. Members of Ye Mystic Krewe of Gasparilla and community leaders received invitations for the January 5, 1954, event to celebrate the long-overdue new Gasparilla ship. After using four smaller schooners the year before to carry krewe members into Tampa, the large and spacious *José Gasparilla* was a welcome addition to the invasion. The previous ship owned by Ye Mystic Krewe of Gasparilla was named *José Gaspar* in honor of the legendary pirate's birth name. To pay homage to his new name that was chosen after he mutinied from the Spanish navy and sailed to Florida to begin a life of piracy, the new ship was named *José Gasparilla*. The ship has stood the test of time and is still in use today. (YMKG.)

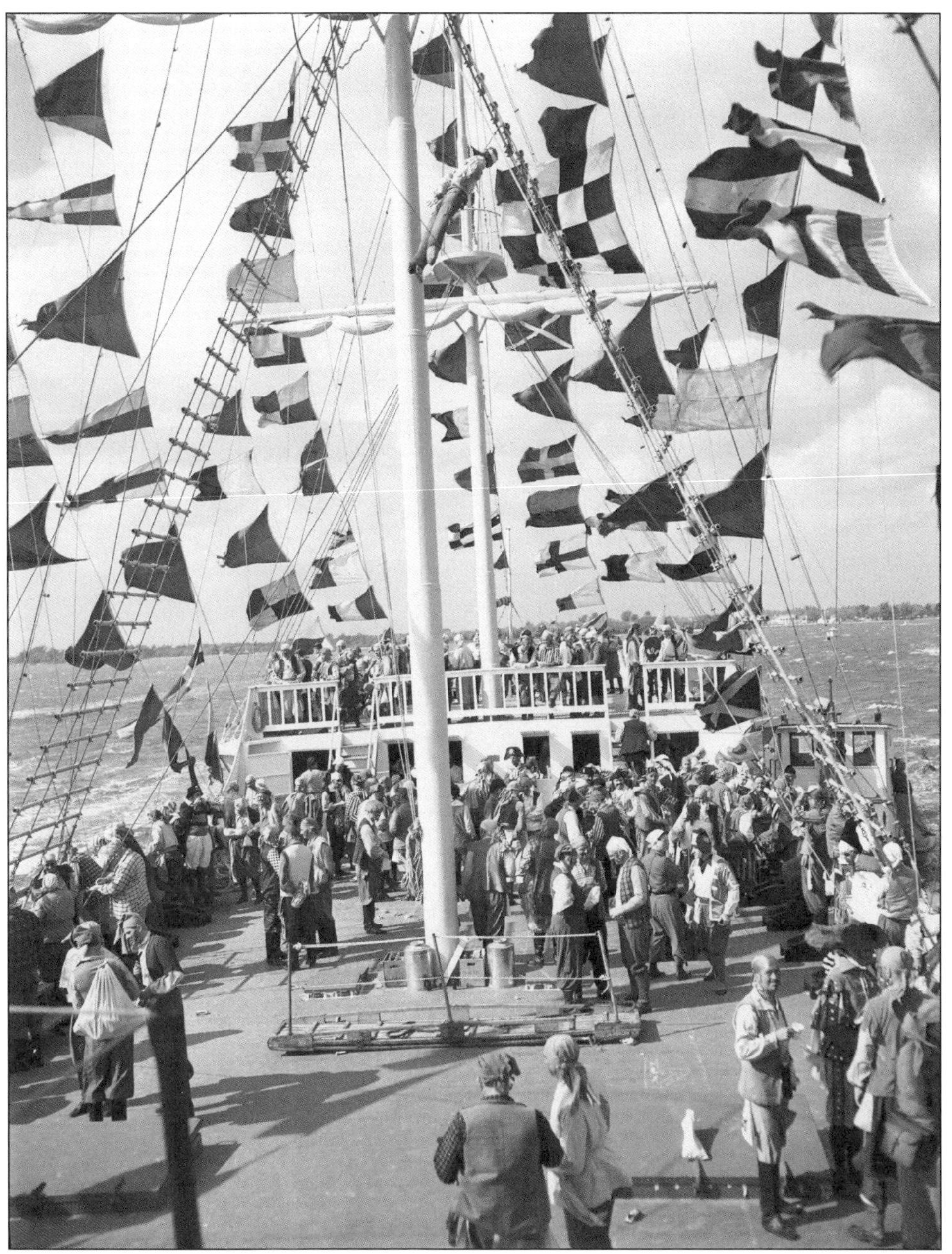

Whitecaps and billowing flags show that the first voyage of the new pirate ship on February 8, 1954, took place on a windy day. Although Gasparilla ships usually left from the Ballast Point Pier to cross Hillsborough Bay, occasional rough seas or high winds required an alternative departure from the estuary near downtown Tampa. This shorter 55-minute trip around the tip of Seddon Island (Harbour Island) avoids the open waters of Hillsborough Bay prior to heading north up the channel along Davis Islands. If the weather cooperates and the ship leaves from the Ballast Point Pier, a flotilla of hundreds of private boats accompanies the ship across the bay and into downtown Tampa. Several hundred pirates aboard the ship announce their arrival with the sound of .38 Special blank guns and 10-gauge salute cannons. The sound of gun and cannon fire adds to the theatrical nature of the invasion and can be heard for miles around the Tampa Bay area. (SAF.)

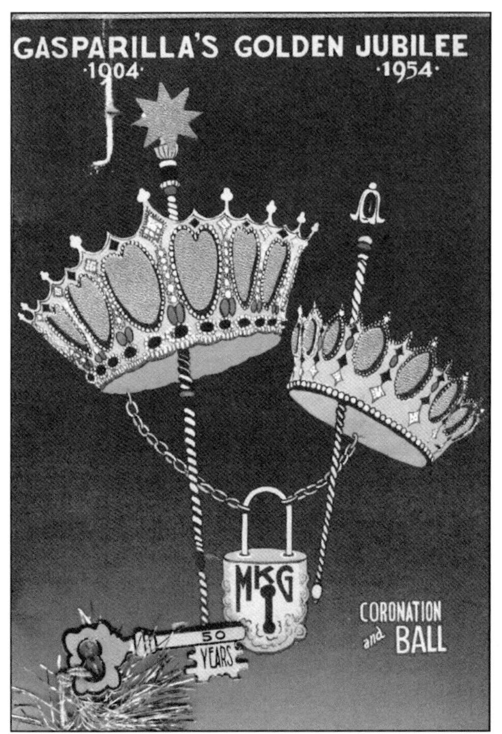

In addition to the inaugural voyage for Ye Mystic Krewe of Gasparilla's new ship, 1954 was also celebrated with a special Golden Jubilee program for the Ye Mystic Krewe of Gasparilla Coronation Ball. This commemorative edition has now become a collector's item and comes with a string-attached key that corresponds to the drawing of the lock. (YMKG.)

The use of cannons to enhance the piratical presence of the ship is a time-honored tradition of the Gasparilla celebration. The specially trained members of the Gunner's Guild of Ye Mystic Krewe of Gasparilla are responsible for firing the cannons aboard *José Gasparilla*. Salute cannons like the one in this 1960s photograph fire 10-gauge shotgun blanks. During the invasion, the 29 cannons on board the ship can fire up to 8,000 rounds. (USF.)

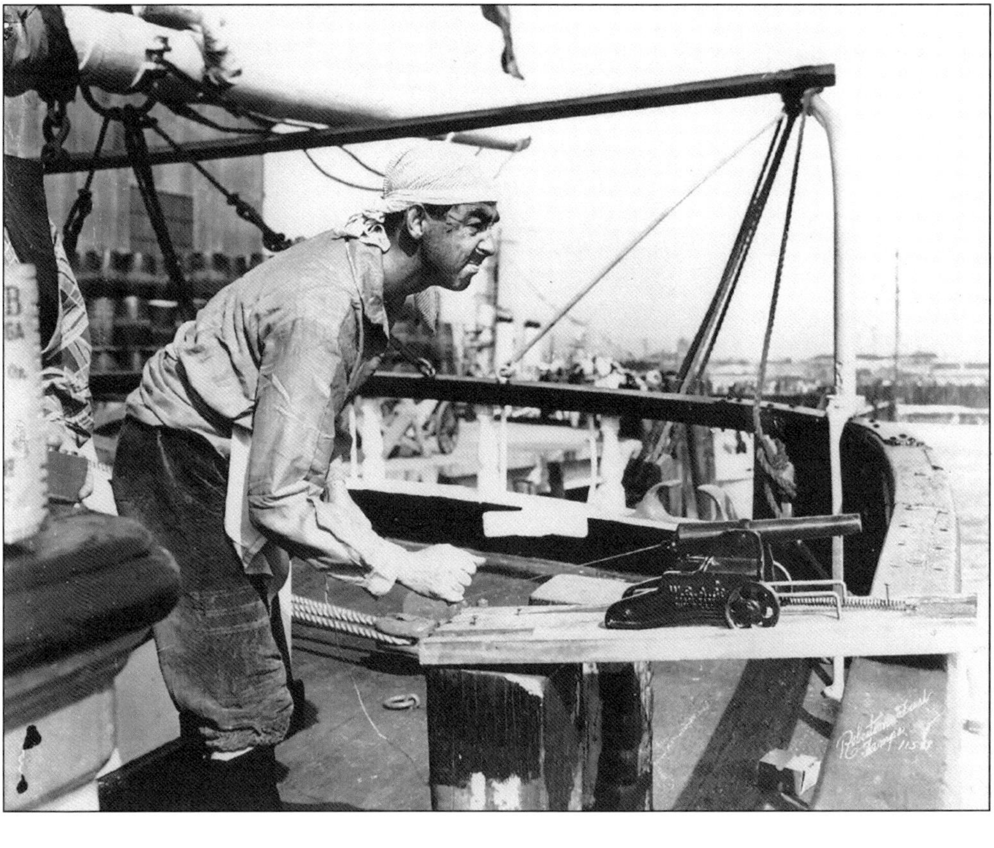

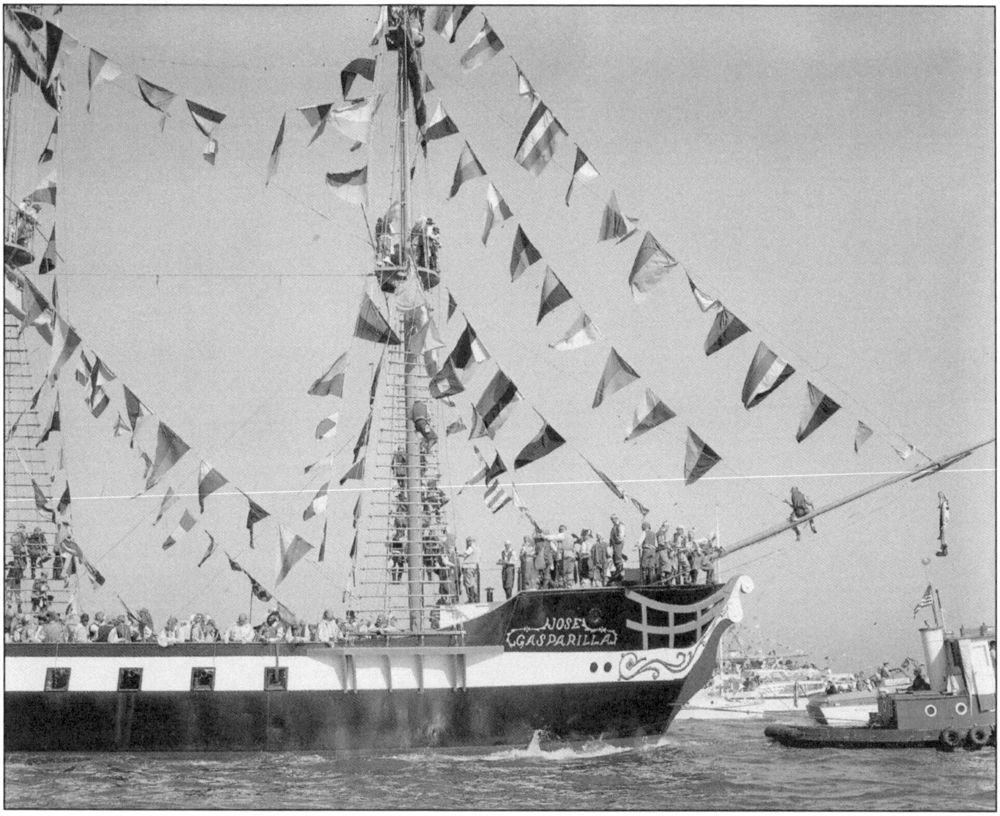

For its maiden voyage in 1954, *José Gasparilla* left from the Ballast Point Pier to make the one-hour fifteen-minute trip across Hillsborough Bay. This new ship had much greater capacity than its predecessors and was more seaworthy. Its flat-bottom design avoided the perils of the area's shallow water. (SAF.)

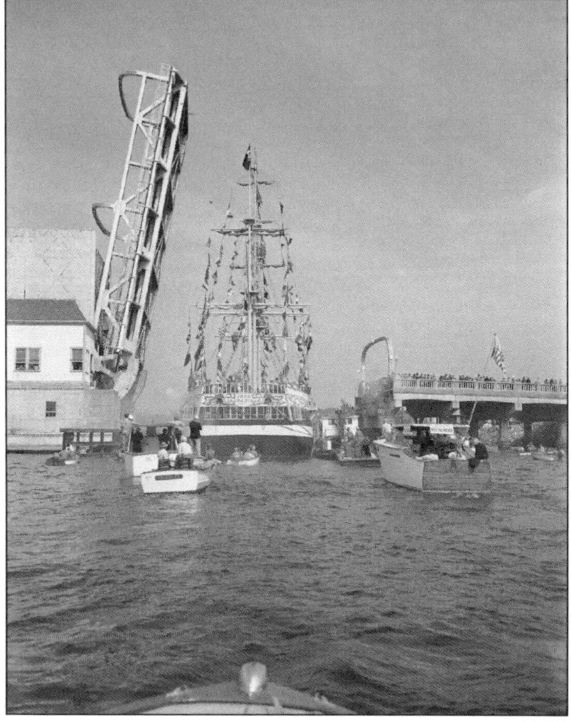

In this 1955 photograph, *José Gasparilla* is moving through the Laurel Street Bridge on its way to dock at the foot of Seventh Avenue, now the site of the Armature Works. The ship has already traveled through the Platt Street, Lafayette Street, and Cass Street Bridges. After 1959, the ship would also go through the Brorein Street Bridge. (SAF.)

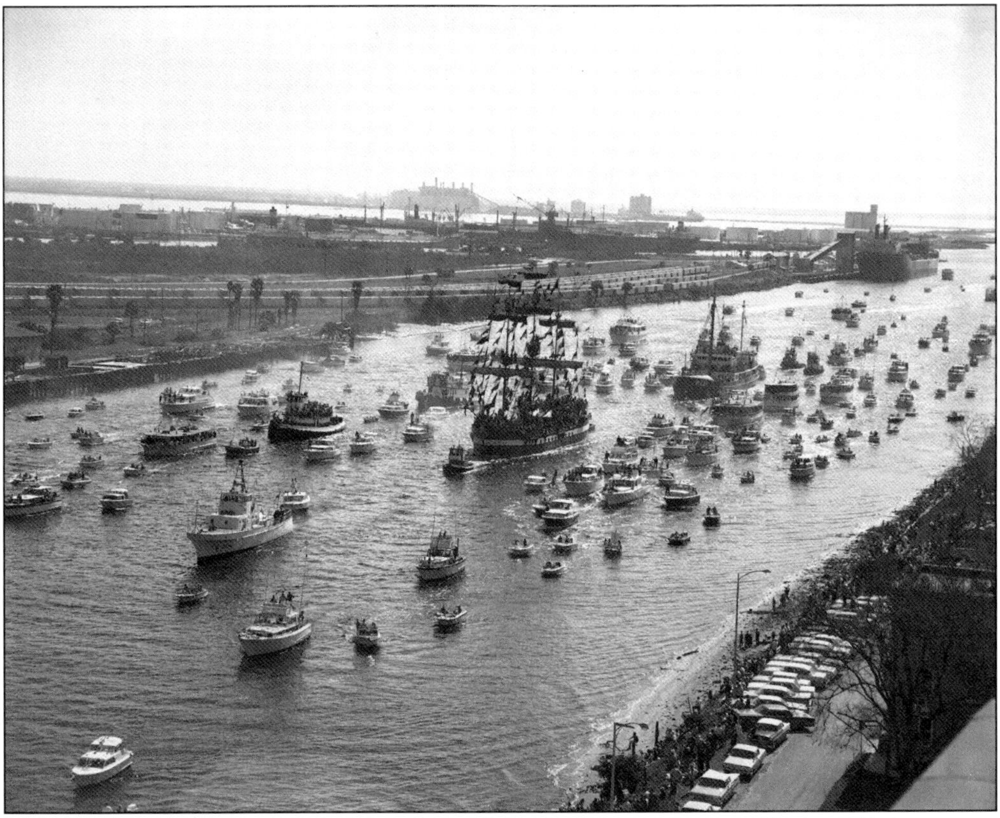

Since the first Gasparilla ship invasion in 1911, pirates of Ye Mystic Krewe of Gasparilla have never sailed alone. As seen in this 1966 photograph, a flotilla of boats accompanies the ship as it makes its way up Seddon Channel into downtown Tampa. This boat parade has become one of the largest in the country, with hundreds of boats participating each year. (SAF.)

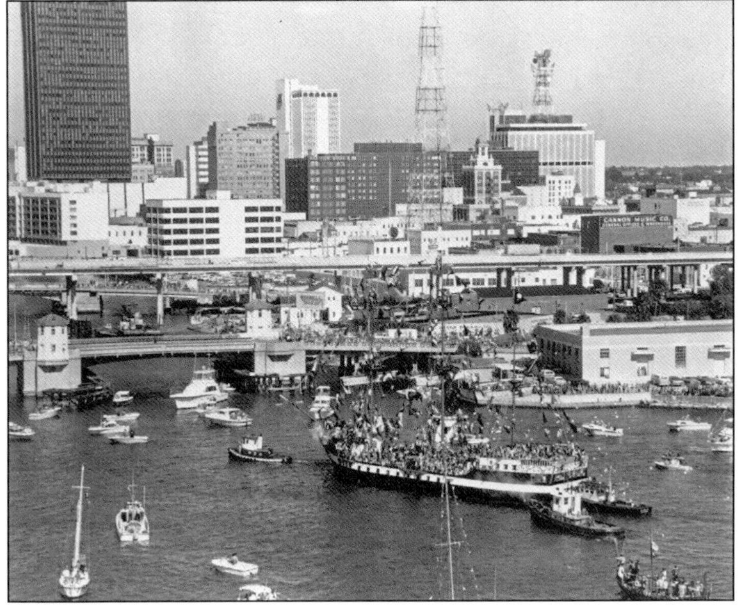

José Gasparilla would last travel up the Hillsborough River in 1975. This 1976 photograph shows the newly constructed and stationary Crosstown Expressway, now the Lee Roy Selmon Expressway, which precluded the ship and its 100-foot masts from entry into downtown Tampa. The Platt Street Bridge can be seen in front of the expressway and the Brorein Street Bridge on the other side. (SAF.)

Four

Get Ready to Be Invaded!

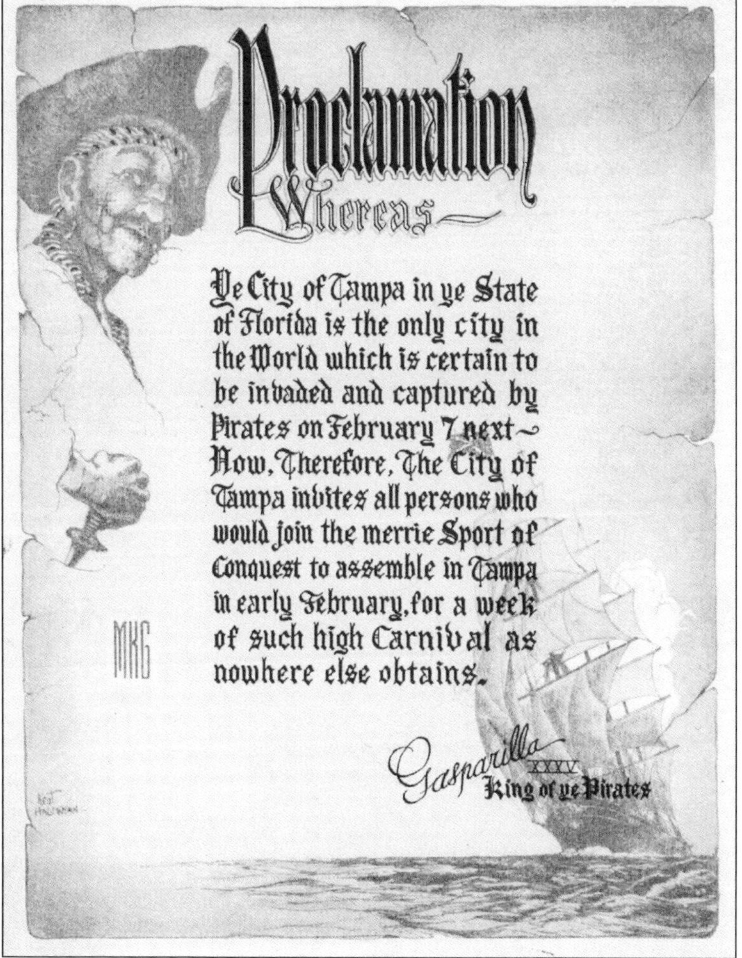
Proclamation

Whereas—

Ye City of Tampa in ye State of Florida is the only city in the World which is certain to be invaded and captured by Pirates on February 7 next—
Now, Therefore, The City of Tampa invites all persons who would join the merrie Sport of Conquest to assemble in Tampa in early February, for a week of such high Carnival as nowhere else obtains.

MKG

Gasparilla XXXV
King of ye Pirates

Before pirates invade Tampa, they offer fair warning. This 1948 proclamation, issued by the "King of the Pirates," is part of the annual Gasparilla tradition in which Ye Mystic Krewe of Gasparilla sends an envoy to city hall to demand the key to the city. When the mayor refuses, the pirates vow to return in full force, launching the storied pirate invasion that has captivated Tampa since 1904. (YMKG.)

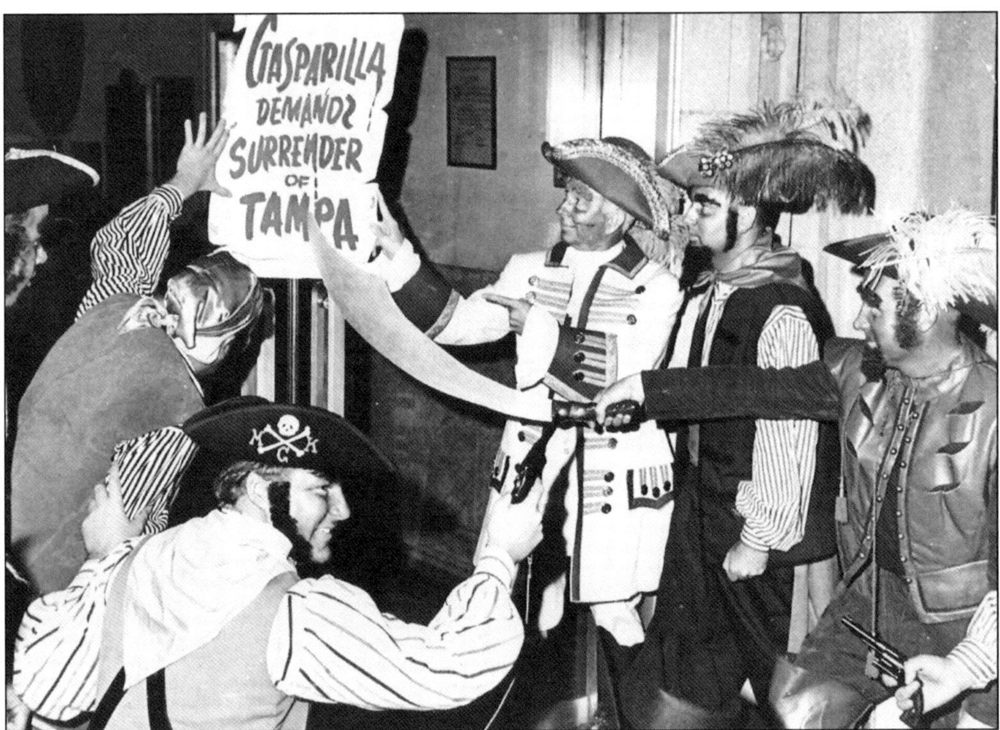

As part of a long-standing tradition, Ye Mystic Krewe of Gasparilla sends an advance group of pirates prior to the invasion to confront the mayor and demand the key to the city. This spirited standoff marks the beginning of Tampa's most celebrated week of revelry and rebellion. As seen above, members of Ye Mystic Krewe of Gasparilla will on occasion bring piratical props to the event. On the day of the invasion, if the mayor hands over the key to the city, as is always the case, Ye Mystic Krewe of Gasparilla stages a celebratory parade instead of attacking the city. In the 1915 photograph below, Mayor D.B. McKay hands over the key to the city as an audience looks on. (Above, YMKG; below, THCPL.)

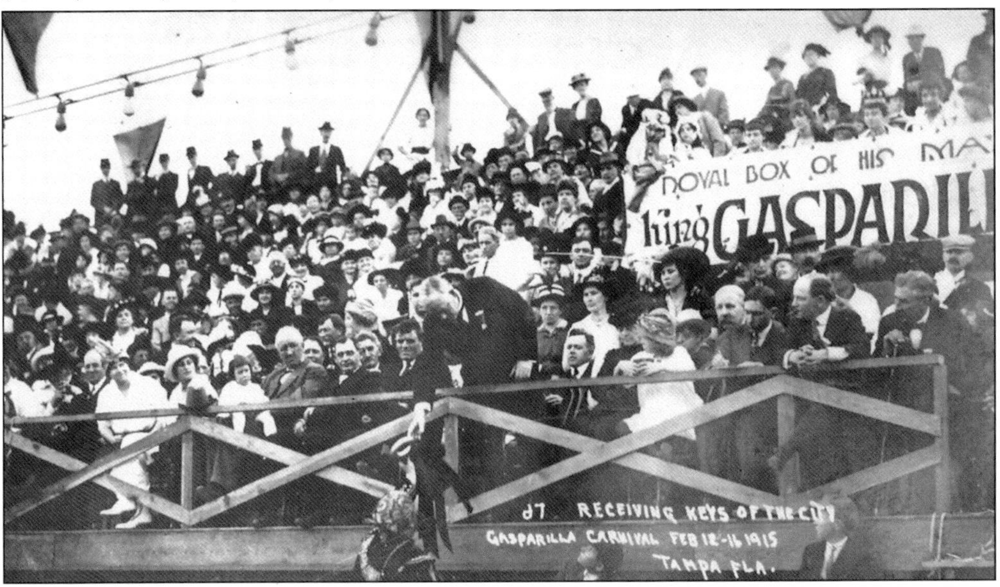

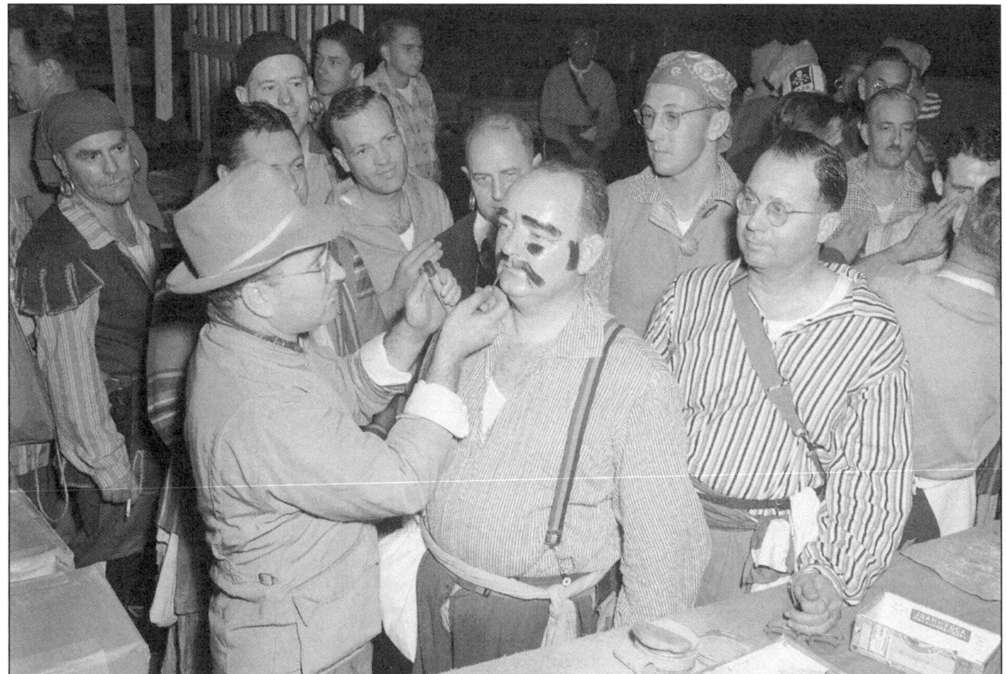

Ye Mystic Krewe of Gasparilla pirates are businessmen, professionals, and civic leaders 364 days a year. On invasion day, they become swashbuckling buccaneers. In the scene above from 1948, makeup artists apply scars, stubble, and theatrical wounds as other members line up to complete their transformation into cutthroat pirates. Founded in 1904, the same year as Ye Mystic Krewe of Gasparilla, the Tampa Yacht and Country Club has served as the official launch point for the invasion for over a century. From the adjacent Ballast Point Pier, the pirates begin their journey to downtown Tampa, kicking off the city's most iconic and enduring celebration. Below is a 1952 aerial view of the Tampa Yacht and Country Club (left) and the long Ballast Point Pier (right). (Both, THCPL.)

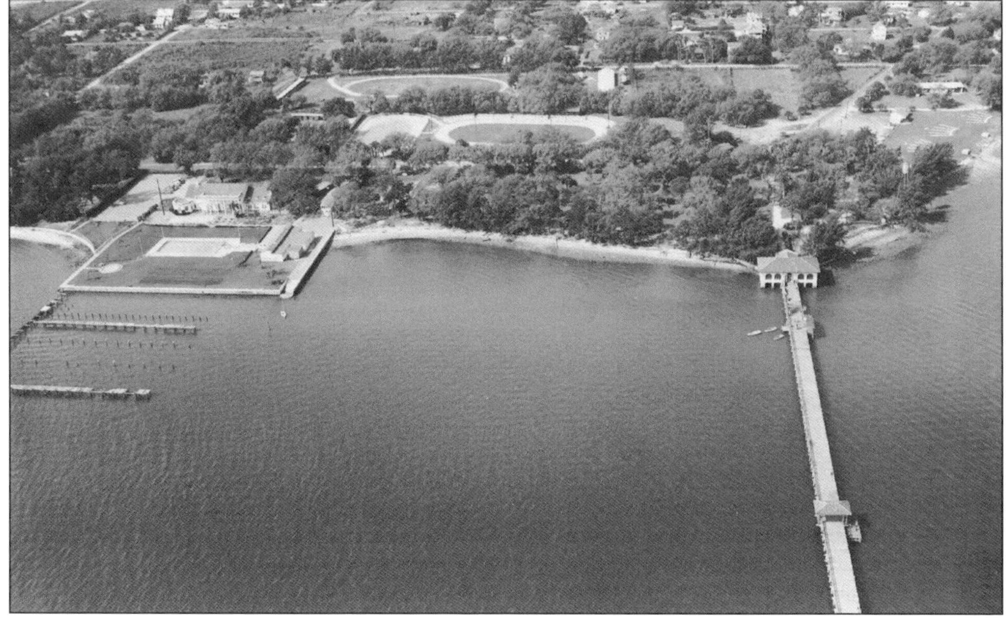

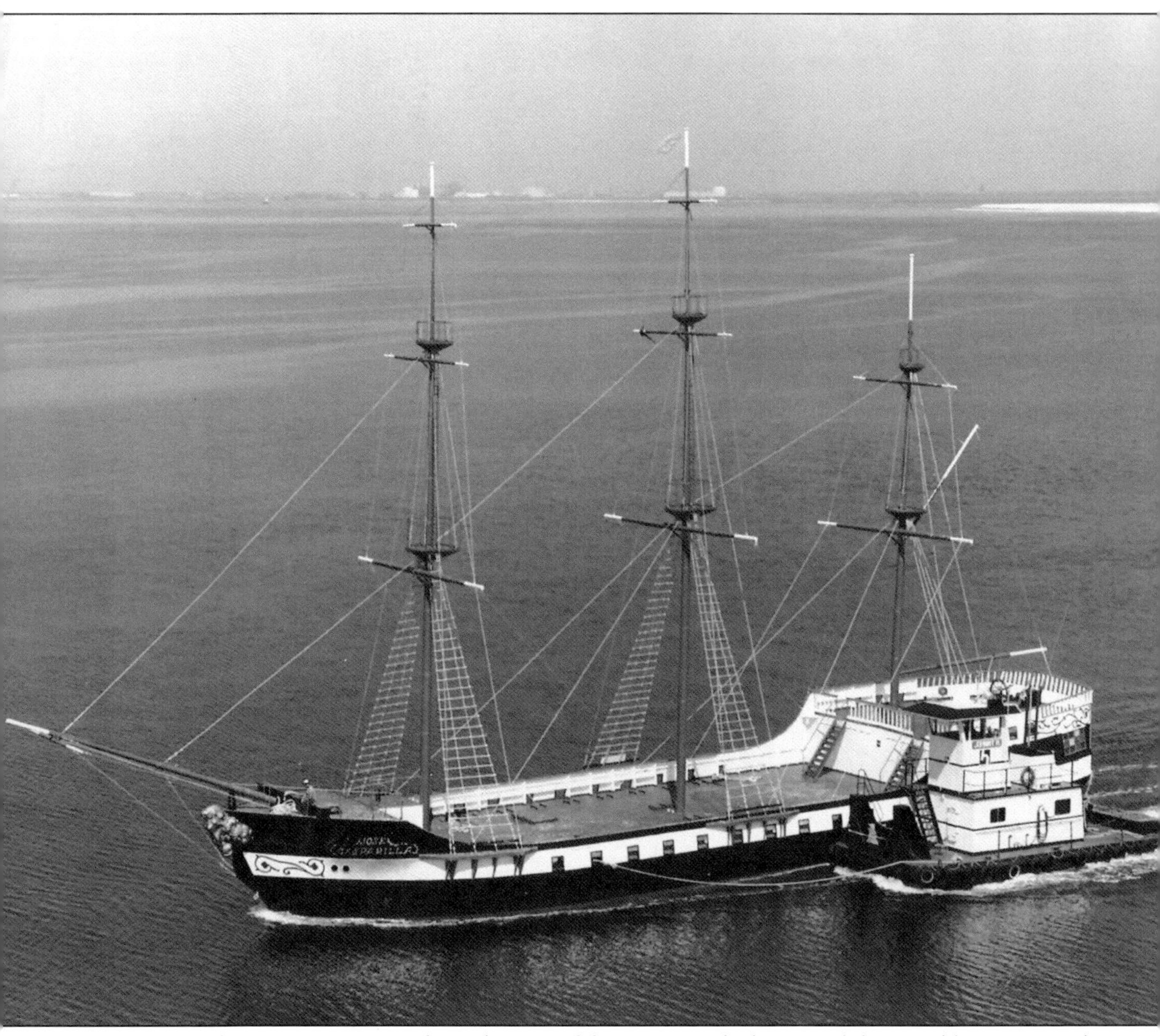

On more than one occasion in the early years of the invasion, the borrowed ship would run aground, and the pirates had to continue their journey to the docking site on the Hillsborough River in rowboats. With prior experiences with borrowed ships running aground in Hillsborough Bay or the Hillsborough River, *José Gasparilla* was designed as a steel flat-bottomed barge. Ye Mystic Krewe of Gasparilla's ship has no motor; instead, powerful tugboats maneuver *José Gasparilla* through the sometimes rough and windy waters of Hillsborough Bay. Pictured here in 1985, the empty ship is being transported to its dock on Bayshore Boulevard. (YMKG.)

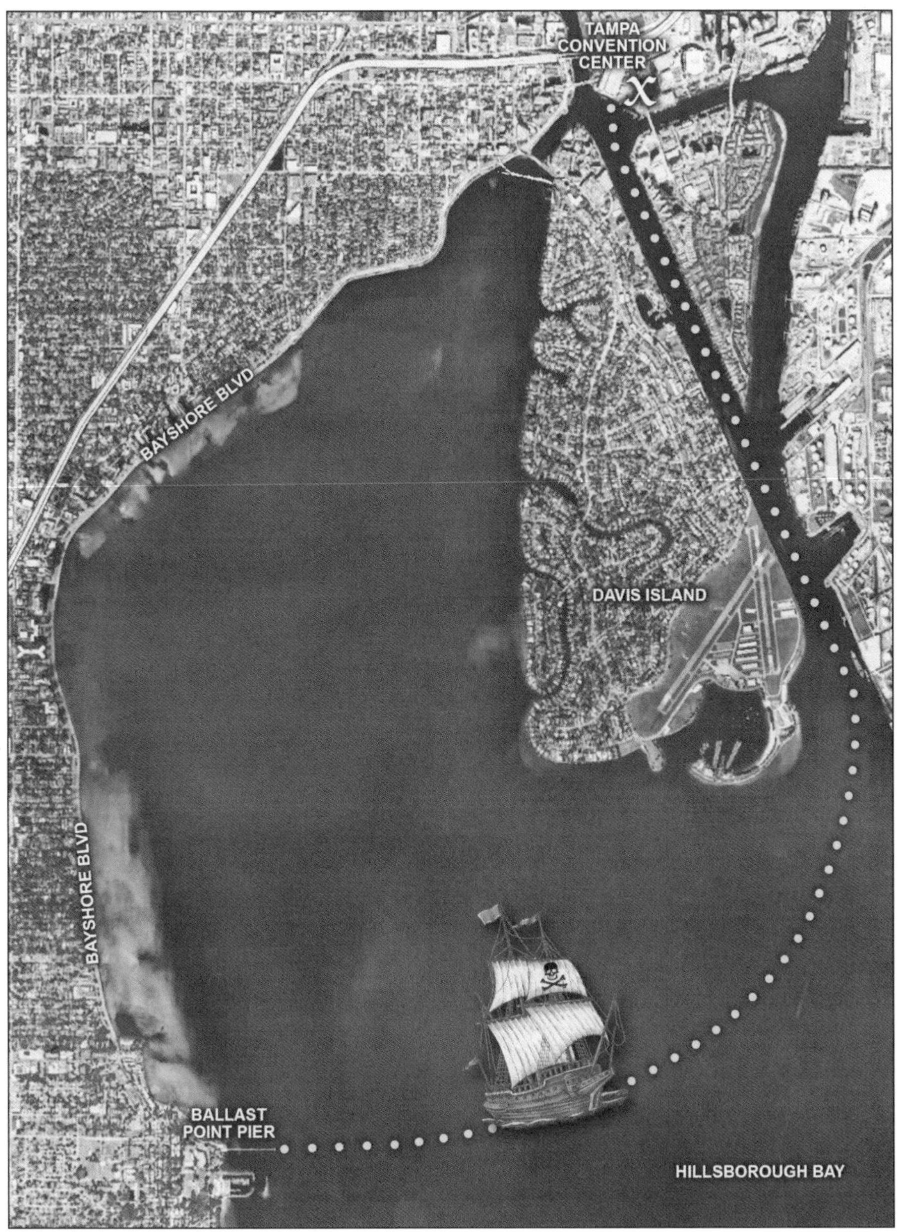

To begin the Gasparilla invasion of Tampa, Ye Mystic Krewe of Gasparilla pirates board *José Gasparilla* at the Ballast Point Pier, adjacent to the Tampa Yacht and Country Club. The voyage crosses Hillsborough Bay then turns north up the Seddon Channel after passing the Davis Island Yacht Club and Peter O. Knight Airport on its way to the Tampa Convention Center. The ship's trip from Ballast Point Pier to downtown Tampa usually takes approximately one hour and fifteen minutes and is accompanied by a flotilla of hundreds of private boats. After docking at the Tampa Convention Center, Ye Mystic Krewe of Gasparilla pirates disembark and are transported to the top of the parade route that begins at Bay to Bay and Bayshore Boulevards. As seen on the left side of the diagram above, Bayshore Boulevard runs along the western shore of Hillsborough Bay. Also paralleling the road and located directly on the water is a four-and-a-half-mile long sidewalk, the longest continuous sidewalk in the world and the ideal location for the Gasparilla parade. (YMKG.)

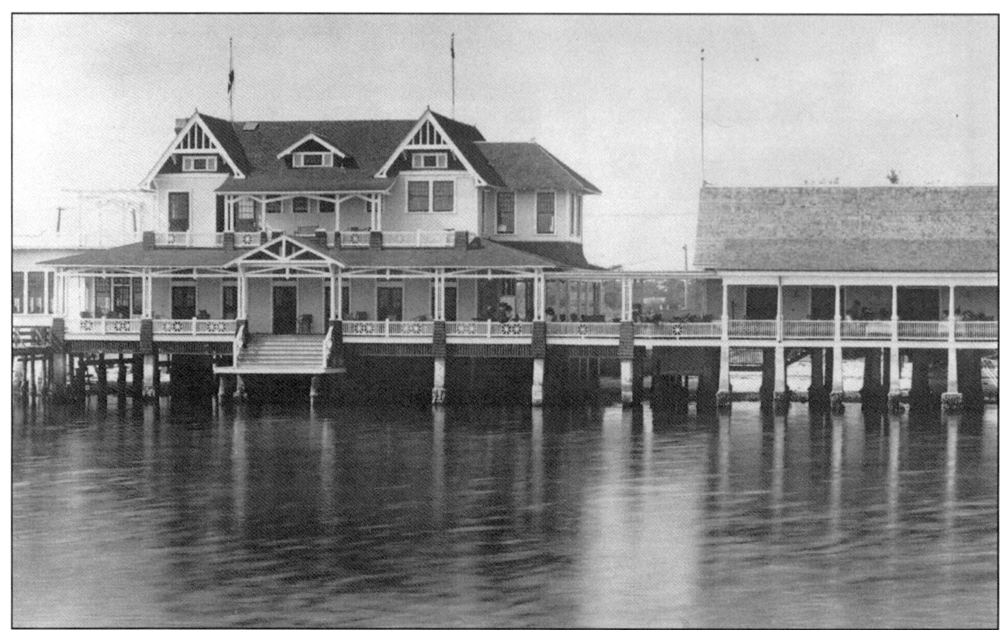

In addition to serving as the launch point for *José Gasparilla*, Ye Mystic Krewe of Gasparilla holds several annual member events at the Tampa Yacht and Country Club. The original club, seen here in 1927, was constructed in 1905 and was destroyed by fire on December 14, 1929. The second building was constructed in 1930 and burned down in December 1938. The present clubhouse was constructed in 1939. (THCPL.)

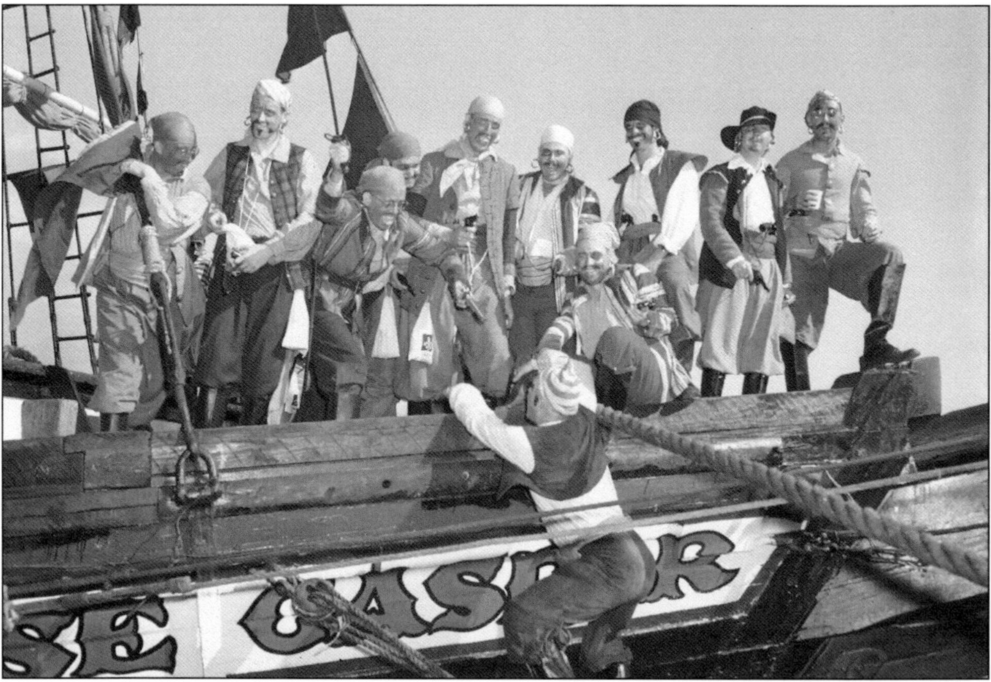

Pictured here are a group of 1940s members of Ye Mystic Krewe of Gasparilla climbing aboard *José Gaspar* as they begin to set sail for the invasion. Built in 1902, this ship was originally named *William Bisbee* until it was transformed into a pirate ship for the 1938 invasion. (USF.)

Five pirates pose for a picture at the bow of *José Gaspar* as they begin the one-hour fifteen-minute voyage across Hillsborough Bay to downtown Tampa. The sail is a celebration in itself, filled with music, drinks, and spirited camaraderie as krewe members prepare for the city's takeover. Outfitted in costumes and makeup depicting rugged deckhands or regal captains, each pirate brings their own personal flair to Gasparilla. (USF.)

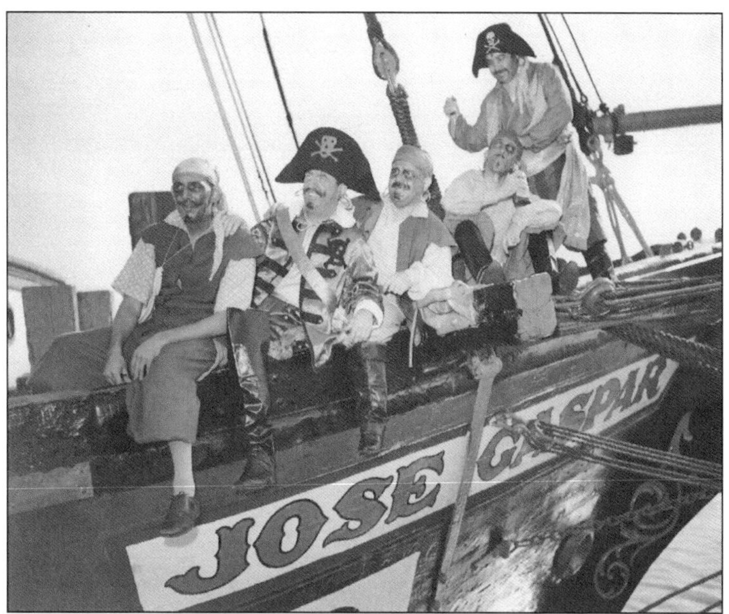

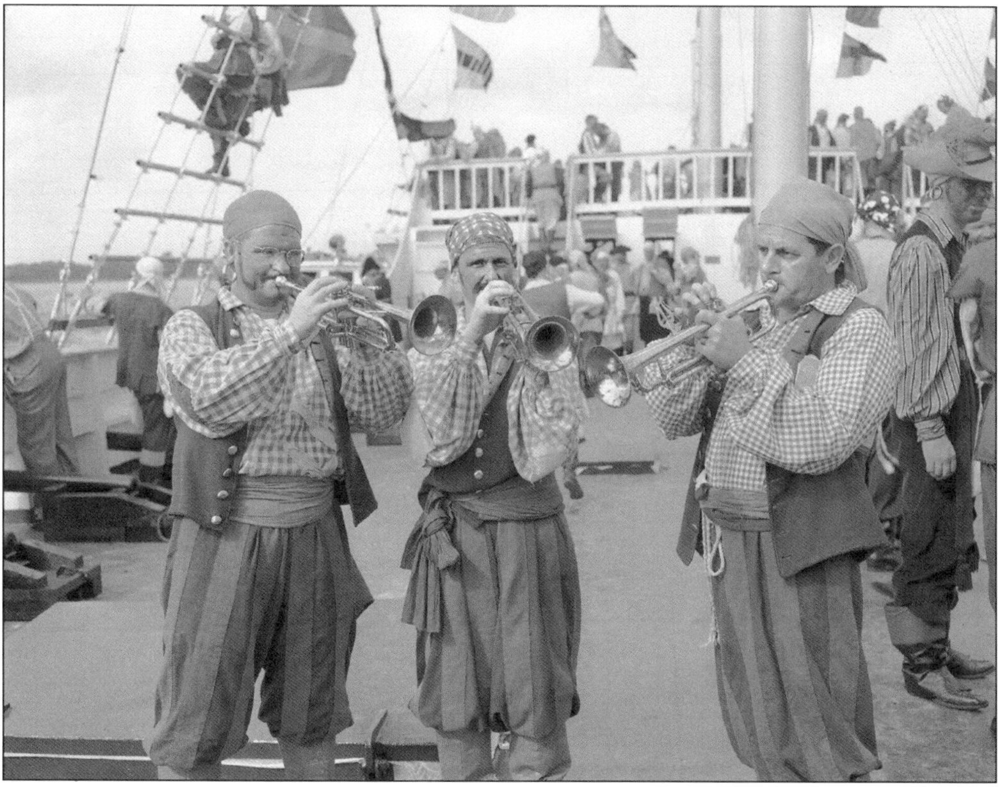

Musicians aboard *José Gasparilla* perform during the 1956 invasion, using live music to rally the krewe as they sail into downtown Tampa. Music has long played a central role in the tradition, helping to energize the pirates and set the rhythm for the flotilla's approach. The trumpet trio pictured here is one of many groups that have helped turn the voyage into a moving celebration before the city's official surrender. (SAF.)

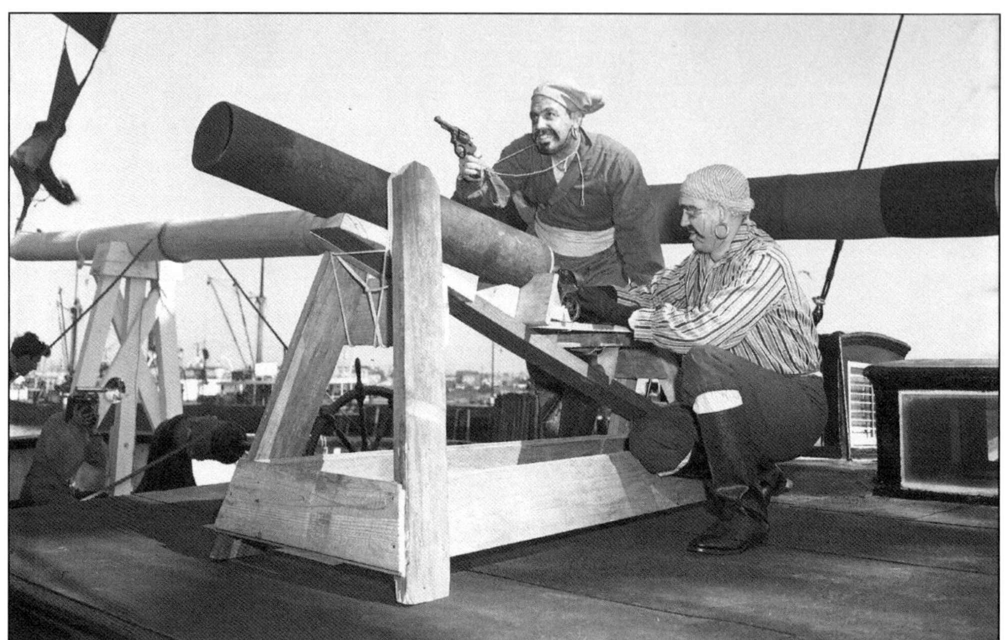

Pirates prepare to make some noise aboard *José Gaspar* during the 1947 Gasparilla invasion. Adding a theatrical component to the invasion, cannon blasts and pistol fire have long been part of the pageantry, announcing the ship's arrival into downtown Tampa. While the fireworks are all in good fun, safety remains paramount, and every Ye Mystic Krewe of Gasparilla member who handles blank-firing weapons is required to complete gun safety training. The 10-gauge salute cannons are fired by a smaller group of members that comprise the Gunner's Guild who have received additional gun safety training. Above, the pirates are firing the salute cannon with the barrel inside of a fake cannon to enhance the theatrical aspect. (Above, THCPL; below, SAF.)

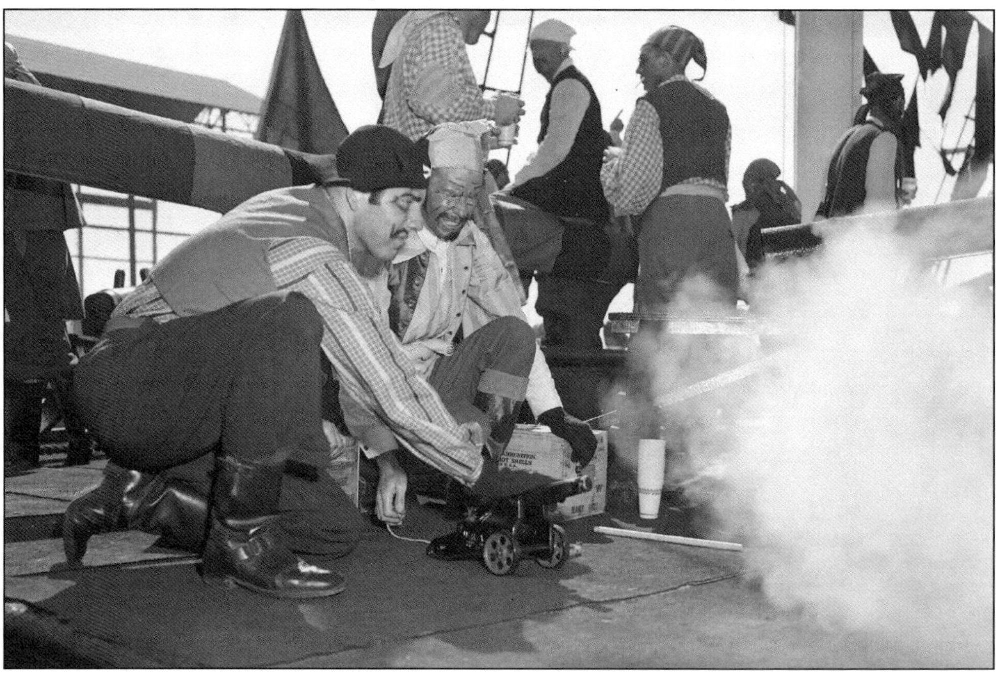

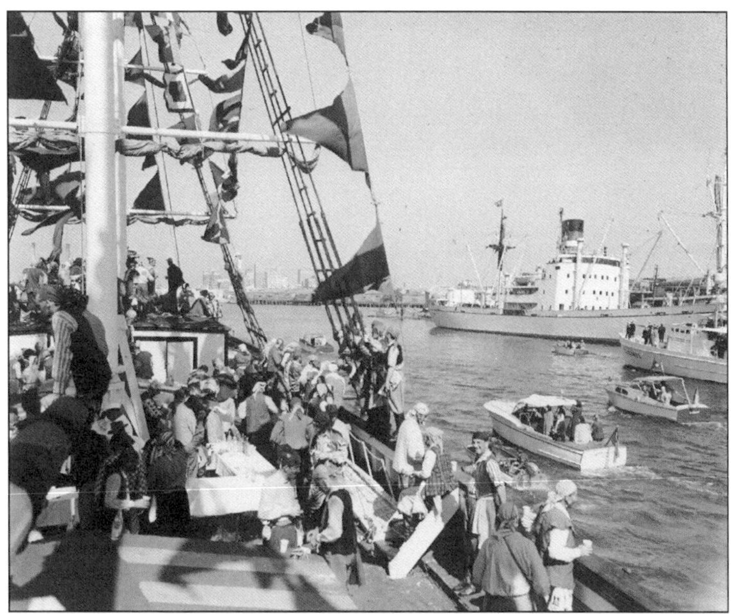

Ye Mystic Krewe of Gasparilla members are pictured aboard *José Gaspar* in 1951 as the ship approaches downtown Tampa, seen in the background. Surrounded by escort boats and the city's working port, the moment captures the blend of tradition and spectacle that has defined Gasparilla for generations. (THCPL.)

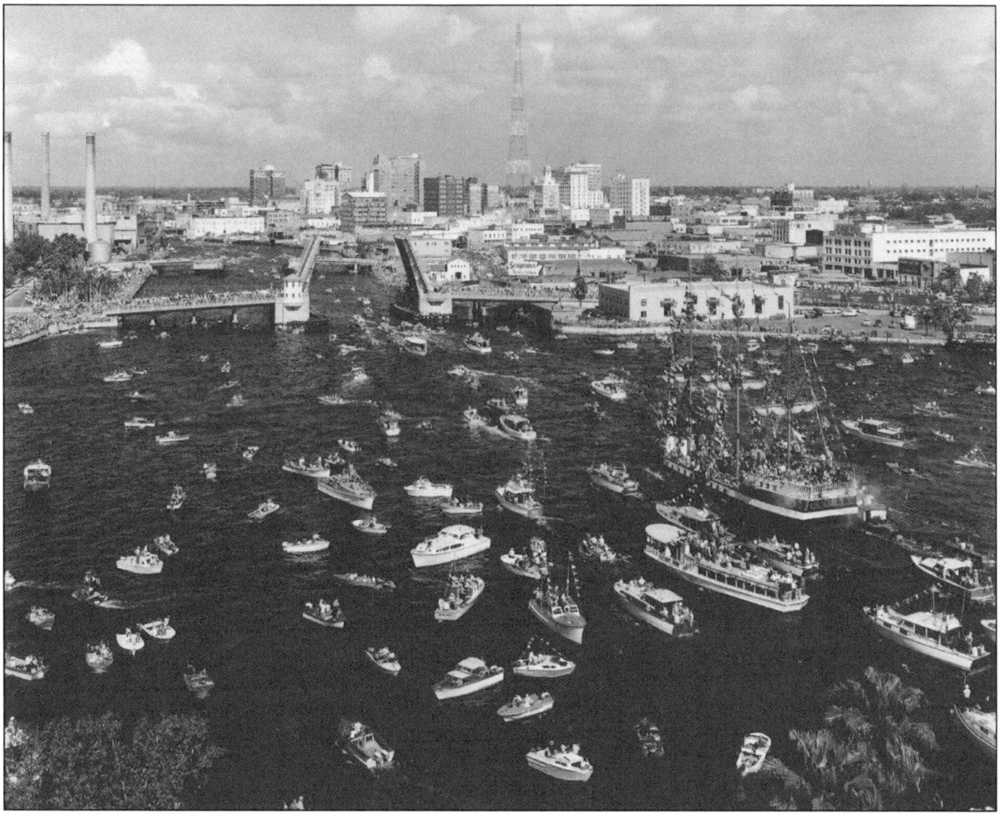

Since the first Gasparilla ship invasion in 1911, pirates of Ye Mystic Krewe of Gasparilla have never sailed alone. As seen in this 1959 photograph, a flotilla of boats accompanies the ship as it makes its way toward the open Platt Street Bridge into downtown Tampa. This boat parade has become one of the largest flotillas in the country, with hundreds of boats participating each year. (THCPL.)

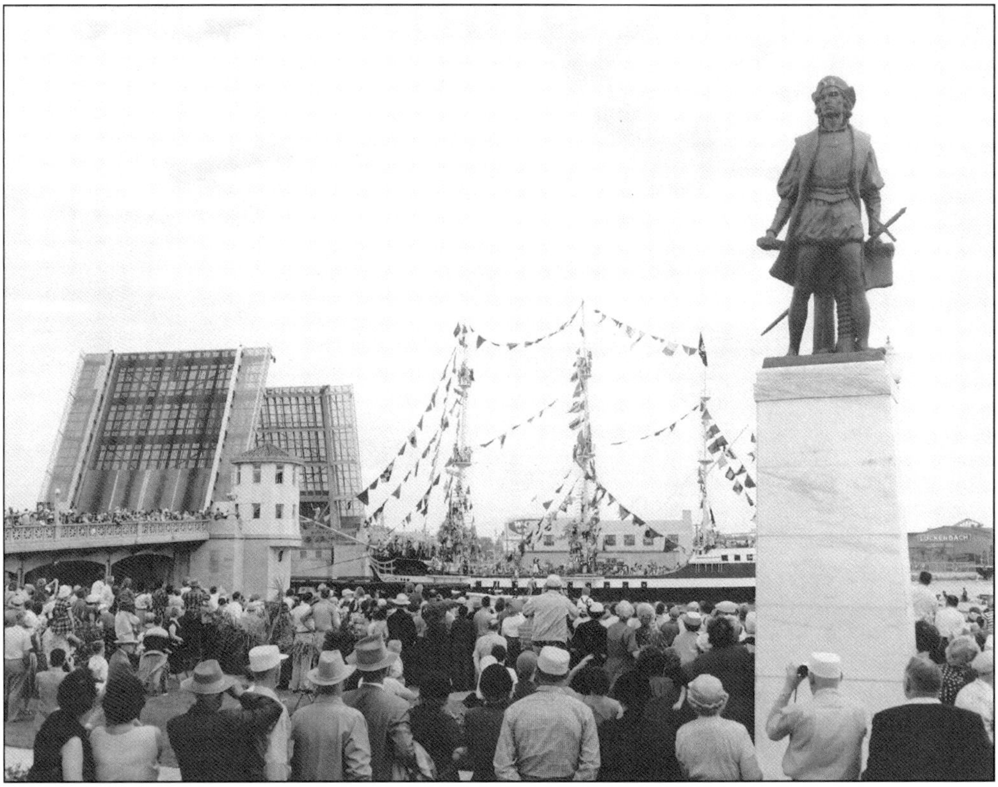

This 1956 photograph shows well-dressed spectators gathered along Bayshore Boulevard to watch *José Gasparilla* maneuver through the narrow Platt Street Bridge. Watching the ship pass through one of the several bridges on the Hillsborough River was always a crowd favorite. A statue of Christopher Columbus is on the right side of the picture. (THCPL.)

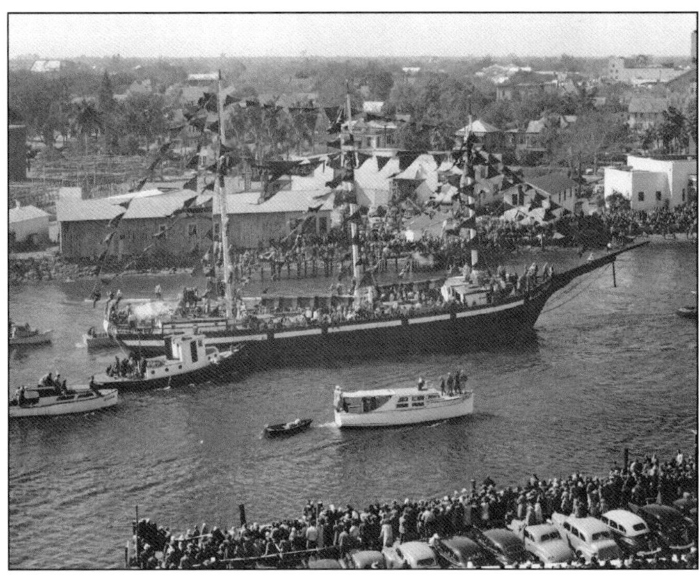

José Gaspar sails past Tampa's Knight & Wall warehouse, once part of a thriving industrial riverfront. In the early 20th century, this stretch of the Hillsborough River was lined with shipping docks, freight depots, and working rail lines. Although parks, museums, and event spaces have replaced the warehouses, the base of the river at the Tampa Convention Center remains the stage of Tampa's longest-running tradition. (THCPL.)

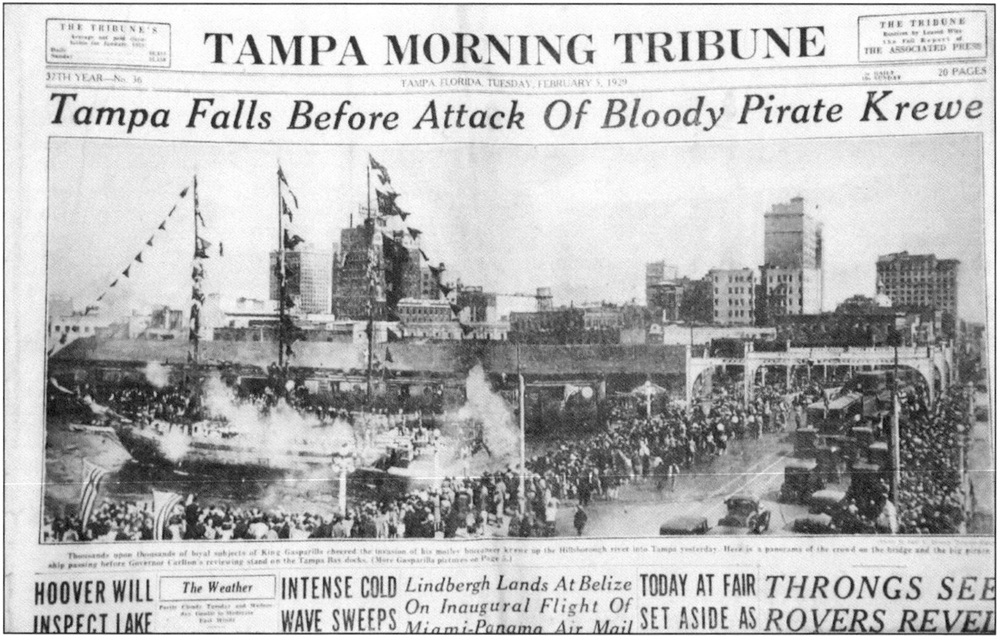

TAMPA MORNING TRIBUNE

37TH YEAR—No. 36 | TAMPA, FLORIDA, TUESDAY, FEBRUARY 5, 1929 | 20 PAGES

Tampa Falls Before Attack Of Bloody Pirate Krewe

HOOVER WILL INSPECT LAKE

The Weather

INTENSE COLD WAVE SWEEPS

Lindbergh Lands At Belize On Inaugural Flight Of Miami-Panama Air Mail

TODAY AT FAIR SET ASIDE AS

THRONGS SEE ROVERS REVEL

The front page of the February 5, 1929, *Tampa Morning Tribune* captures the theatrical triumph of Ye Mystic Krewe of Gasparilla's annual invasion above. "Pirates Capture City in Dazzling Sun!" is a more subdued headline in the February 5, 1957, edition below. Heralding the start of Tampa's beloved Pirate Festival Week, the newspaper's special edition celebrated the spectacle of costumed buccaneers, decorated ships, and festive crowds that turned the city into a stage for swashbuckling pageantry. Prior to the advent of social media, newspapers were the primary source of information and photographs of Gasparilla. Looking at the morning paper the day after a Gasparilla invasion was always popular, as parade-goers would scan the photographs to possibly get a glimpse of themselves. (Both, YMKG.)

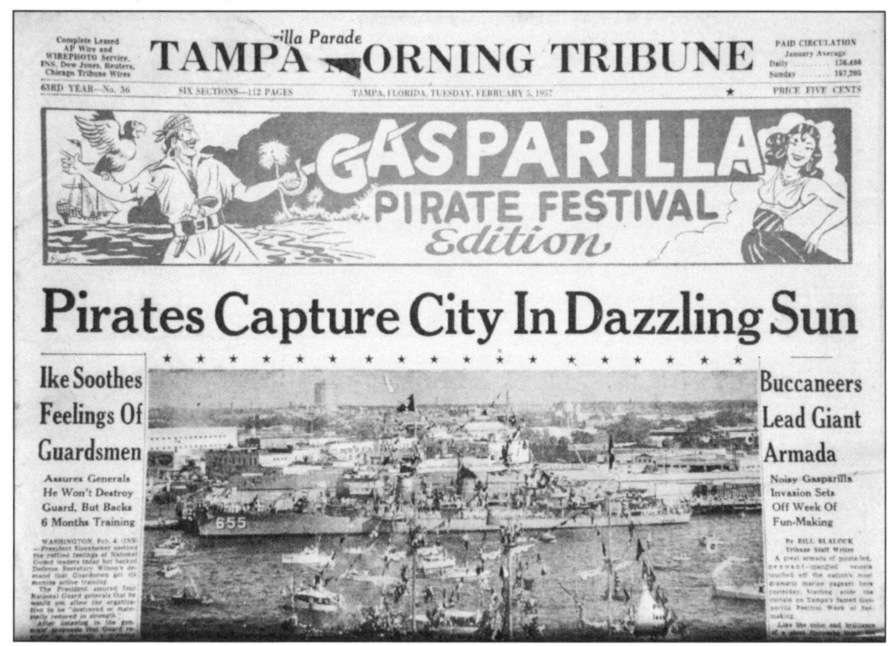

Complete Leased AP Wire and WIREPHOTO Service, INS, Dow Jones, Reuters, Chicago Tribune Wires

TAMPA MORNING TRIBUNE

PAID CIRCULATION January Average Daily 136,486 Sunday 157,205

63RD YEAR—No. 36 | SIX SECTIONS—112 PAGES | TAMPA, FLORIDA, TUESDAY, FEBRUARY 5, 1957 | PRICE FIVE CENTS

GASPARILLA PIRATE FESTIVAL Edition

Pirates Capture City In Dazzling Sun

Ike Soothes Feelings Of Guardsmen

Assures Generals He Won't Destroy Guard, But Backs 6 Months Training

WASHINGTON, Feb. 4 (INS)—President Eisenhower soothed the ruffled feelings of National Guard leaders today but backed Defense Secretary Wilson's demand that Guardsmen get six months active training.

The President assured four National Guard generals that he would not allow the organization to be "destroyed or materially reduced in strength."

Buccaneers Lead Giant Armada

Noisy Gasparilla Invasion Sets Off Week Of Fun-Making

By BILL BLALOCK
Tribune Staff Writer

A great armada of pirate-led, pennant-spangled vessels touched off the nation's most dramatic marine pageant here yesterday, blasting aside the curtain on Tampa's famed Gasparilla Festival Week of fun-making.

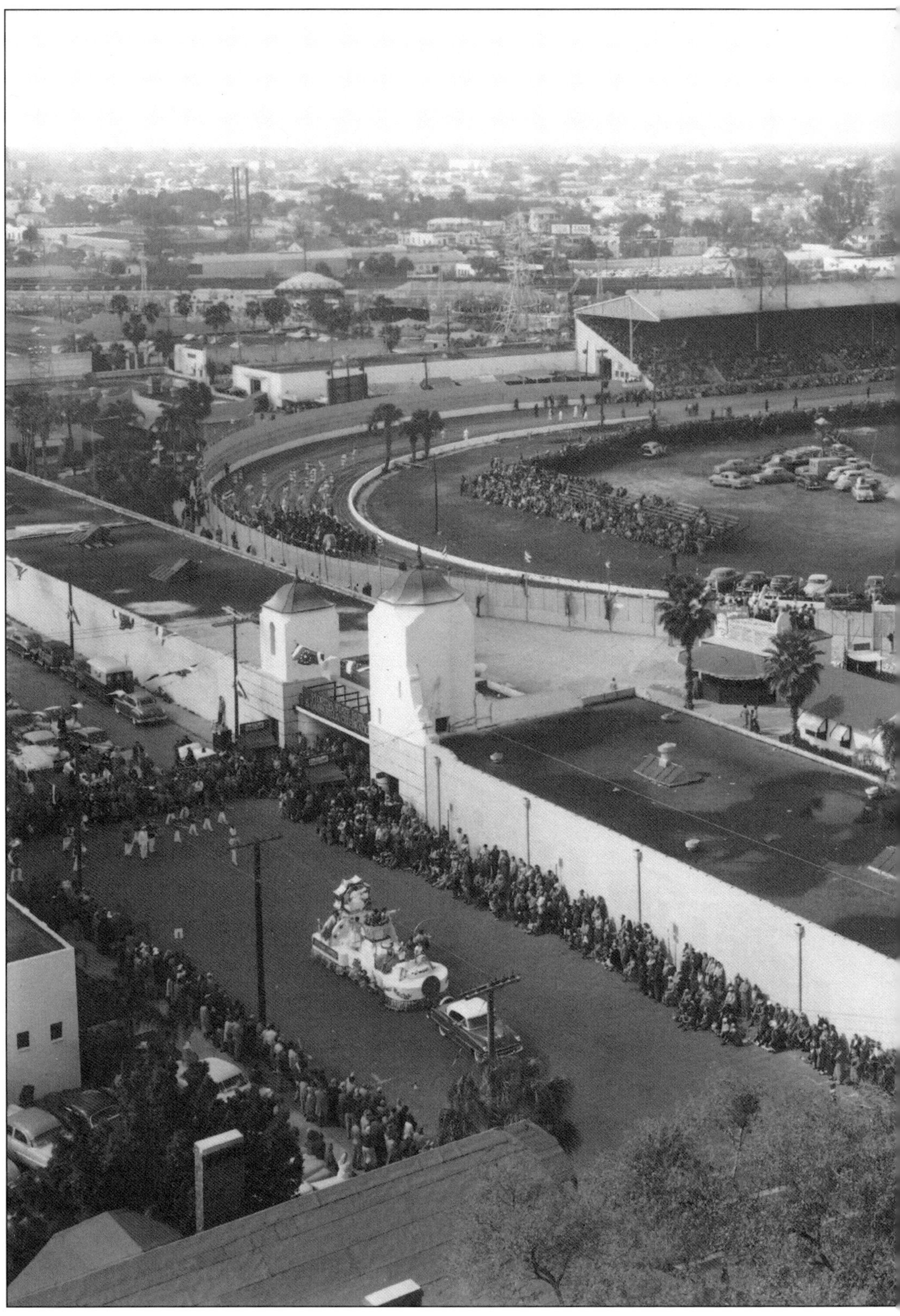

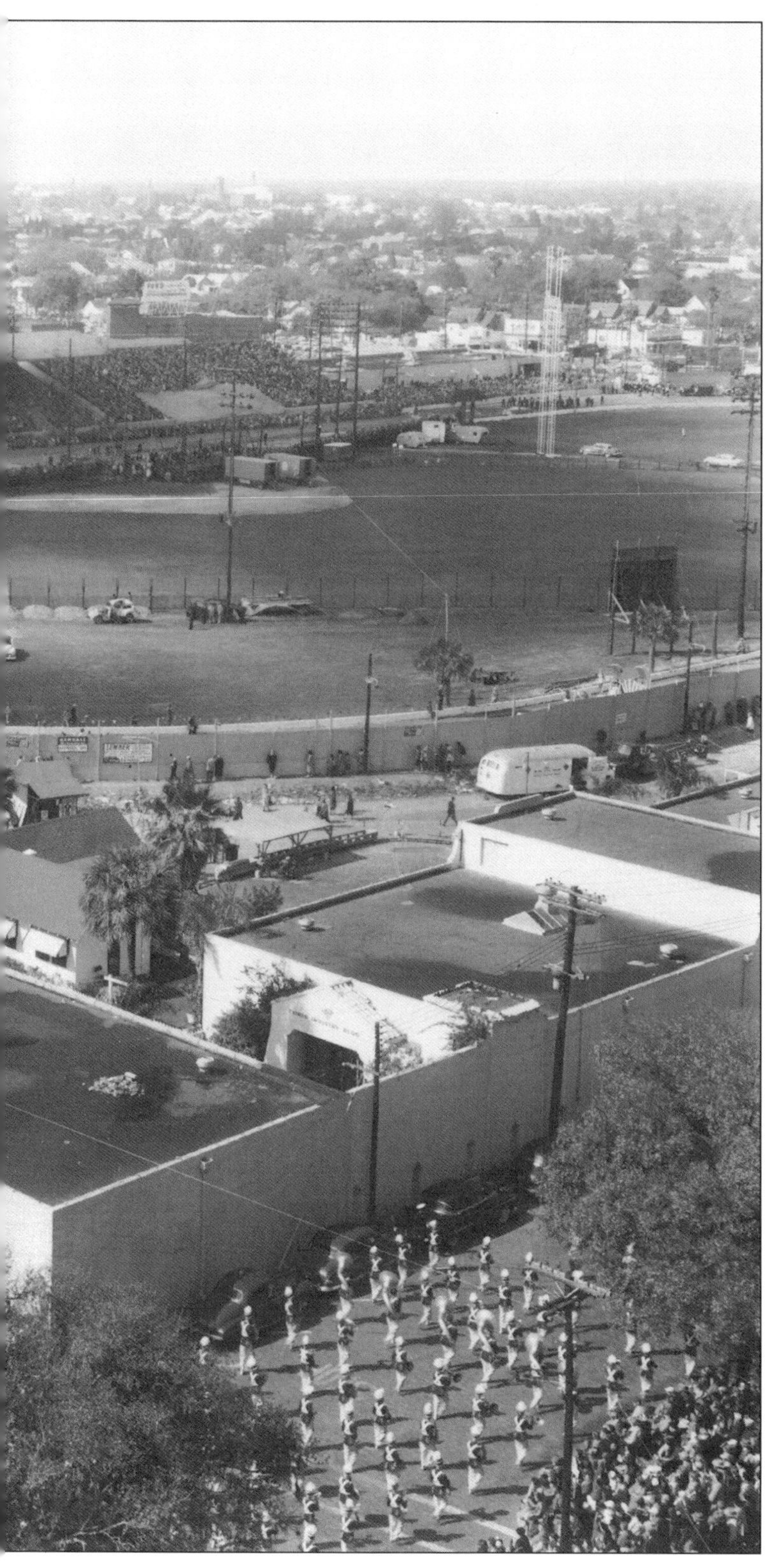

Ye Mystic Krewe of Gasparilla marked its 50th anniversary in 1954. A grand invasion and parade were staged at the Florida State Fairgrounds near Plant Park and the historic Tampa Bay Hotel, now Plant Hall at the University of Tampa. In this scene, civic organizations, elaborate floats, and marching bands gather, ready to join the city's most anticipated celebration. For many years, the parade ended by circling the track in front of the grandstands. While early parades ended at the fairgrounds, today's festivities stretch along Bayshore Boulevard, ending downtown and drawing crowds in the hundreds of thousands for Tampa's iconic pirate celebration. (THCPL.)

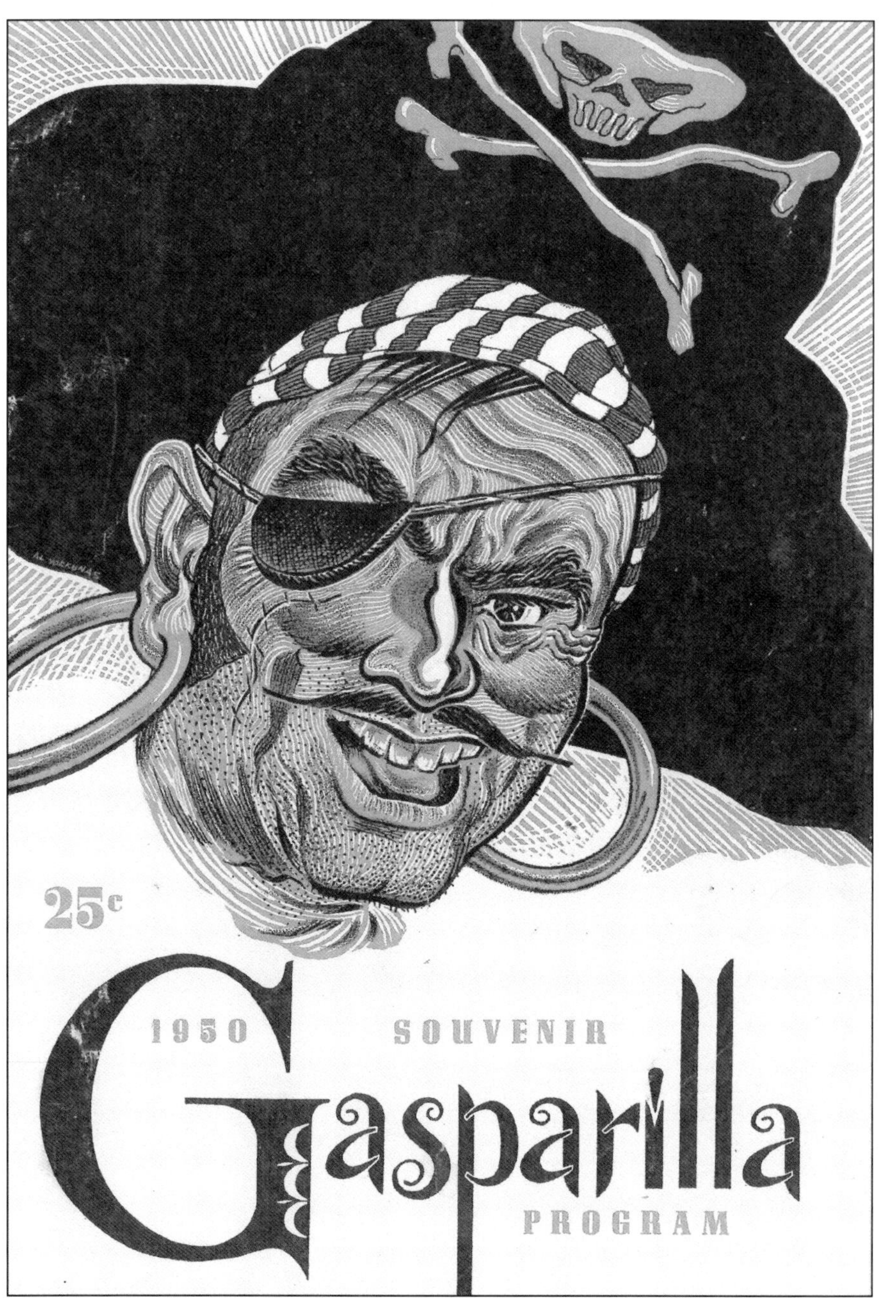

This 25¢ souvenir program from the 1950 Gasparilla parade shows one of the many ways in which the pirate Gasparilla has been depicted through the years. At times, Gasparilla was depicted as jovial, while at other times, he was illustrated as cutthroat. These years of artwork have added to the lore of Gasparilla. The pirate became so associated with Tampa culture that artist Lamar Sparkman created the iconic "Bucco Bruce" in 1976 as the original logo for the new National Football League franchise Tampa Bay Buccaneers. These programs were very popular with local merchants, who ran special Gasparilla advertisements that would generate more customers. These illustrated programs, filled with event details and whimsical artwork, have since become cherished collector's items, chronicling the Gasparilla festival's theatrical history and civic pride. (YMKG.)

Five

Pirates on Parade

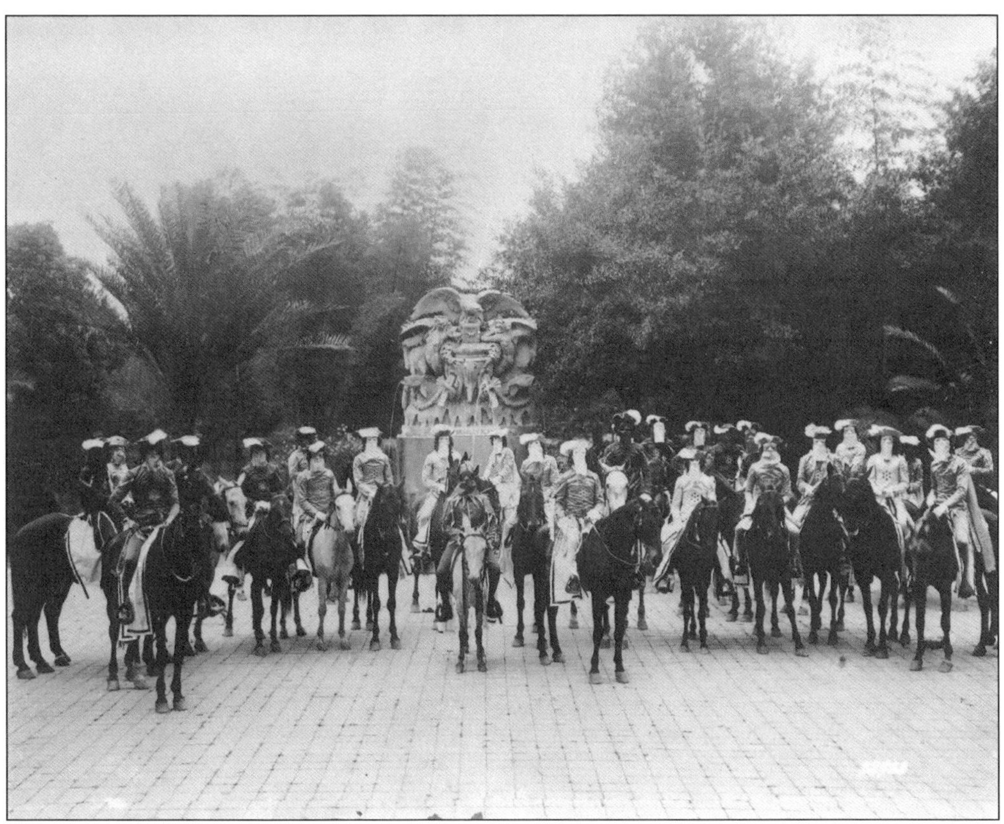

Ye Mystic Krewe of Gasparilla made its first parade appearance in the 1904 Floral Parade, one event of a weeklong May Festival celebration. Pictured here are 26 of the original 50 members who invaded Tampa on horseback and, according to the *Tampa Morning Tribune* account, "took for themselves a place among our ladies in the Floral Parade." This photograph was taken on the grounds of the Tampa Bay Hotel. (YMKG.)

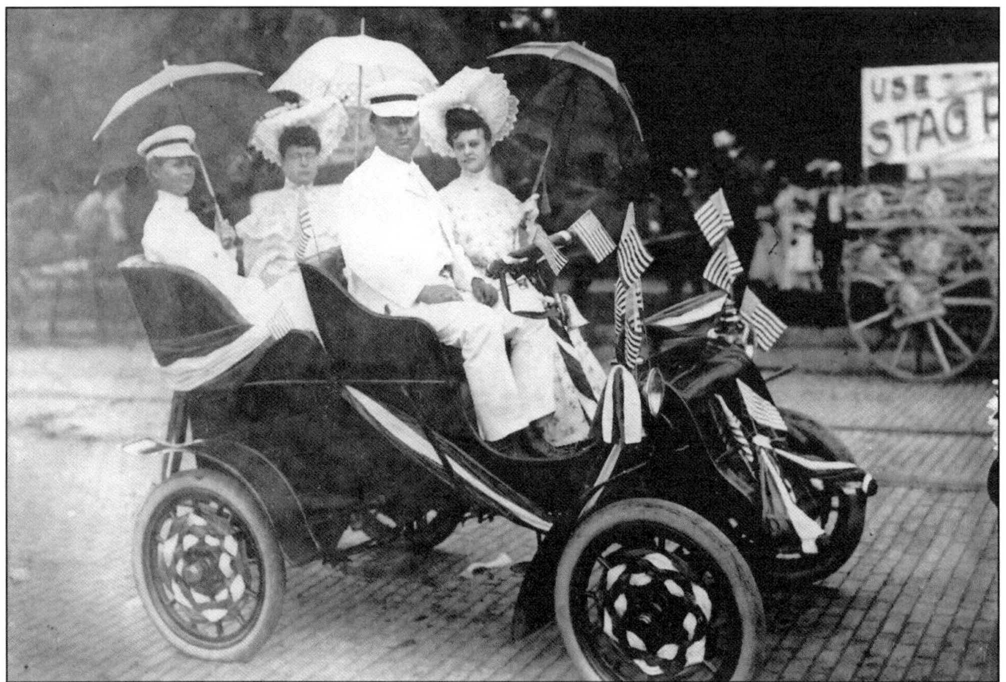

The automobile has always been a popular feature of Gasparilla parades. This 1904 photograph shows the first car to participate in the parade, and it was no doubt a novelty. It was noted by a disappointed *Tampa Morning Tribune* writer that only three of the city's 60 registered cars participated in the parade the following year. (THCPL.)

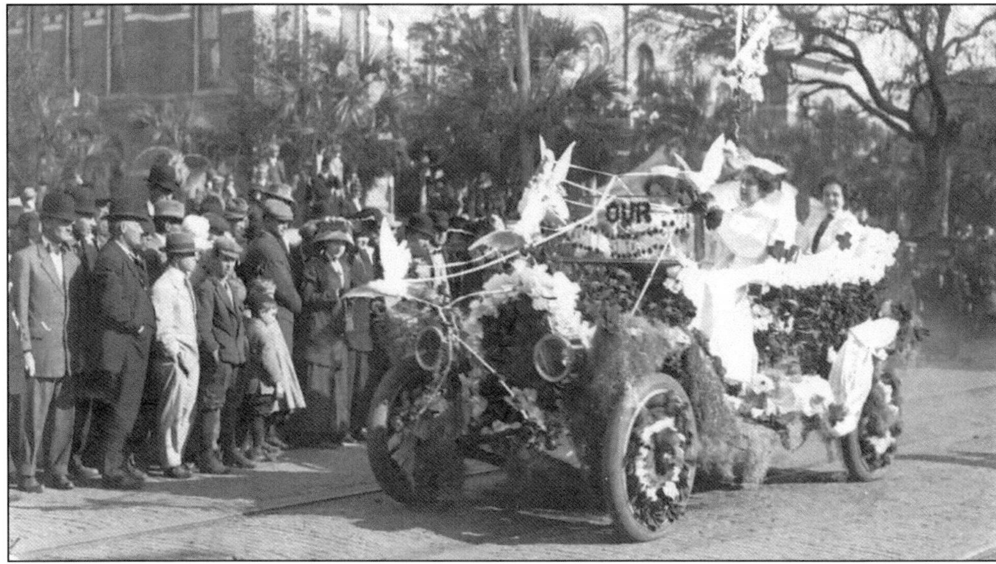

The automobile in this 1910 photograph clearly illustrates the connection to the parade's original theme as the May Festival Floral Parade. Early *Tampa Morning Tribune* accounts describe many of the floats as "decked in all the fragrant flora of the Flowery Land." The occupants of this vehicle all appear to be Red Cross nurses. The vehicle is draped with Spanish moss and covered in magnolia leaves, beautiful white flowers, and white doves, the symbol for peace often associated with the International Red Cross. (SAF.)

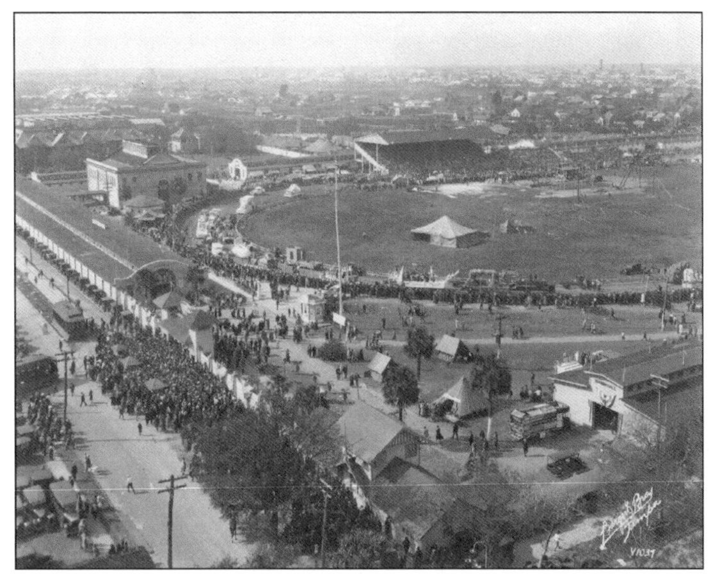

Originally created to feature horse races for the adjacent Tampa Bay Casino, a racetrack was converted to a half-mile dirt oval track in 1921 to take advantage of the rising popularity of automobile racing. The casino and racetrack were two of the most popular attractions at Henry B. Plant's Tampa Bay Hotel. In this photograph, the parade is circling the track in front of the grandstand as a crowd of people awaits entry into the celebration. (THCPL.)

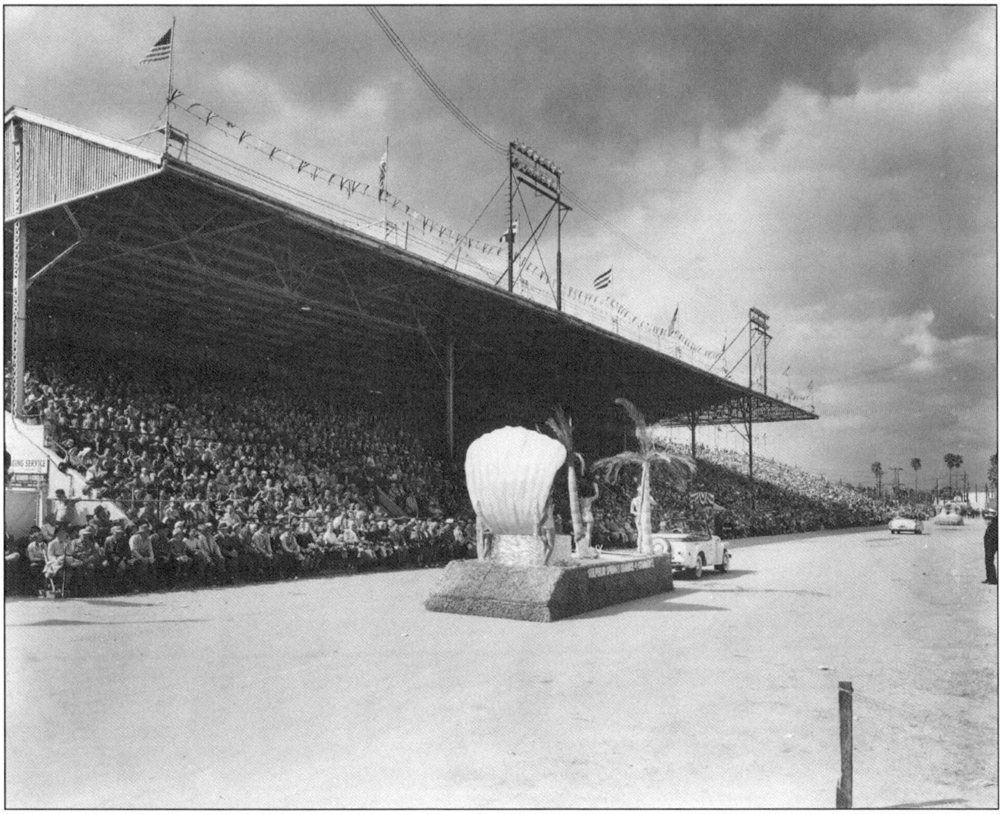

From 1905 through 1975, the Gasparilla parade concluded at the fairgrounds, located on North Boulevard, now the site of the University of Tampa. As parade participants entered the fairgrounds, they would finish the parade with a lap around the racetrack past the reviewing stand. Beginning in 1906, parade judges would award prizes to the year's top participants, including the award for best float. (THCPL.)

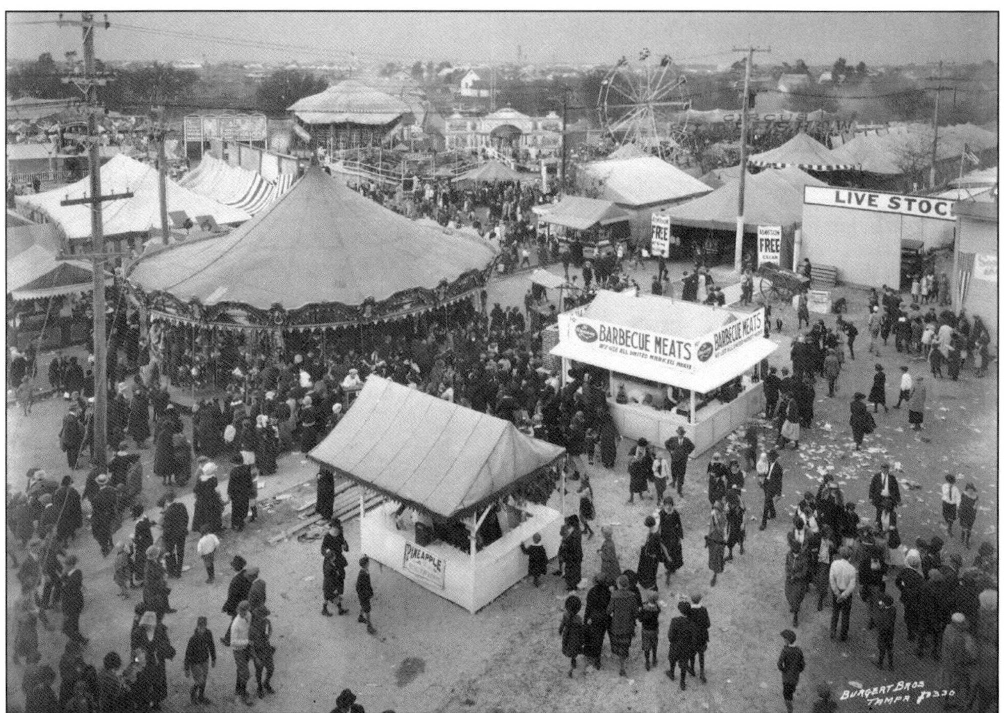

For 70 years, the Gasparilla parade ended at the fairgrounds on North Boulevard. Royal American Shows, which promoted itself as "The World's Largest Midway," operated the fair and came to Tampa for several weeks each year to coincide with the Gasparilla festival. This photograph shows the Florida State Fair midway in 1924. (THCPL.)

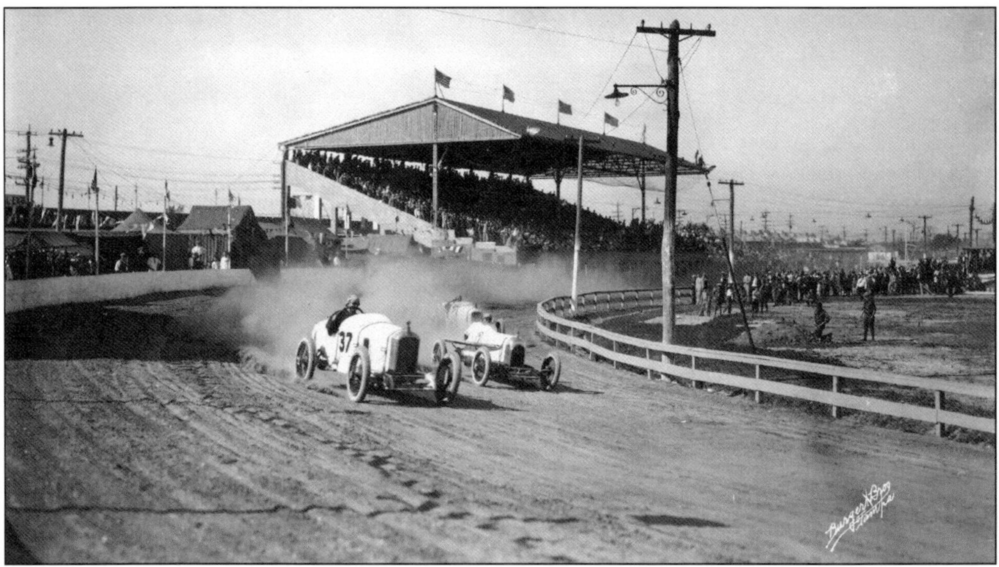

In addition to its popular midway and exhibits, the Florida State Fair also held car races on the dirt track. This 1927 photograph shows the sprint model of race car with its open driver's cockpit affording little protection. The cars were very loud and could be heard for several city blocks during the race. In the 1950s and 1960s, the cars became faster and would also occasionally throw dirt over the track walls when going around the turns. (SAF.)

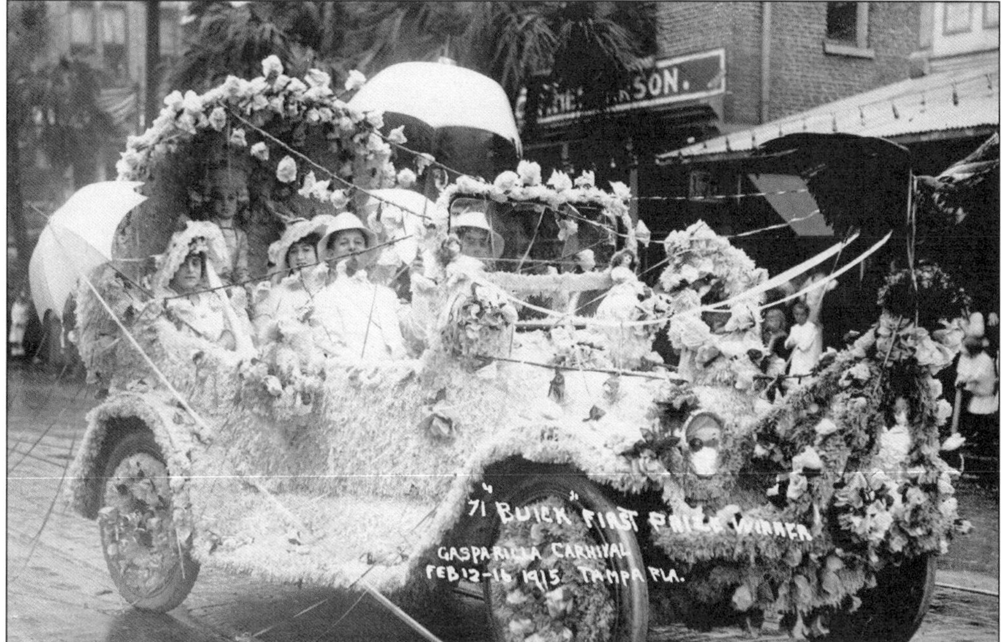

The 1915 first prize winner for the Gasparilla parade was a spectacular floral-festooned Buick, described by the *Tampa Morning Tribune* as "beautifully decked in white chrysanthemums." The flowers covered nearly every inch of the car, including its wheels. Even the women in the car are wearing hats adorned with flowers. Passengers in the car are carrying umbrellas for protection from the falling rain. (SAF.)

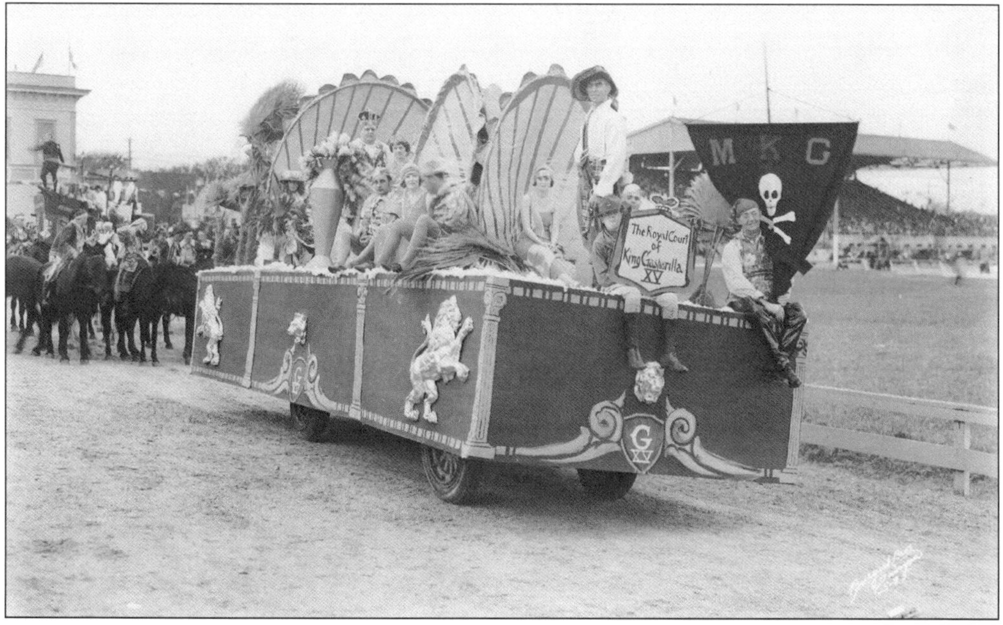

Traditionally, the Gasparilla Royal Float leads the parade. Seen here, the 1918 court of King Gasparilla XV, including the queen, maids, and courtiers, rides a final lap around the racetrack toward the reviewing stand, where the parade ends. Notice how the float is listing slightly to the left with the pitch of the racetrack. (THCPL.)

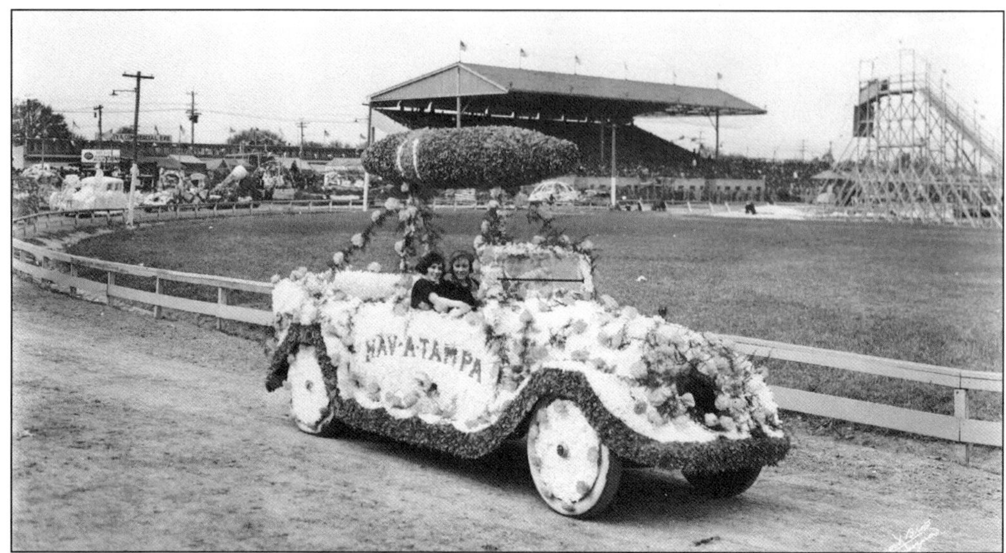

In the first several years of Gasparilla, there were as many as six different parades during the week for the city to enjoy. Initially, floats representing Tampa businesses were relegated to separate parades, but they eventually also participated in the Gasparilla parade. Shown here, a Hav-A-Tampa decorated car is an example of one of the many floats representing Ybor City's vibrant cigar industry. (SAF.)

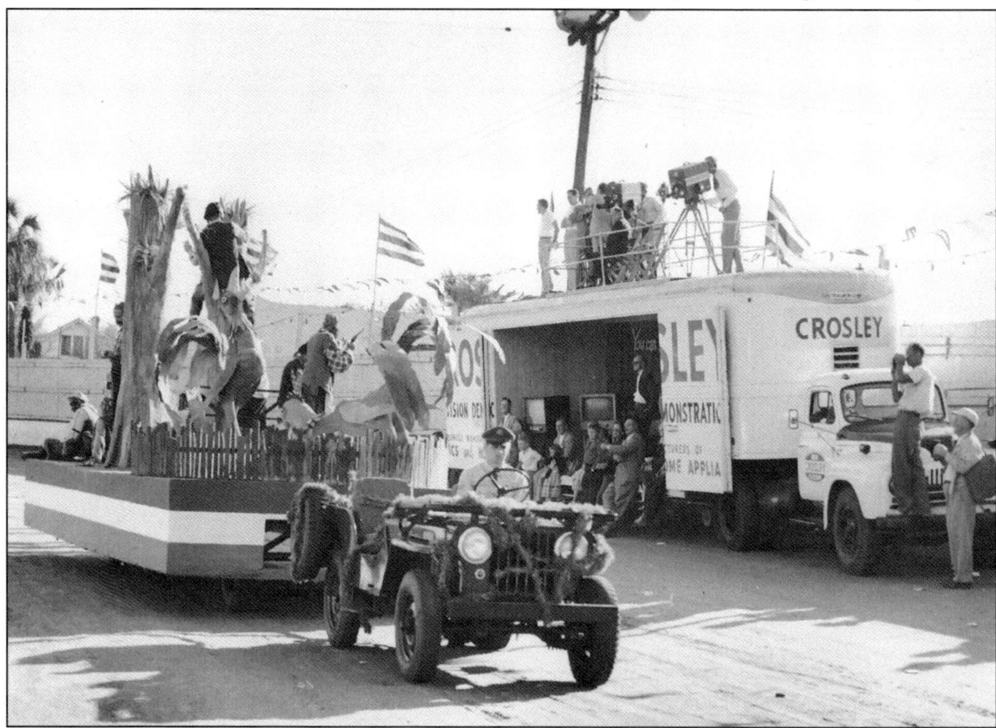

On Monday, February 14, 1955, the Gasparilla parade was televised for the first time on live television. Tampa's first television station, WFLA Channel 8, set up a mobile unit at the corner of Franklin and Washington Streets with one camera atop the mobile unit and a second on a 17-foot hoist. The transmission signal bounced off the Lykes Brothers building then the Knight & Wall building en route to the tower. Viewers from Fort Myers to Orlando enjoyed a perfect picture. (YMKG.)

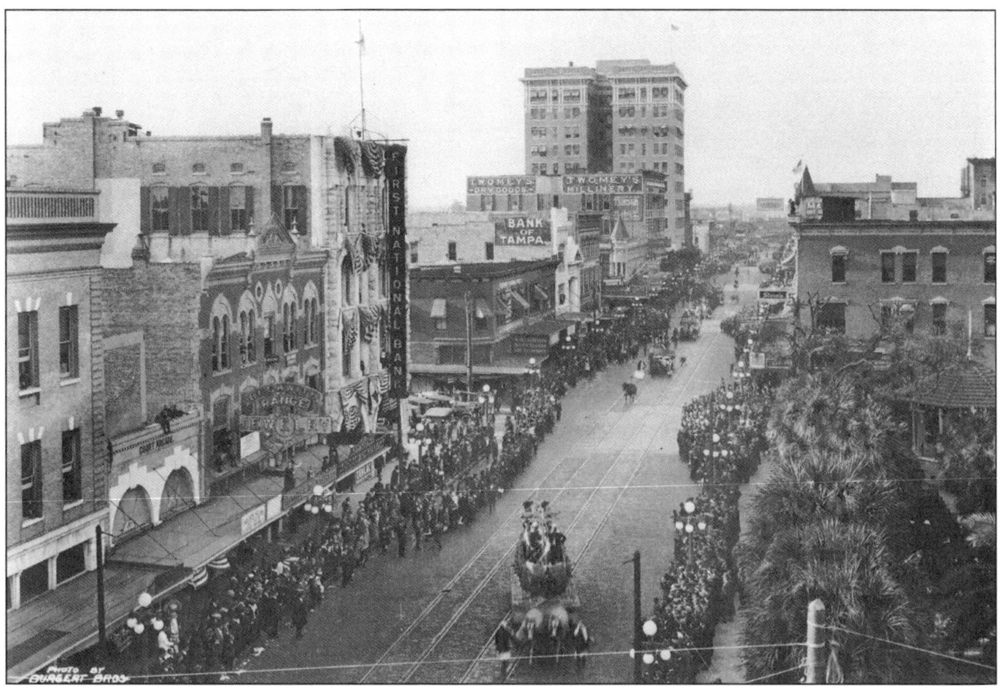

The Gasparilla parade route has always included portions of downtown Tampa. For many years, the parade began downtown, where *José Gaspar* or *José Gasparilla* ended their voyage. For today's Gasparilla, after the ship lands at the Tampa Convention Center, Ye Mystic Krewe of Gasparilla pirates are transported to the beginning of the parade route on Bayshore Boulevard with the parade ending downtown. Above is an early Gasparilla parade traveling through downtown. Notice the well-dressed spectators as well as the Bank of Tampa and First National Bank buildings on the left. The photograph below, taken in 1924, also shows well-dressed spectators but now shows more automobiles lining the streets. Also notice the sign pointing to the fairgrounds. (Both, THCPL.)

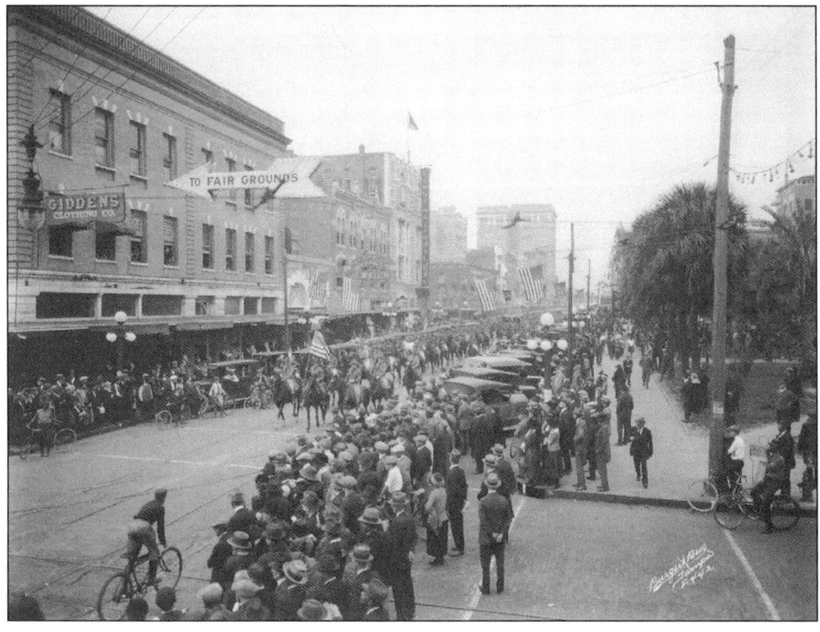

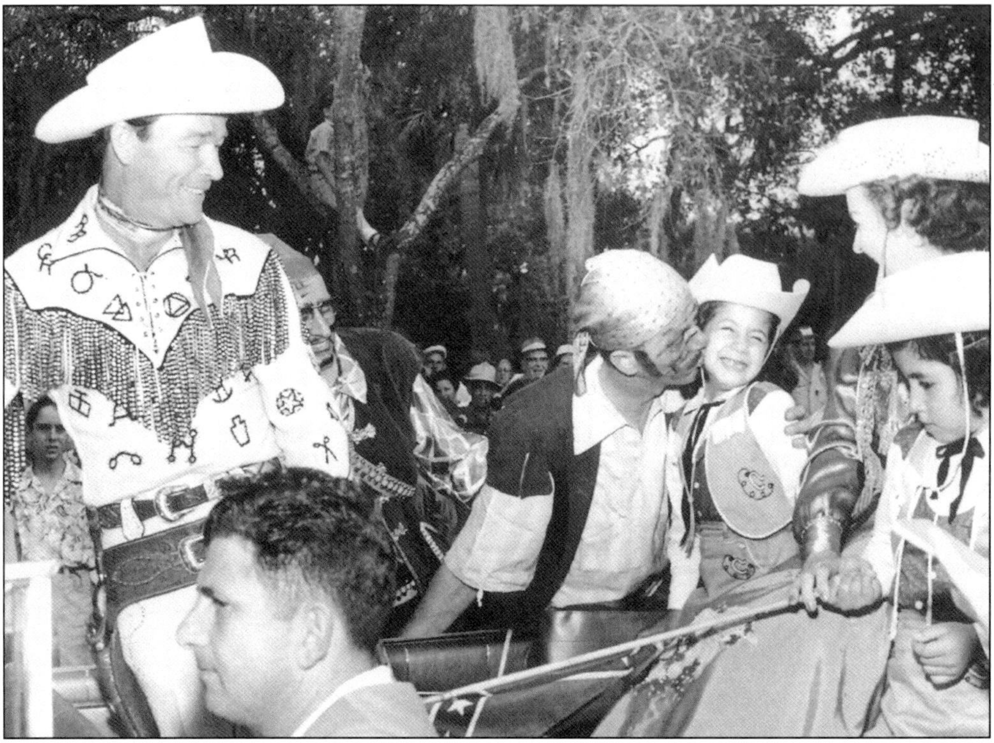

Gasparilla has a long history of having a grand marshal lead the parade. There have been politicians, professional athletes, war heroes, and world-famous actors. Above in 1959, singing cowboy Roy Rogers and his wife and fellow performer, Dale Evans, led the Gasparilla parade. Rogers appeared in almost 90 movies and, between 1951 and 1957, hosted *The Roy Rogers Show* on television. He often appeared with Dale Evans; his golden palomino horse, Trigger; and his German shepherd dog, Bullet. Rogers is best remembered for his signature song, "Happy Trails." The signage on the horse trailer, "Headed for the Florida State Fair," was great advertising for the event. (Both, YMKG.)

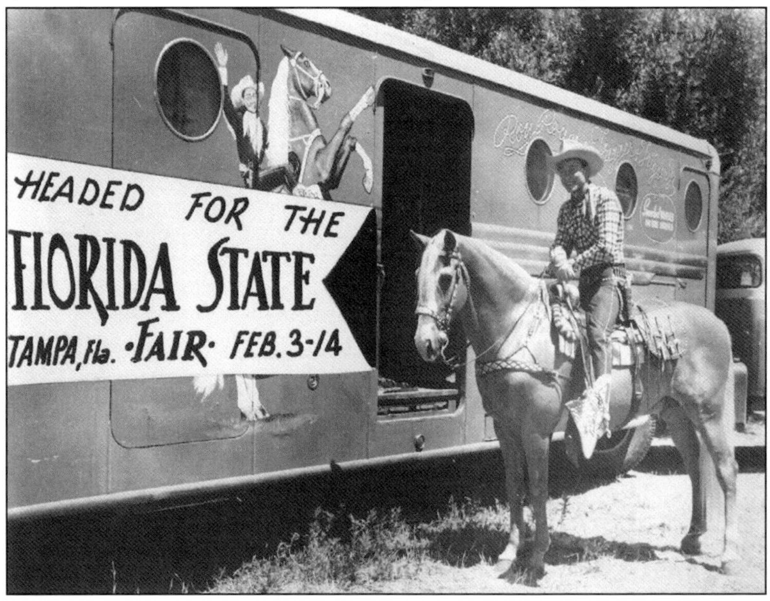

Through the years, talented artists have depicted the pirate Gasparilla in varying and interesting ways to create memorable program illustrations. In the 50¢ commemorative program at right from 1958, Gasparilla is depicted as a jovial pirate with a steady hand on the ship's wheel. In earlier drawings, such as the 1915 Gasparilla Carnival poster below, the maniacal cutthroat pirate is seen holding a bloody cutlass. By 1976, the pirate had become so associated with Tampa culture that artist Lamar Sparkman created the iconic "Bucco Bruce" as the original logo for the Tampa Bay Buccaneers. Sparkman's version was a dashing, swashbuckling pirate with a plumed hat and Errol Flynn good looks. (Both, YMKG.)

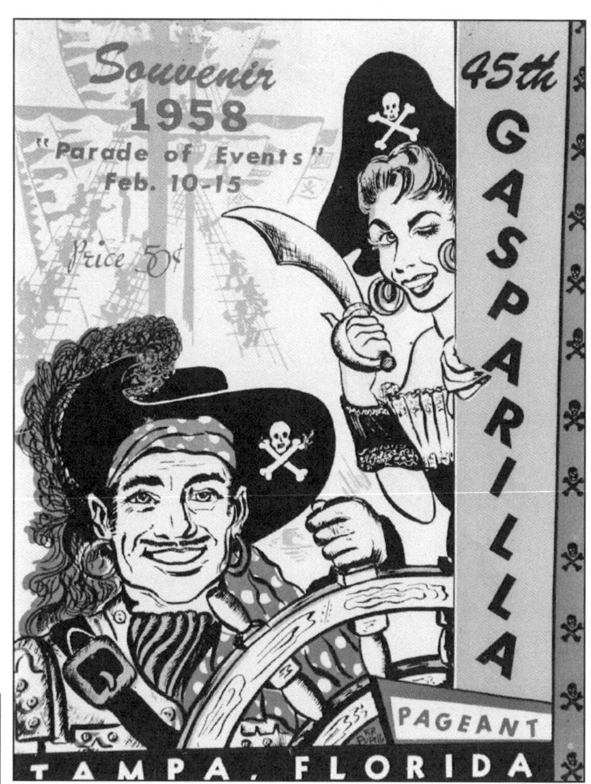

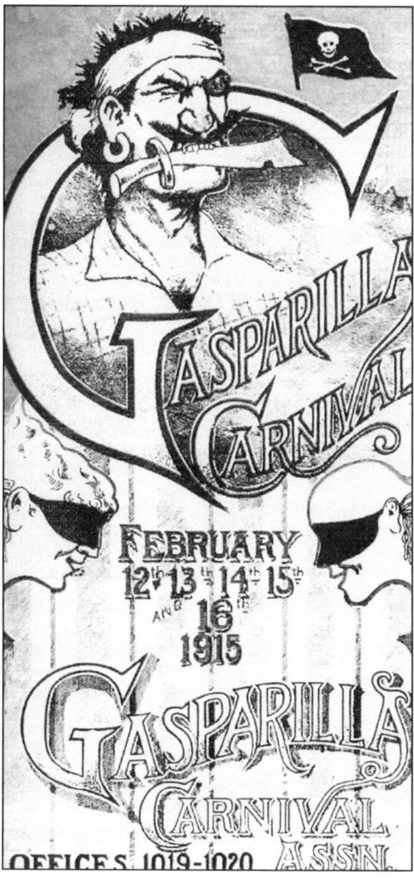

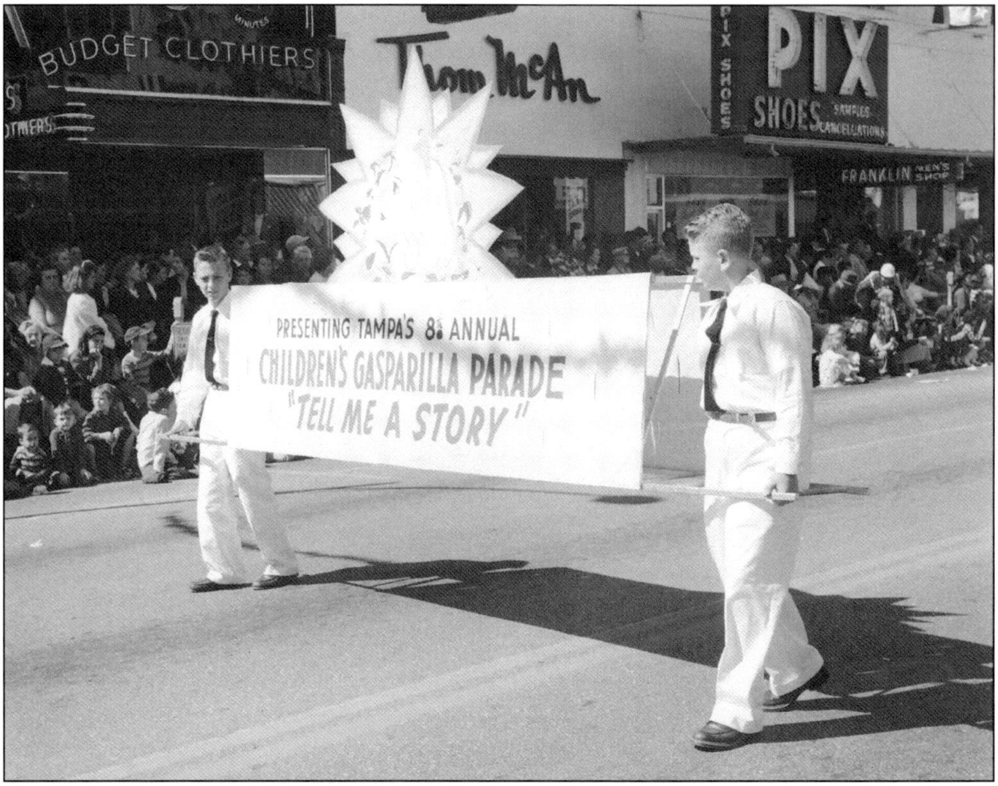

In 1947, Ye Mystic Krewe of Gasparilla began lending its name to the Children's Gasparilla Parade, now known as the Gasparilla Children's Parade. In early years, participation was limited to children. School marching bands, Scout troops, boys' and girls' clubs, and themed floats were typical of children's parade participants. Today's family-oriented Gasparilla Children's Parade ranks as the largest parade for children in the United States. (USF.)

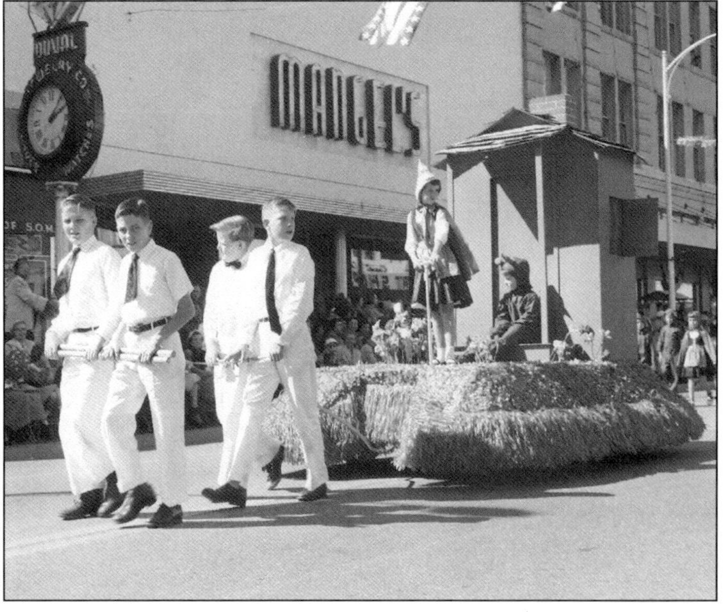

The eighth Children's Gasparilla Parade, themed "Tell Me a Story," featured floats depicting scenes from beloved children's stories. This float features characters from "Little Red Riding Hood." Other floats included "Aladdin's Lamp," "Jack and the Beanstalk," "The Tortoise and the Hare," "Three Blind Mice," "Peter Pan," Knights of the Round Table," "Jonah and the Whale," "Humpty Dumpty," and "Rapunzel." (USF.)

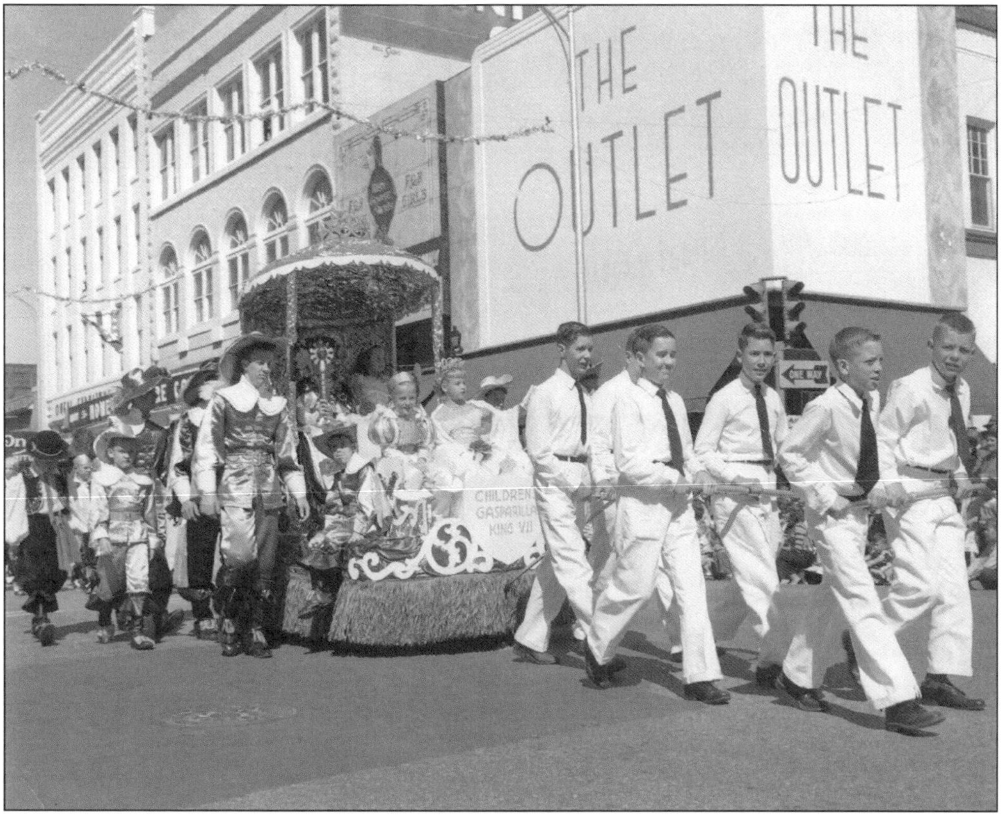

In this photograph, the Children's Gasparilla Parade's royal court float is hand drawn by young boys dressed in all white with black ties. Older children towed all of the floats in the early years of the Children's Gasparilla Parade, while younger children dressed the parts of the parade theme. (USF.)

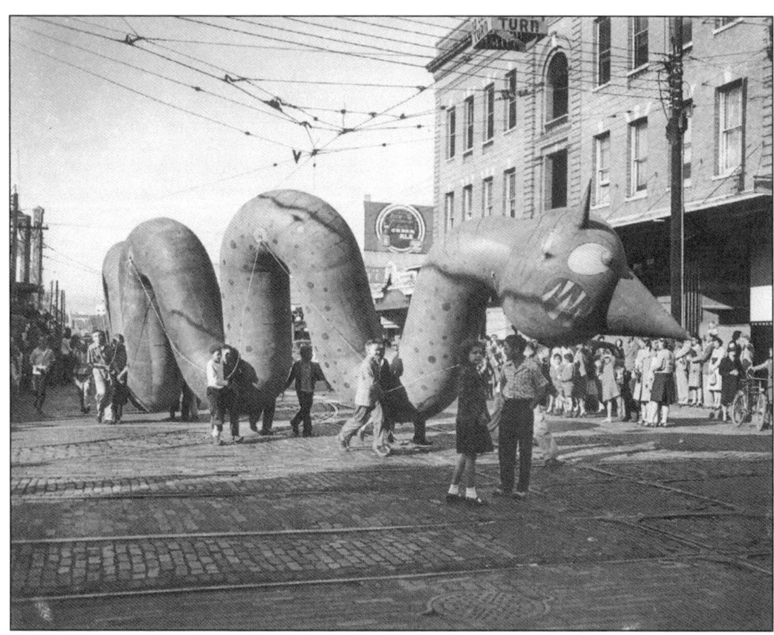

The fabulous sea monster was a great early example of an inflatable balloon float. Children carry the creature by the rope handles on each side, careful to keep the float from touching the electrified overhead lines of the Tampa streetcar system. Helium gas floated these great character balloons, allowing them to hover just above street level. (USF.)

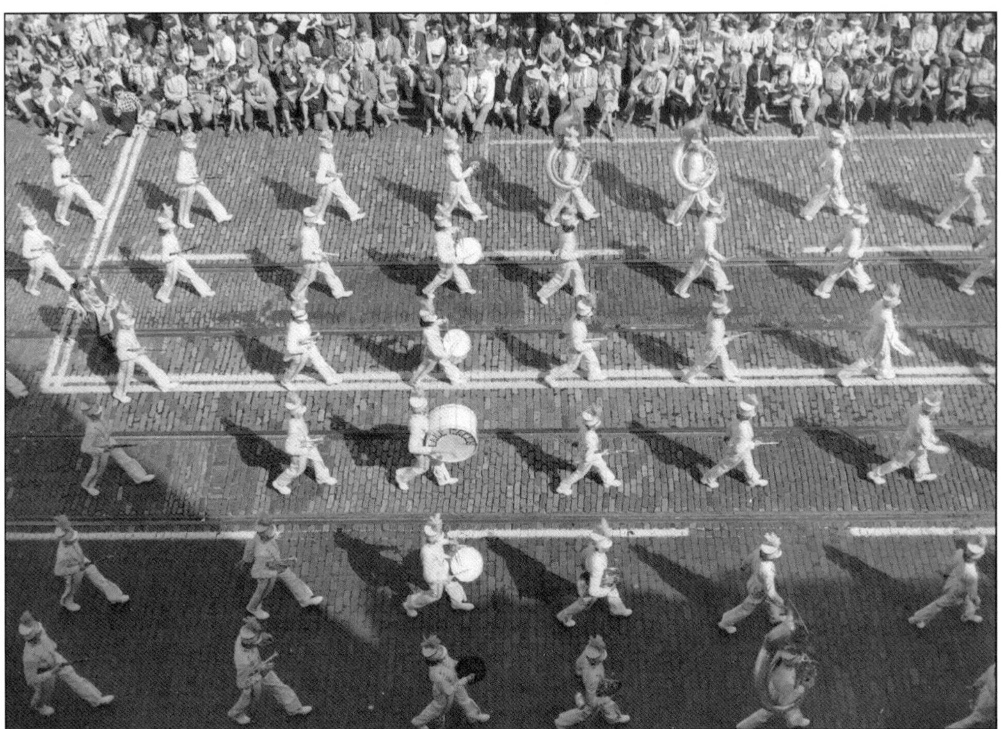

Beginning with the first Gasparilla parade, marching bands have been a popular fixture in the celebration, with groups coming from all parts of Florida to participate. The photograph above shows a full band marching in neat columns down the brick streets of downtown Tampa. Their ordered arrangement against the grid of bricks and traffic lines creates a beautiful composition. The photograph below shows the marching band from DeLand High School entertaining the crowd in front of the Exchange Bank on Franklin Street downtown with the iconic Tampa Theatre sign in view. Notice the letters spelling "DeLAND" displayed over the bells of the five giant sousaphones. Each year, numerous high schools send their bands to represent them in the Gasparilla parade. (Above, YMKG; below, SAF.)

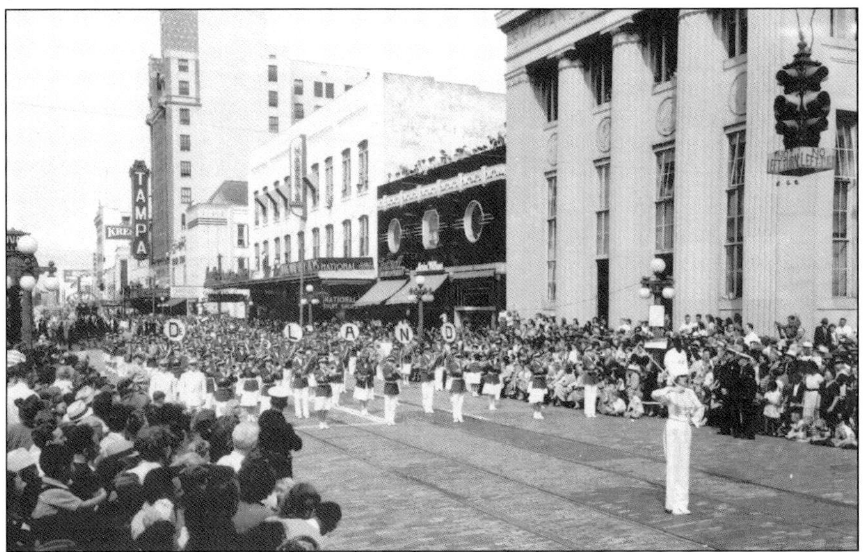

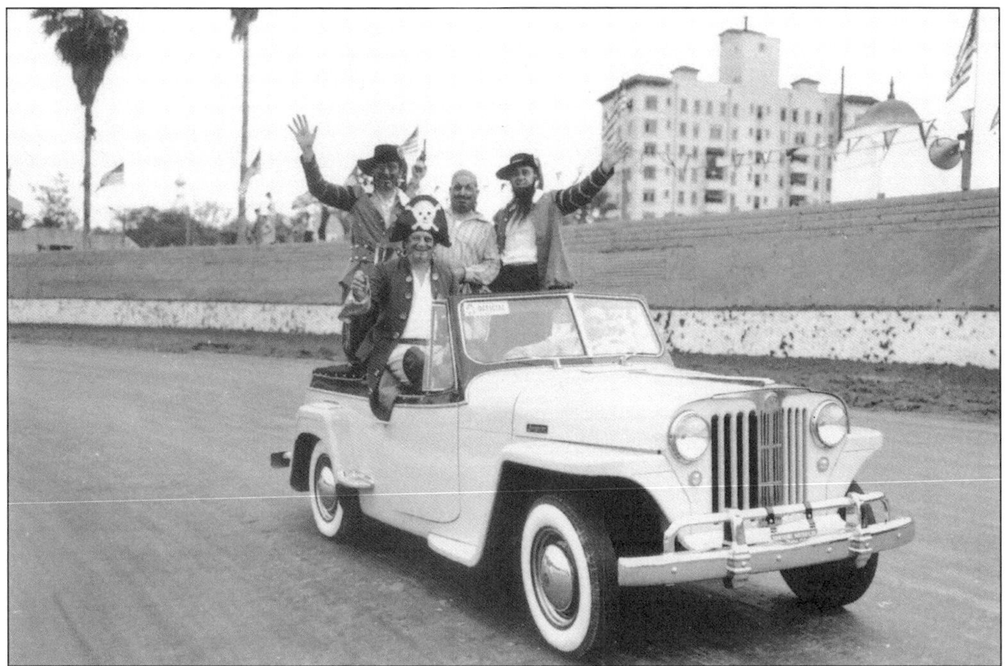

The automobile has always been prominently featured in the Gasparilla parade with local car dealerships displaying their latest models. The Jeep rose to icon status during World War II, when Willys-Overland produced the 4x4 light reconnaissance vehicle for the US Army. Following the war, Willys-Overland produced the wildly popular Jeepster for civilian use. Above, pirates of Ye Mystic Krewe of Gasparilla enjoy the parade in this 1949 Willys-Overland Jeepster phaeton. Mayors, governors, and other politicians, along with local dignitaries, traveled the parade route in the most stylish automobiles of the day. Below, the alcalde (mayor) of Ybor City waves from the back seat of a Buick LeSabre. (Above, USF; below, THCPL.)

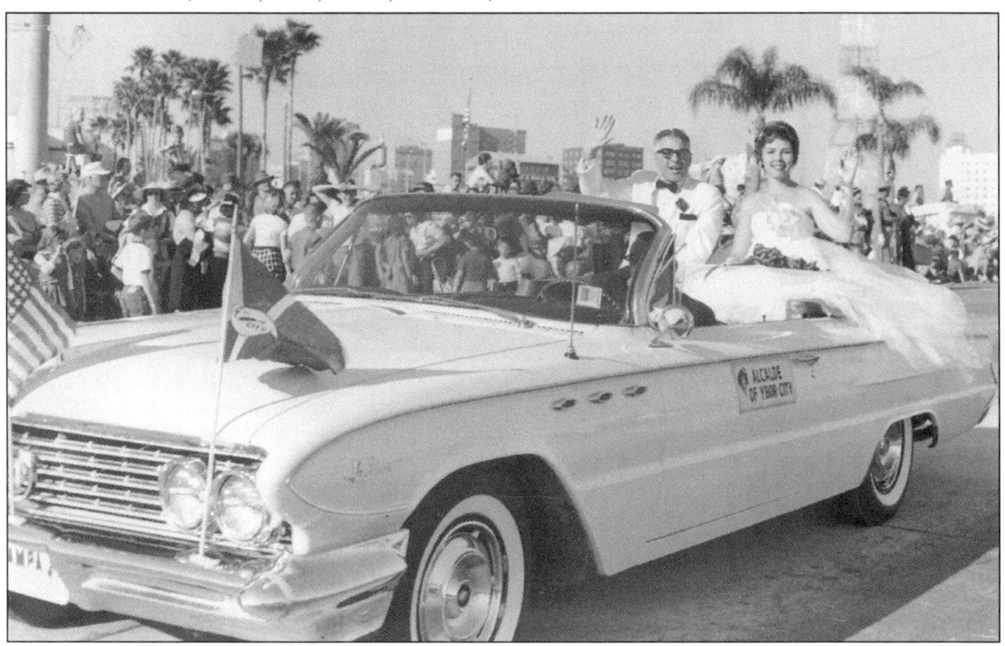

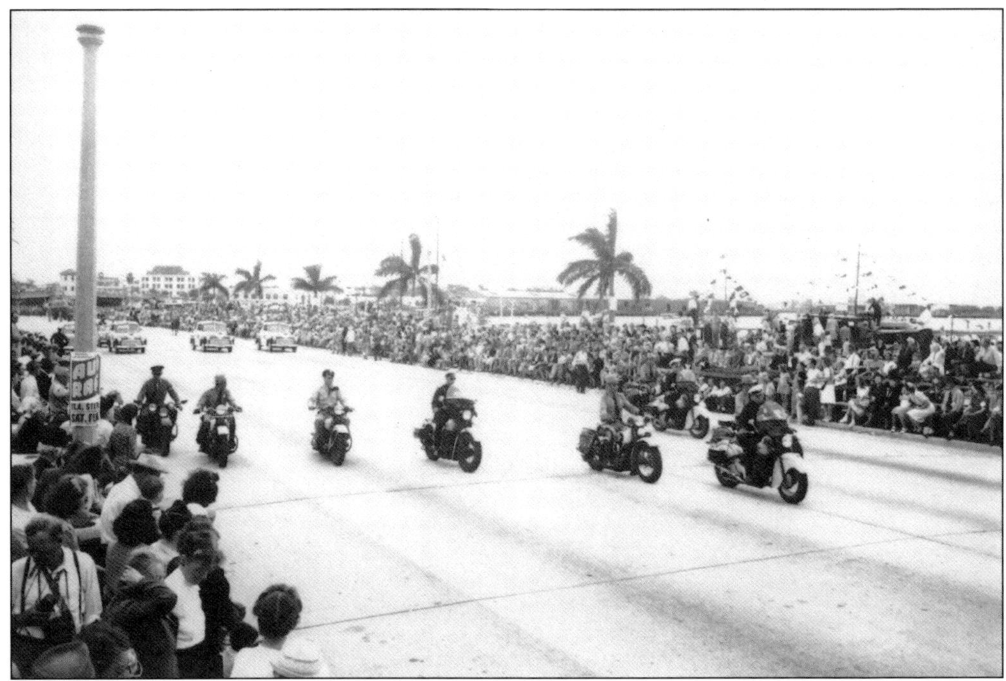

Beginning with the first parade, law enforcement has played a prominent role in Gasparilla, traditionally leading the event in the early years. Accounts from 1905 describe a mounted police force leading the parade from their rallying point in Ybor City. In later years, police motorcycles and cruisers replaced the horse. The rumbling troop of police motorcycles above would loudly announce the commencement of the parade. Below, four 1940s police cruisers span the width of the parade route. Police forces from neighboring municipalities also joined the Tampa Police Department. Also, bleachers were now being used for spectators. (Both, USF.)

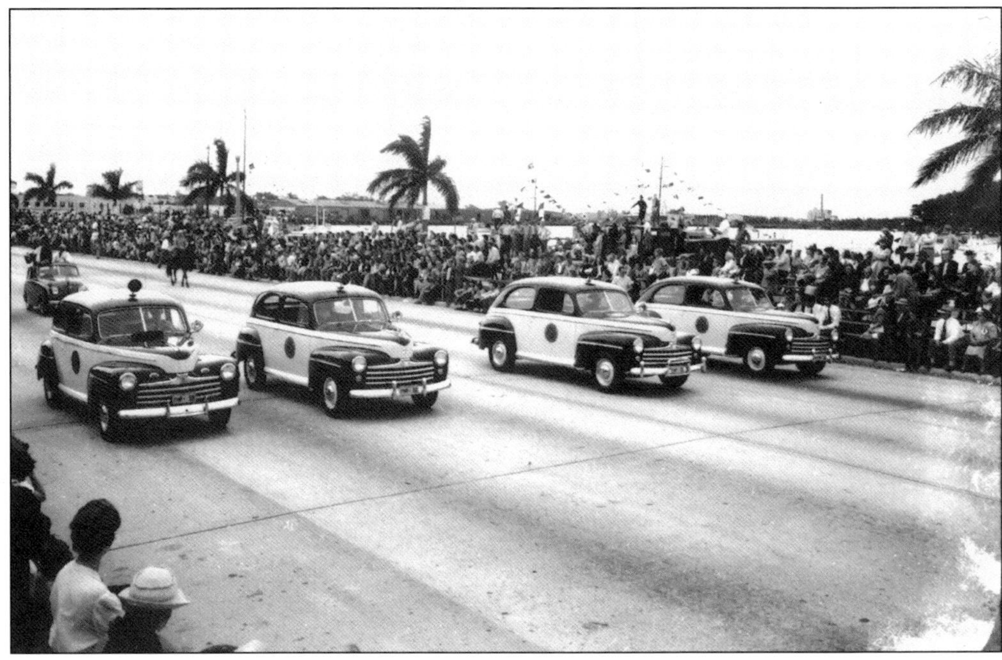

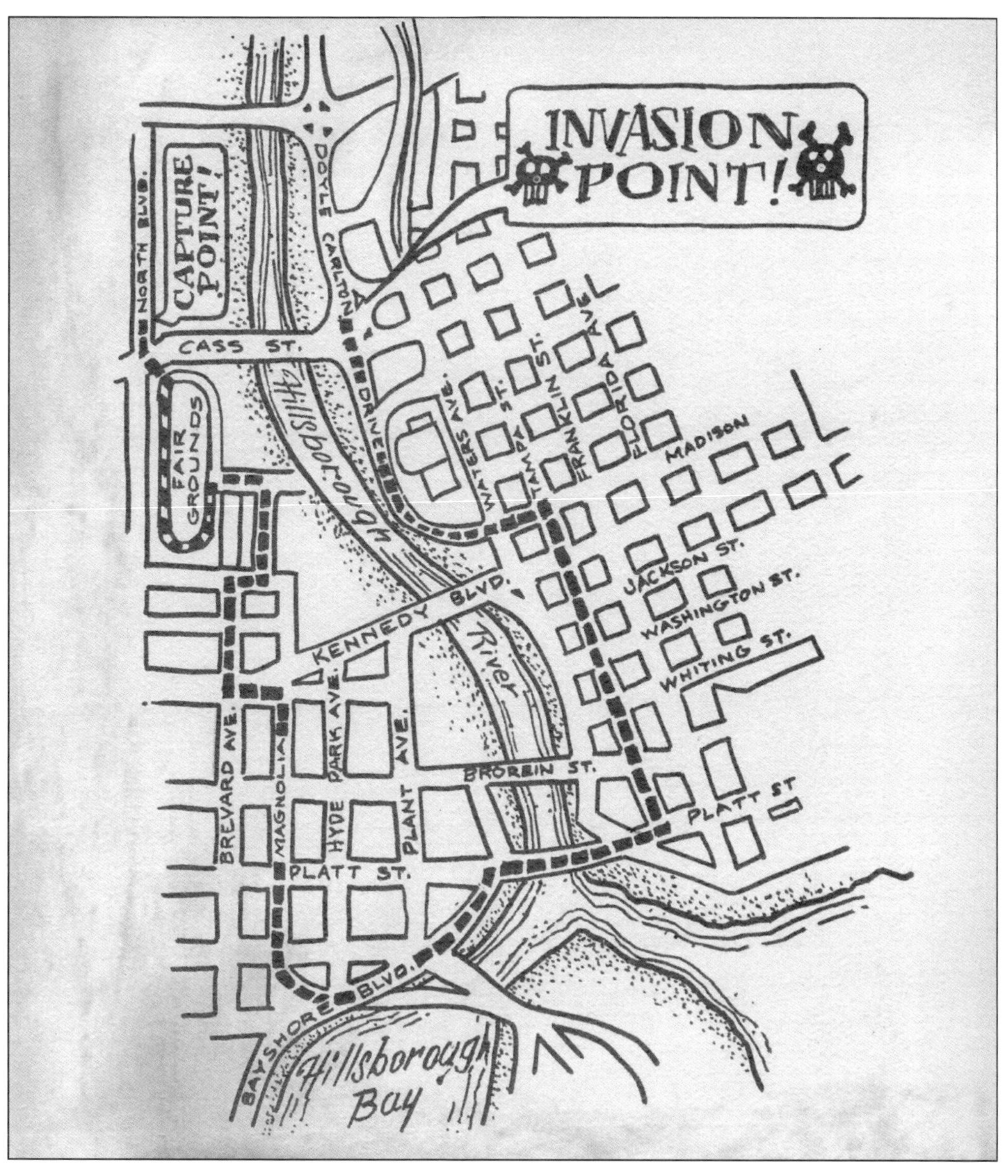

The property where Henry B. Plant built his Tampa Bay Hotel played an integral role in the first 72 years of the Gasparilla parade. The 1904 parade began at Tampa Bay Park on the grounds of the Tampa Bay Hotel, now Plant Hall at the University of Tampa, and concluded downtown at Courthouse Square, where the Hillsborough County Courthouse stood from 1892 until 1953. The parade route has evolved through the years, as shown by this 1969 map, which shows the parade starting near the Cass Street Bridge at the old Curtis Hixon Convention Center, which opened in 1965. Throughout the years, the ship used various landing sites along the Hillsborough River, which was where the parade usually began. As seen above, the parade then moved into downtown Tampa, south on Tampa Street, across the Platt Street Bridge, and included just a small section of Bayshore Boulevard. The route then turned north up Magnolia Avenue to North Boulevard, the site of the Florida State Fair in 1969 and now the site of the University of Tampa. (YMKG.)

PARADE
STARTS HERE

FRANKLIN

Ye Mystic K

PRESENTS T

THE PARADE

FEBRUARY

OFFICIAL ORDER OF MARCH

(Note: Ten official cars of notables will precede Parade by ten minutes.) Note also that crack Drill Teams from High School and College ROTC units will execute maneuvers along Parade Route, beginning at Cass and Franklin Streets at 12:20 p.m. Included will be prize platoons from Plant, Hillsborough and Jefferson High Schools, Tampa; Pershing Rifles, Stetson University; Florida Southern College Drill Team; and the Colonial Ancient Fife and Drum Corps, Bethpage, Long Island.

SECTION I

Police Escort
State Highway Patrol Cars
Sheriff's Cars
Color Guard, MacDill AFB
Pirate Flags and Girls
Pirate Grand Marshal, Charles P. Lykes
Drums and Bugles, U. S. Marines
MacDill AFB Ceremonial Squad
Pirate Captain's Car
King Gasparilla Float
Charlotte County Float
Hialeah High School Band

SECTION II

Marshal Arthur Spencer
Lee County Possettes
Edison Pageant Float
Eastern Air Lines Float
Palatka High School Band
General Telephone Float
Royal Castle Float
Longwood Lyman High School Band
DeSoto County Possettes
National Airlines Float
Publix Markets Float
Orlando Colonial High School Band
Atlantic Coast Line Float
Schlitz Brewing Float
Orlando Maynard Evans Band
Florida National Guard Unit

SECTION III

Marshal Sam F. Davis
Fairyland Baby Elephant
Tampa Electric Float
University of Tampa Band
Seaboard Air Line Float
Maas Bros. Float
Turkey Creek High School Band
Anheuser-Busch Float
Gainesville Indian Horses
Tropical Gas Float
King High School Band
Florida Confederate Army Unit
Zendah Grotto Unit
Tampa Coca-Cola Float
Sarasota High School Band
Sarasota Possettes

FAIR GROUNDS

SECT

Marshal Francis
Largo High Schoo
Lakeland Chambe
Hillsborough Cou
Jefferson High Sc
Tampa Merchants
Renegades' Horse
Middleton High S
Hillsborough Cour
Ballantine Beer F
Plant High Schoo
Ybor City Chamb
Alcalde of Ybor

NOTE: CERTAIN SPECIAL FEATURES SUCH AS GIANT HEADS, BABY ELEPHANT, CLOWNS, ETC., WILL NOT MAINTAIN FIXED POSITIONS AFTER PARADE STARTS.

32

From 1905 through 1975, the Gasparilla parade took varying routes, but it always concluded at the state fairgrounds on the site of Henry B. Plant's racetrack on the west side of the Tampa Bay Hotel. As seen in this 1966 map, the parade started downtown on Franklin Street, then crossed the Platt Street Bridge and included only a small section of Bayshore Boulevard. The parade then took a

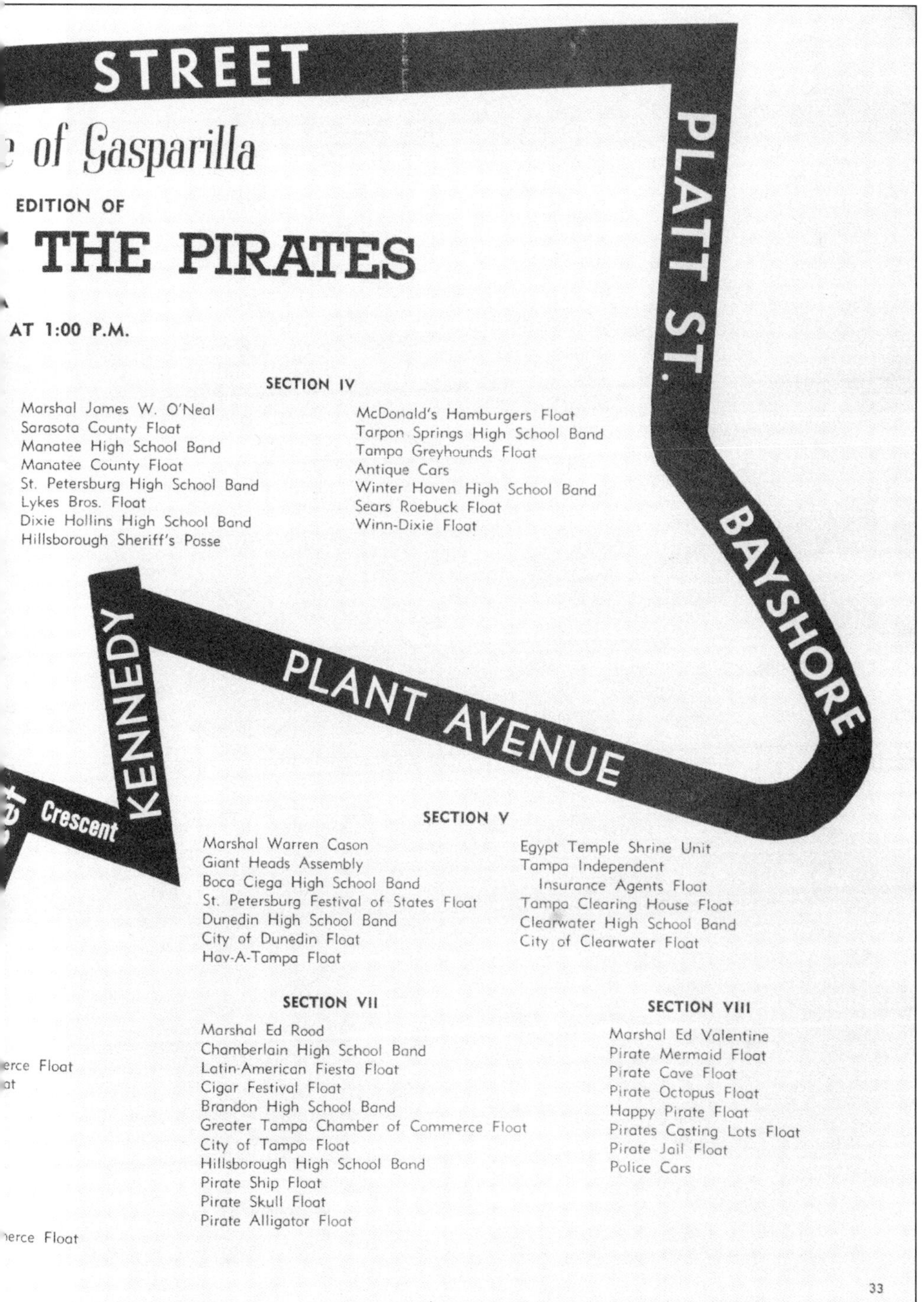

circuitous route that included Plant Avenue, Kennedy Boulevard, Crescent Street, and B Street and then ended at the Florida State Fair on North Boulevard. The modern route of the parade begins on the south end of the city's iconic and scenic Bayshore Boulevard bordering Hillsborough Bay and heads north to end in downtown Tampa. (YMKG.)

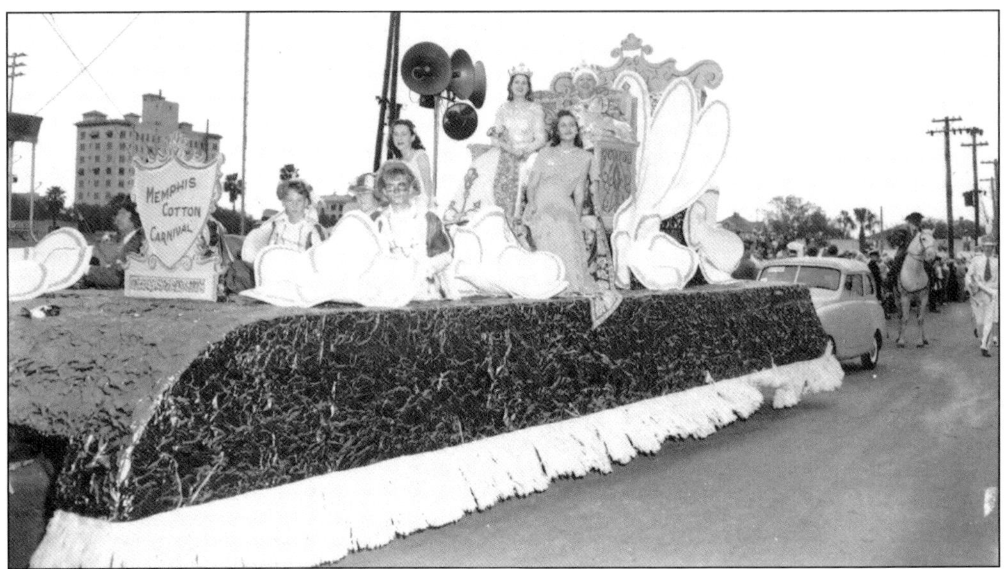

In addition to participating in other local parades, Ye Mystic Krewe of Gasparilla regularly sent envoys to the Memphis Cotton Carnival, the New Orleans Mardi Gras Rex Parade, the Minneapolis Aquatennial Torchlight Parade, the St. Paul Ice Carnival, and the Havana Carnival. This photograph shows the Memphis Cotton Carnival float in the Gasparilla parade. Recognizing the economic impact that Gasparilla produces, the City of Tampa continues to promote Gasparilla at the national level. (USF.)

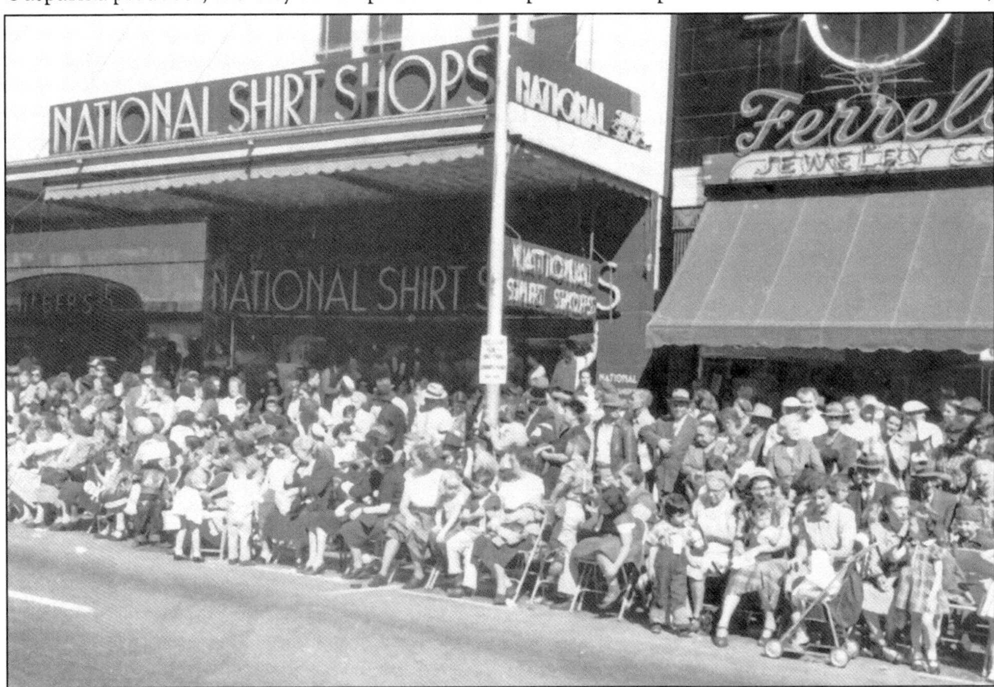

A great seat for the Gasparilla parade is a precious commodity. This photograph, taken in downtown Tampa on Franklin Street, shows parade patrons who paid $1 for a reserved seat in the yellow ticket section. Notice the signs for National Shirt Shops and Ferrell Jewelry Company, two of Tampa's former successful businesses. For today's Gasparilla, parade-goers pay handsomely for reserved seats to watch the parade from their favorite locations. (USF.)

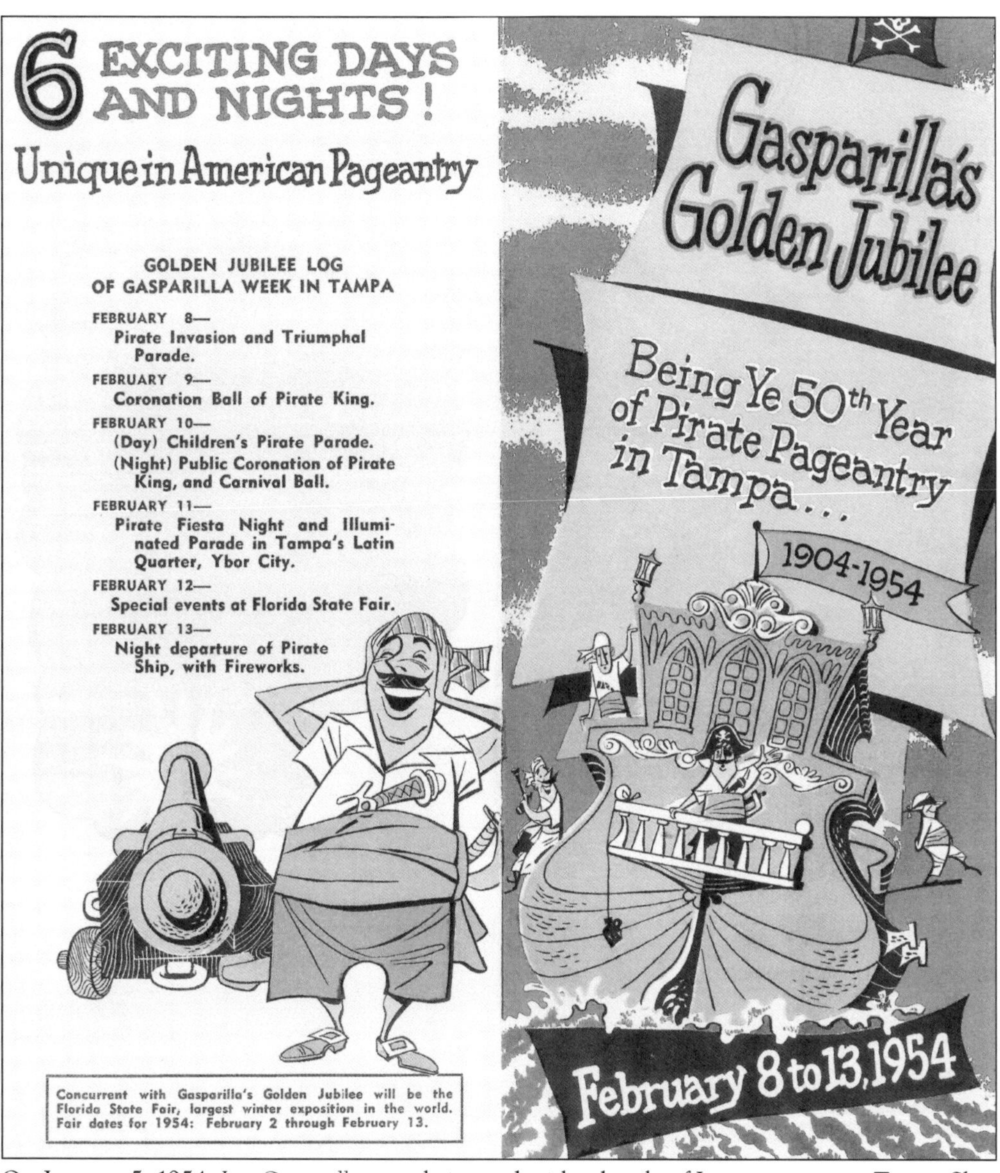

On January 5, 1954, *José Gasparilla* was christened with a bottle of Jamaican rum at Tampa Ship Repair and Drydock Company. It was the first ship built for and owned by Ye Mystic Krewe of Gasparilla and is still used today for the invasion. This year was also the Golden Jubilee celebration of the krewe's founding in 1904. The program seen here lists the weeklong events that were planned for February 8–13, 1954. The event started on Monday, February 8, with the invasion of the new *José Gasparilla* and ended with a night departure of the ship on Saturday, February 13. A fireworks display was also planned for the night festivities. At the bottom of the brochure, the Florida State Fair was advertised as the "largest winter exposition in the world." (YMKG.)

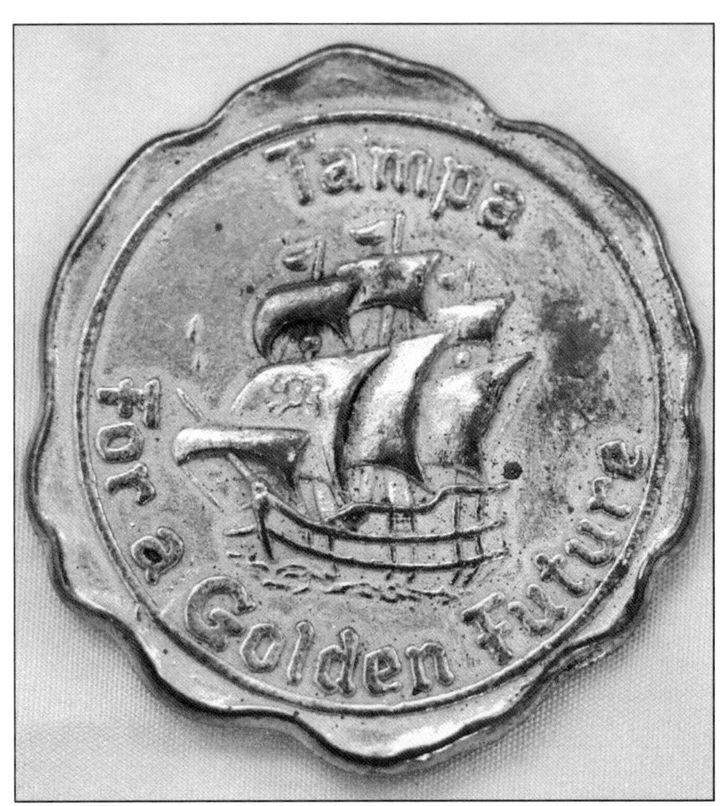

For many years, Ye Mystic Krewe of Gasparilla handed out thick doubloon coins or empty blank shell casings along the parade route. The coins were especially cherished items for the thousands of spectators who collected them for years. The photograph at left shows the usual coin, which displayed a picture of the pirate ship and was engraved "Tampa—For a Golden Future." For the 1954 Golden Jubilee, a special coin (below) was minted and engraved with "50 Years of Pirate Pageantry, 1904–1954, Feb. 8." Ye Mystic Krewe of Gasparilla still gives out coins as souvenirs, but beads are much more popular. (Both, YMKG.)

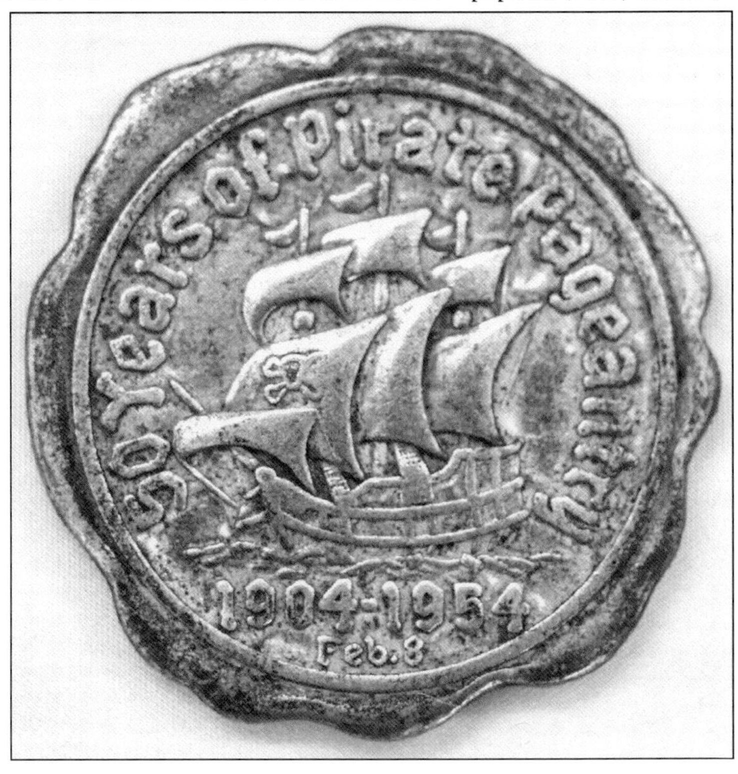

Six

The Floats

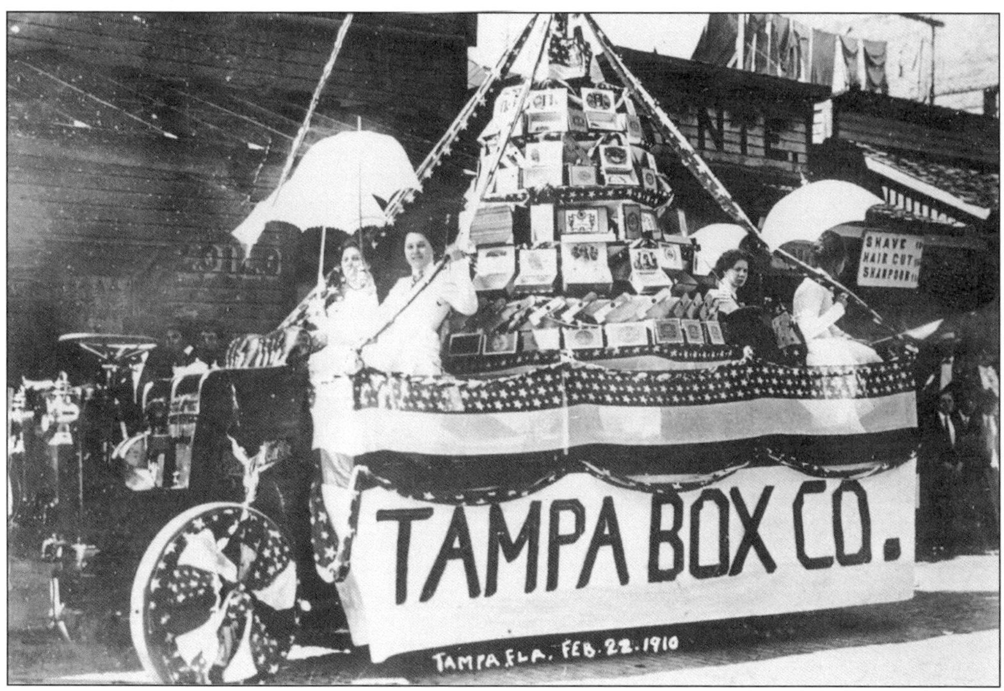

A float sponsored by the Florida Box Company was part of the Gasparilla parade in 1910. The float features cigar boxes that are representative of Tampa's large cigar industry of that era. The float was built atop a truck, which was the custom at that time. The trucks of those days were not always reliable, resulting in frequent delays to the parade. (USF.)

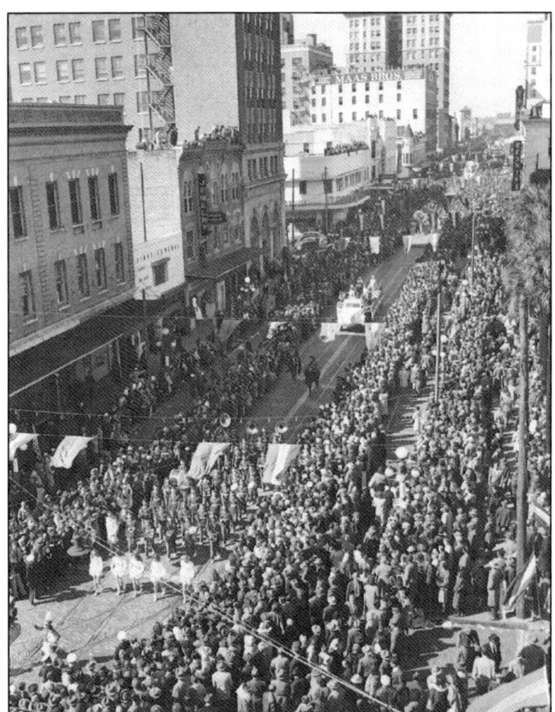

In this 1947 photograph, a white truck pulls a float through the huge crowd that attended the first Gasparilla parade following the end of World War II. In addition to the crowded sidewalks, also notice the spectators on the rooftops of the buildings. Seen on the left side of the photograph is the Maas Brothers department store, an extremely popular and successful business at the time. (THCPL.)

Large crowds in 1923 observe as floats head west over the Hillsborough River on the Lafayette Street Bridge, now Kennedy Boulevard. In the background is the Atlantic Coast Line railroad depot, which was a fixture on the river until it burned to the ground in 1943. Note that at this time the floats continued to be built atop truck chassis. (THCPL.)

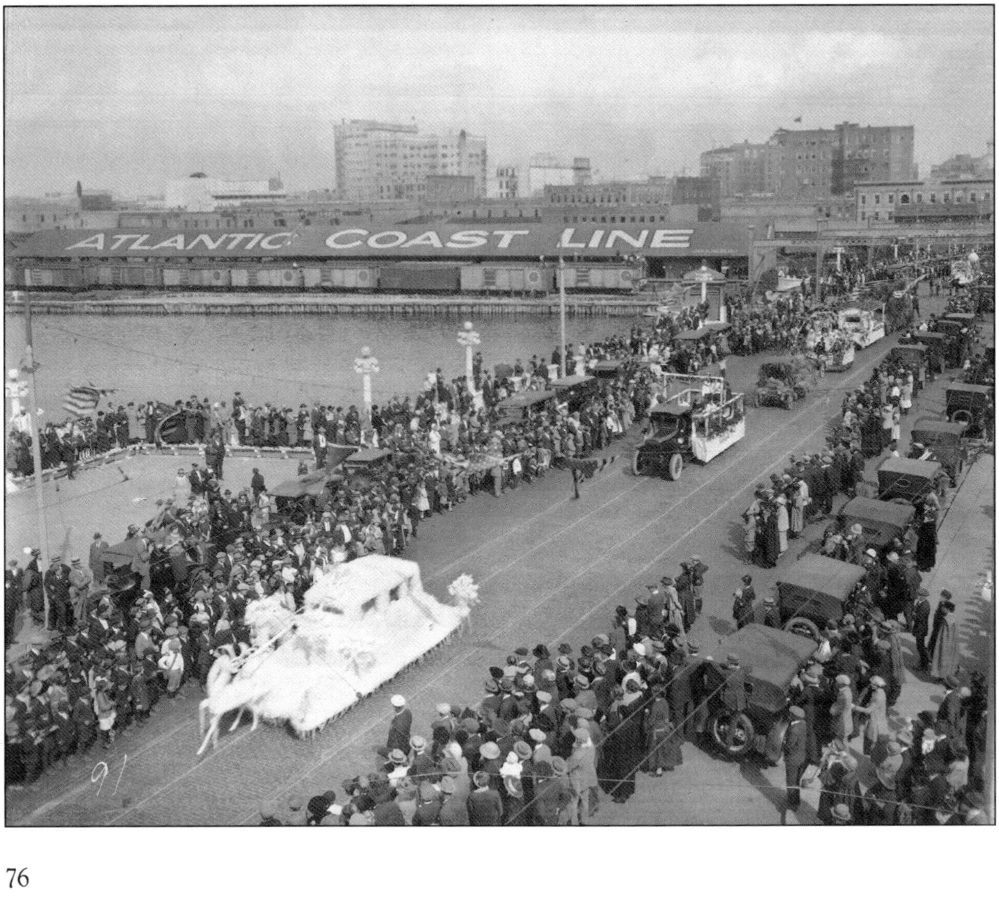

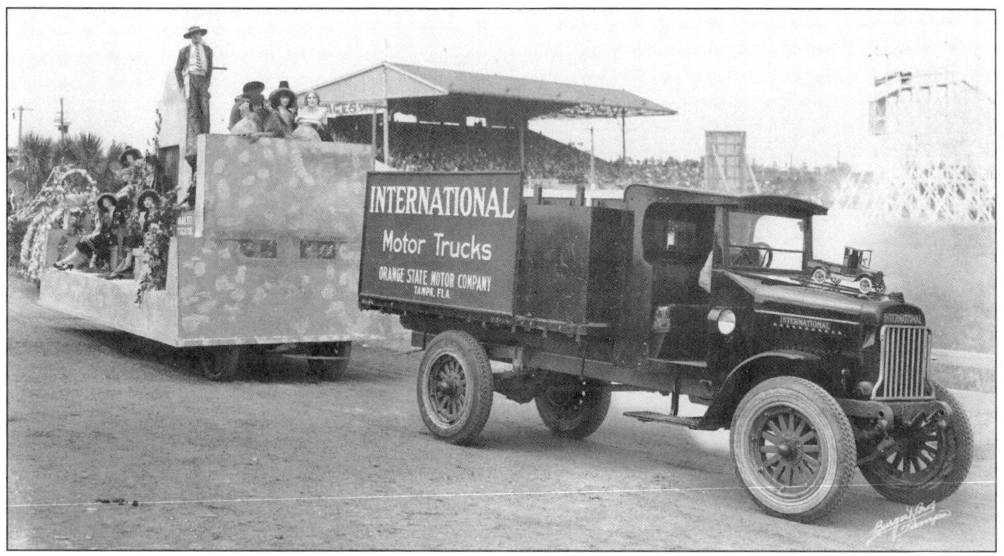

In 1924, a truck-drawn float from the Orange State Motor Company circles the Plant Field track at the old Florida State Fairgrounds on North Boulevard, pulling a float sponsored by the Rialto Theater. Visible in the background are both the grandstand, now part of Pepin Stadium at the University of Tampa, and a thrill ride constructed for the midway at the fair. (THCPL.)

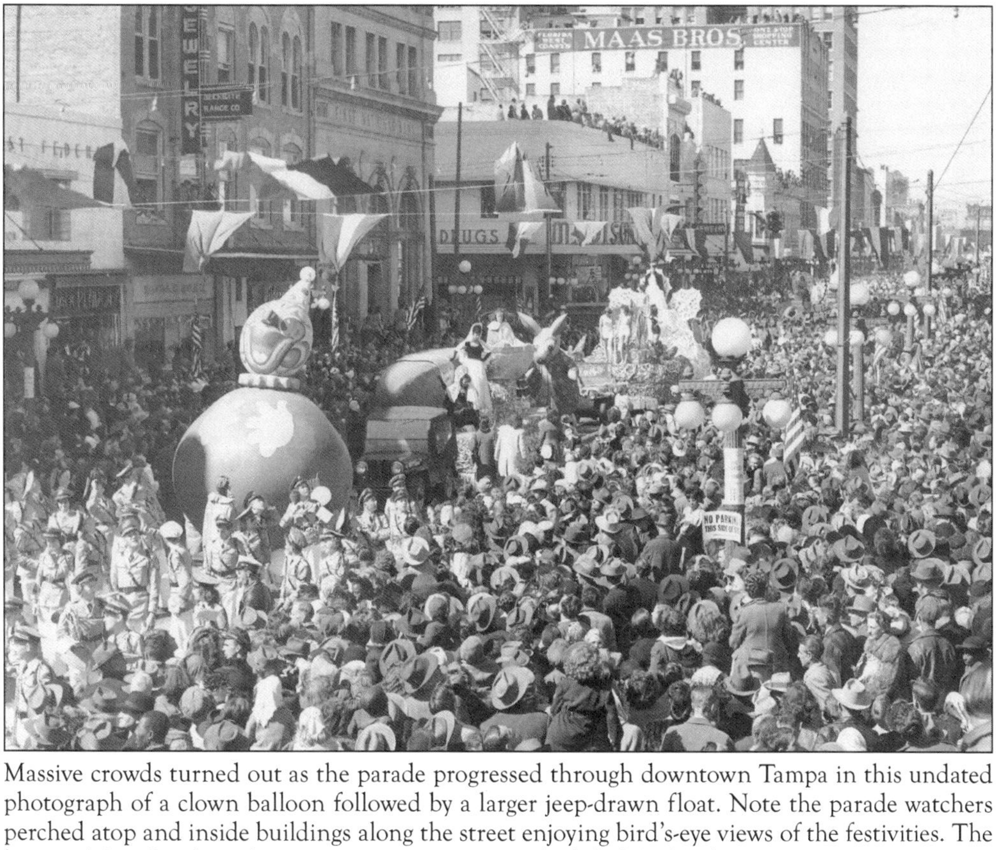

Massive crowds turned out as the parade progressed through downtown Tampa in this undated photograph of a clown balloon followed by a larger jeep-drawn float. Note the parade watchers perched atop and inside buildings along the street enjoying bird's-eye views of the festivities. The historic Maas Brothers department store is seen on the left. (THCPL.)

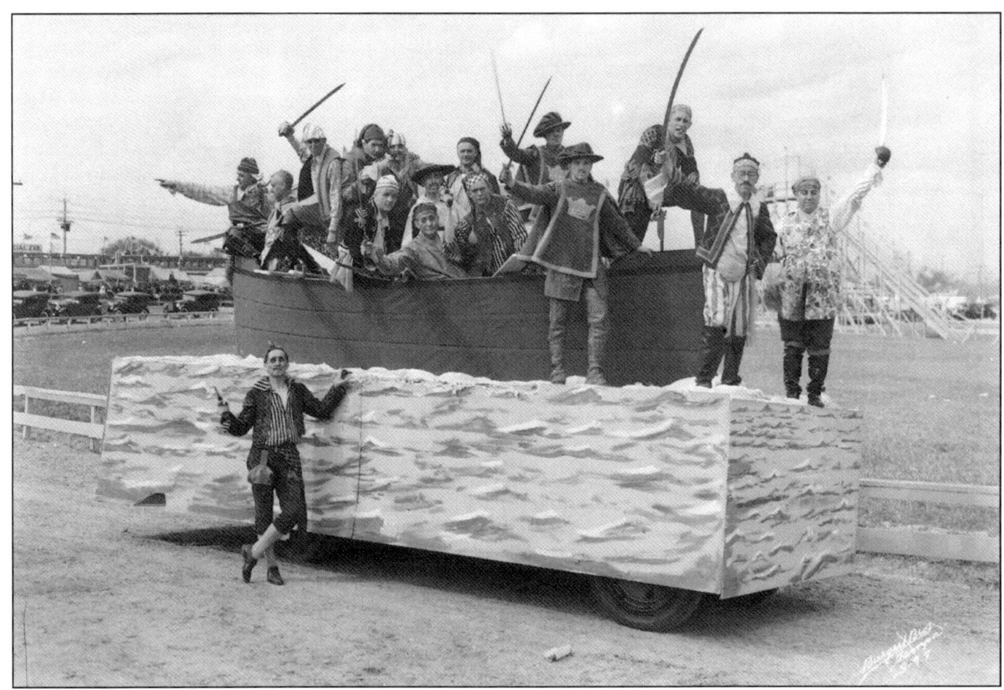

Ye Mystic Krewe of Gasparilla pirates crowd a small pirate ship perched atop this float circling the track at Plant Field at the Florida State Fairgrounds, now the site of the University of Tampa athletic field. Costumes worn at this time were quite different from those worn in the modern-day parade. (THCPL.)

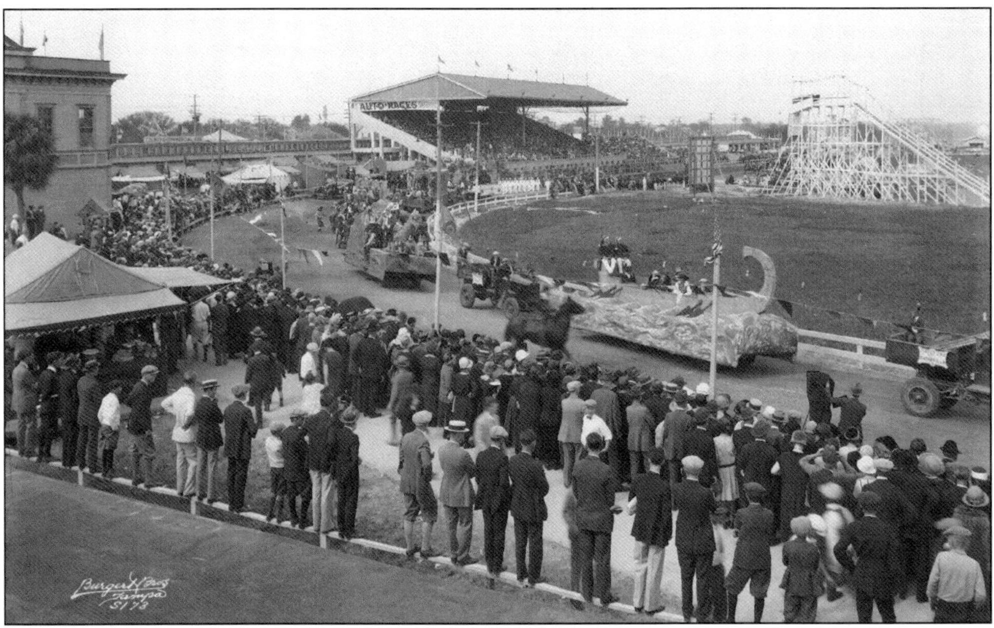

This 1925 view shows how the auto-racing track at Plant Field was used for the floats in the parade. The corners of the racetrack were slightly banked, so the floats lean ever so slightly to the left as they negotiate this turn. Notice the well-dressed spectators in hats, coats, and dresses, quite different from modern-day Gasparilla attire. (THCPL.)

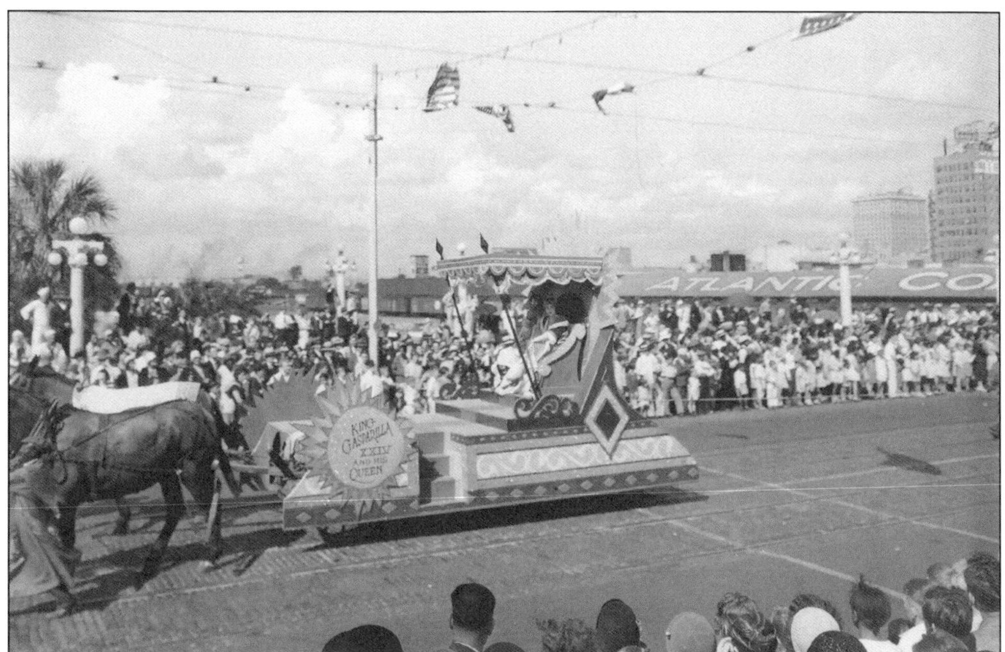

In the 1932 parade, the King and Queen of Gasparilla rode in the horse-drawn Royal Float. In the modern Gasparilla parade, the current king and queen still ride a royal float in the parade, but the entire royal court now joins them. Here, the float is exiting the Lafayette Street Bridge in front of Plant Park, now on the grounds of the University of Tampa. (THCPL.)

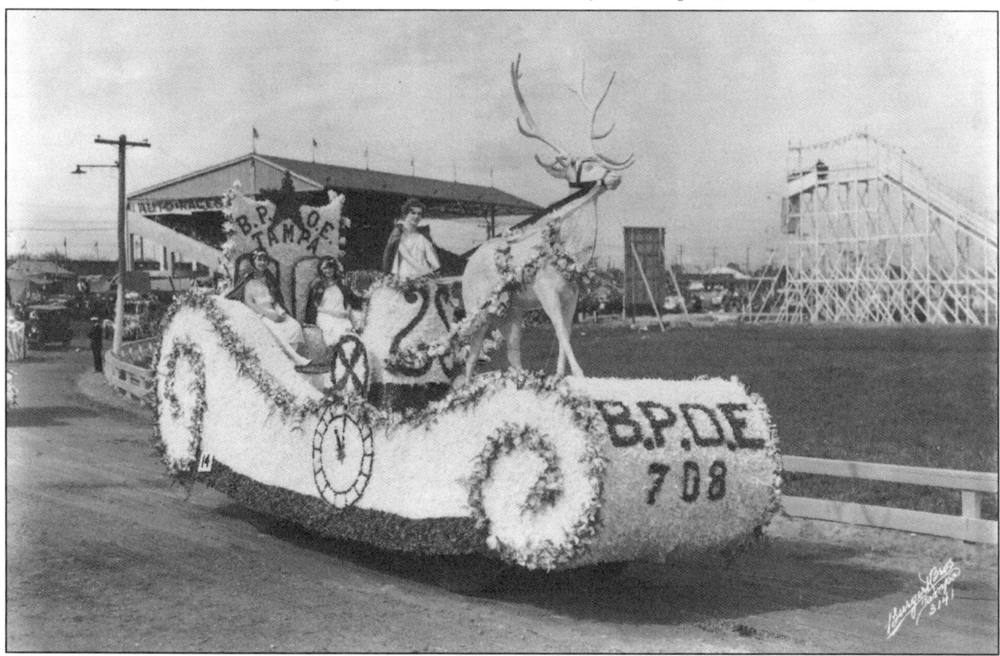

Many Tampa-area fraternal organizations have participated in Gasparilla parades. In 1925, a float sponsored by the Elks Club Lodge 708 makes its way around the racetrack at Plant Field. This float is particularly fancy for the times with an elk statue atop it. In the back of the float are three caped women representing the club. (THCPL.)

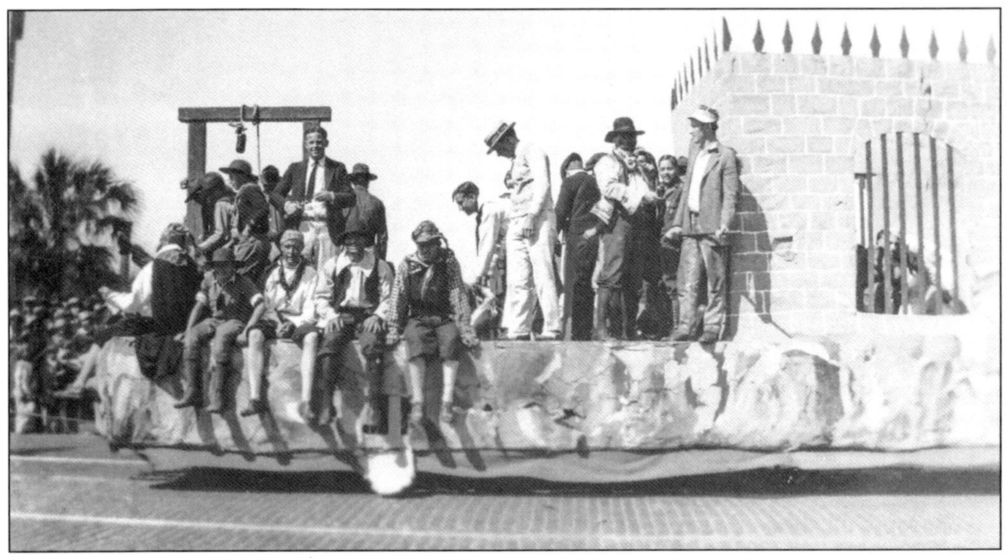

Ye Mystic Krewe of Gasparilla's Jail Float is customarily the final float in the Gasparilla parade. It provides transportation for members who do not want to be left behind when the parade is over. In the first Gasparilla following World War I, this 1920 photograph shows several pirates riding the Jail Float on its way to the fairgrounds. (SAF.)

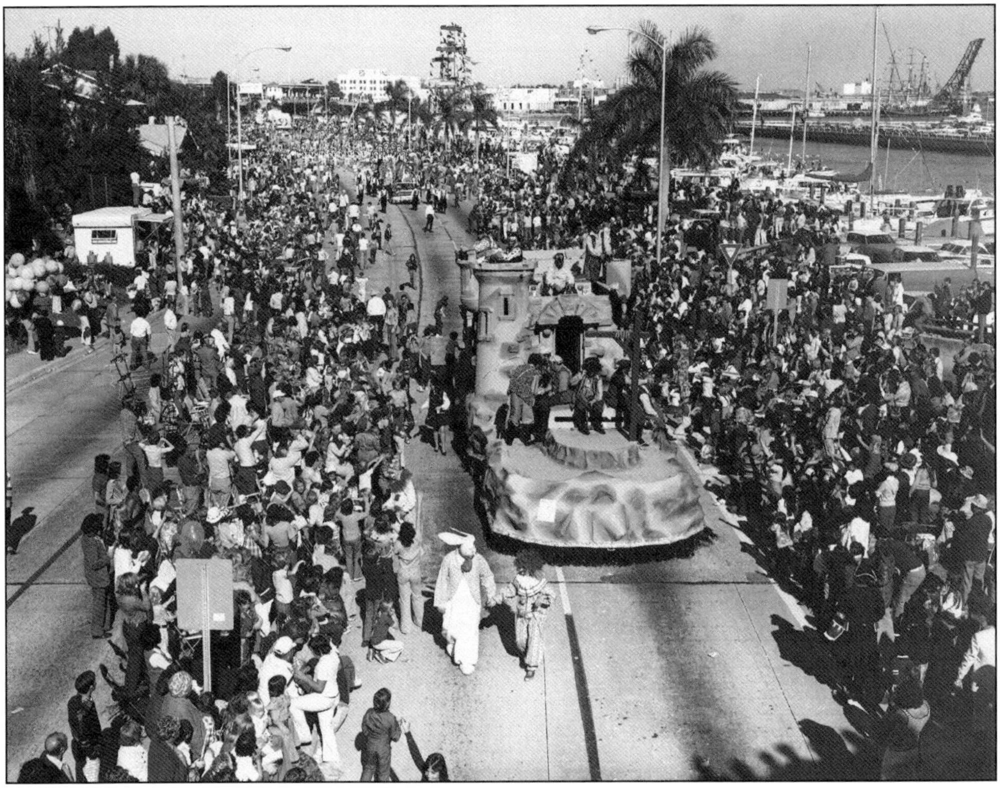

The two-story Castle Float makes its way south along Bayshore Boulevard in the 1946 Gasparilla parade. *José Gaspar* can be seen moored in the background of this photograph. Although Tampa was a much smaller city at the time, the parade crowds were quite large, as seen here. (THCPL.)

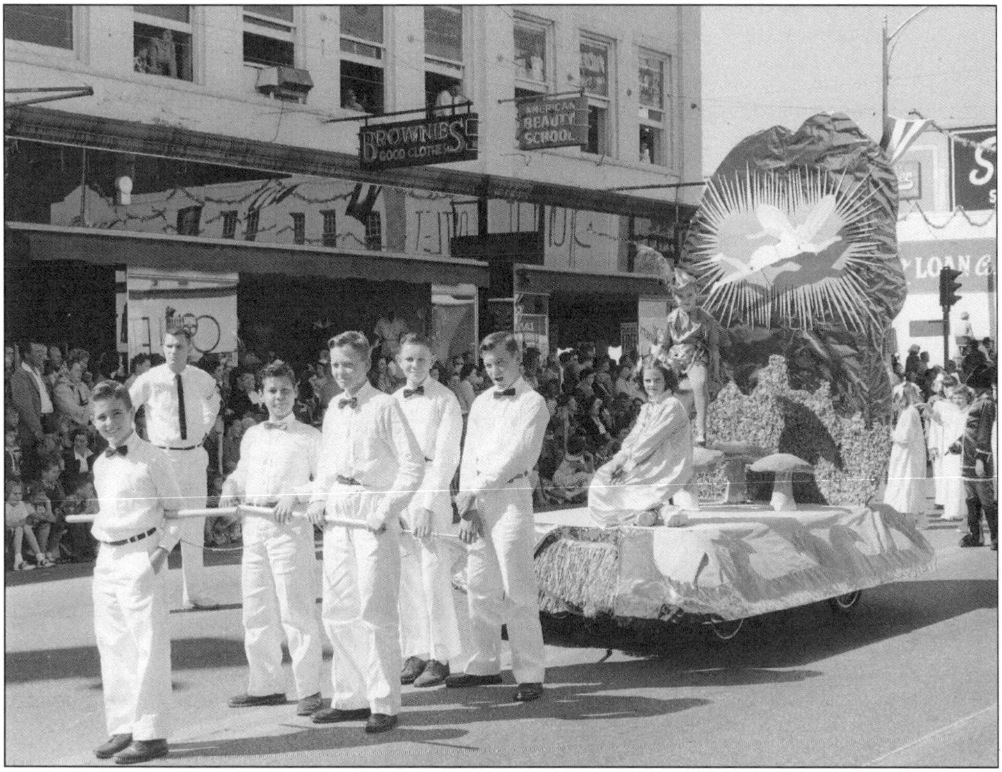

Mules, horses, trucks, and tractors did not pull all the floats in Gasparilla parades. In the 1956 version of the Children's Gasparilla Parade, a group of boys pulls a float featuring Peter Pan. The Children's Gasparilla Parade was begun in 1947 (after a two-year war hiatus for the larger Gasparilla parade). Now called the Gasparilla Children's Parade, the family-oriented event is staged along Bayshore Boulevard and attracts crowds of several hundred thousand. (USF.)

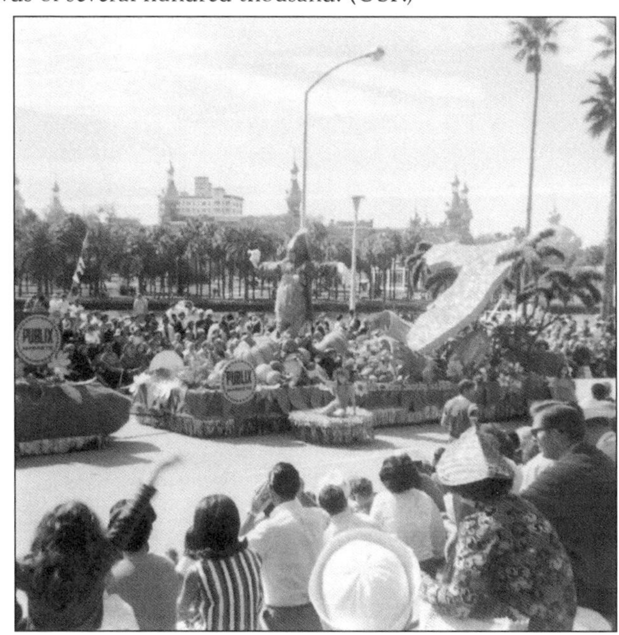

Between 1904 and 1965, Ye Mystic Krewe of Gasparilla was the only krewe participating in the Gasparilla parade. There have always been many businesses and civic organizations with floats in the event. A scarecrow standing in a field of vegetables is pictured in this 1969 Publix supermarket float. In the background are the minarets of Plant Hall on the campus of the University of Tampa. (USF.)

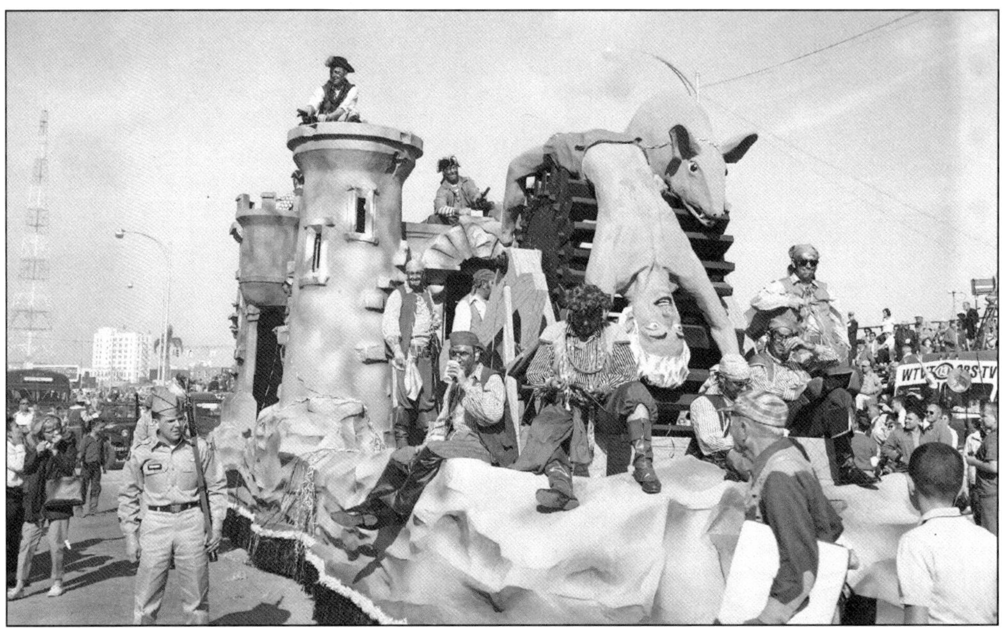

This 1964 Ye Mystic Krewe of Gasparilla float shows a more theatrical side of the festival, as an apparent captive is on some sort of torture device. Notice the disproportionately huge rat to the right of the victim. Two pirates on top of the float are shooting 10-gauge salute cannon blanks. (USF.)

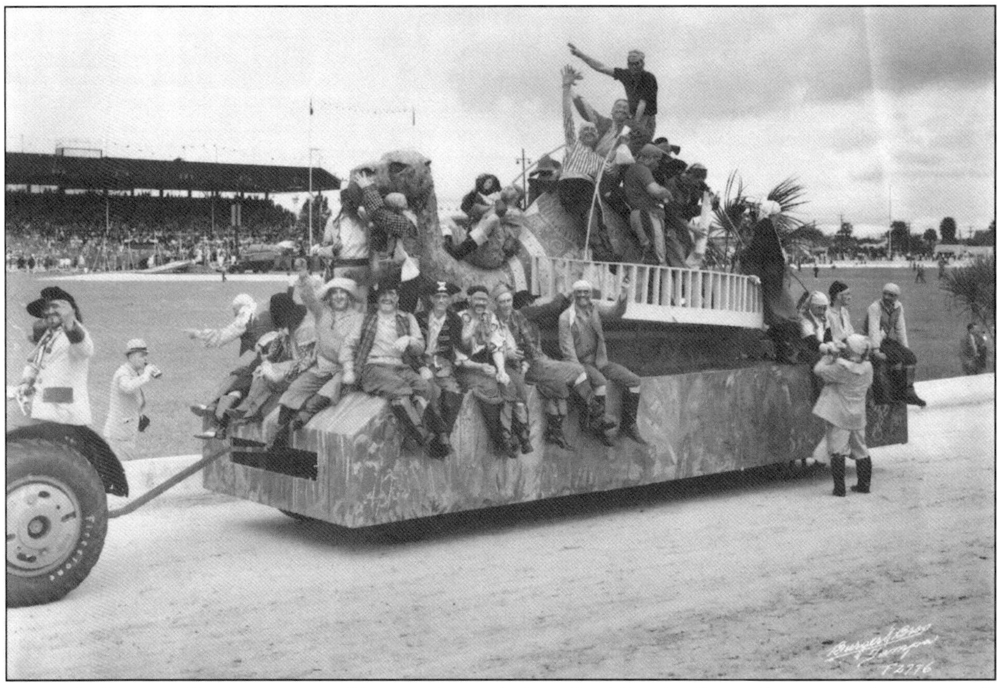

From 1905 to 1975, the Gasparilla parade ended at the Florida State Fairgrounds on North Boulevard, now the site of the University of Tampa. The floats would circle the dirt track in front of the grandstand at the end of the parade. This February 1, 1937, photograph shows a group of Ye Mystic Krewe of Gasparilla pirates precariously sitting on a float that is being pulled by a tractor. (THCPL.)

Seven

More than a Black Eyepatch

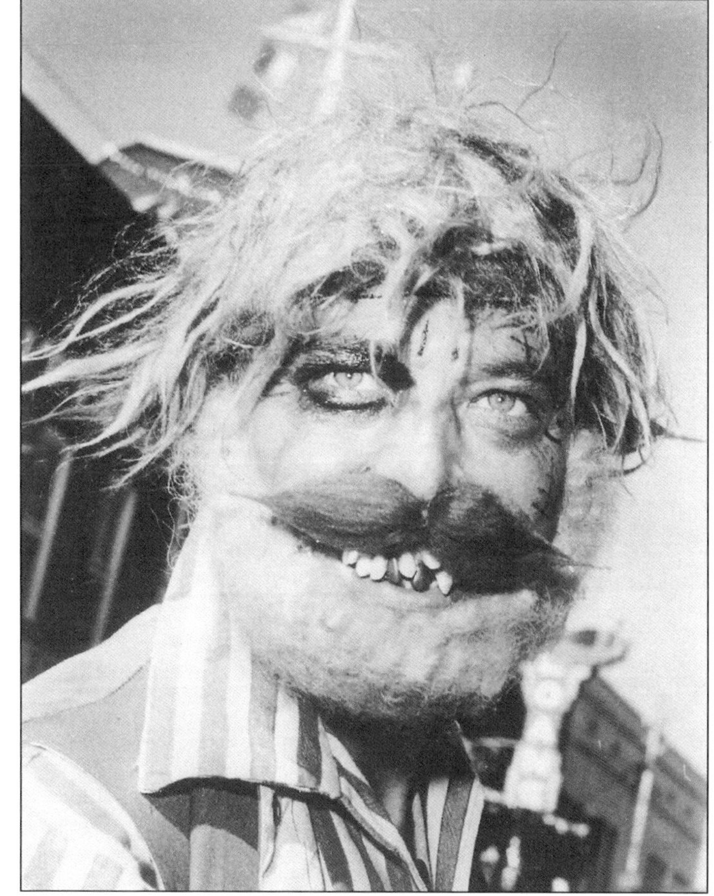

On invasion day, members of Ye Mystic Krewe of Gasparilla transform into full-fledged pirates with ornate costumes and professional makeup. Some choose to adorn themselves with mainstream piratical outfits such as long jackets, headgear, boots, feathered hats, and foul weather gear, while others wear more customized costumes. On this one day, many pirates become completely unrecognizable to the local community. (YMKG.)

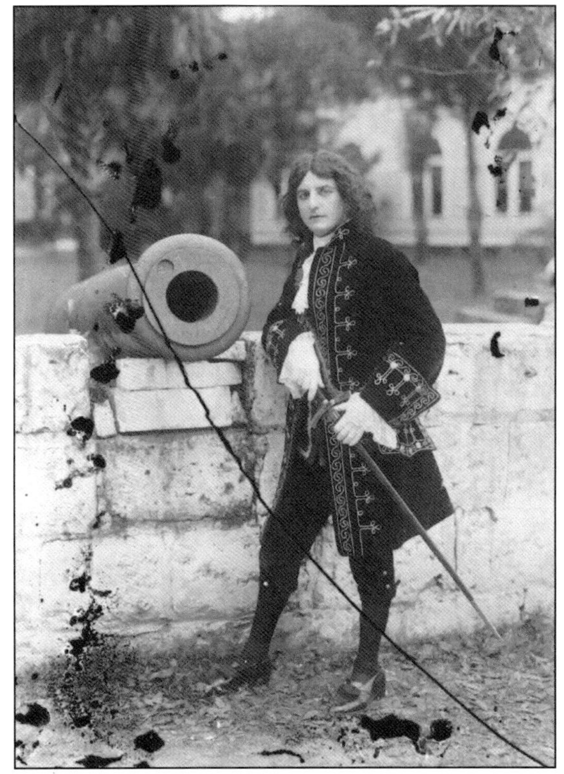

In 1917, the Gasparilla Festival was held in conjunction with the South Florida Fair, now called the Florida State Fair. Due to World War I, Gasparilla would not be held again until 1920. At left, a Ye Mystic Krewe of Gasparilla pirate wears an intricate embroidered coat, much like New Orleans Mardi Gras attire, which is more formal than what a traditional pirate would have worn. Pirates participating in the festivities then began wearing more common-day seaworthy costumes that "real" pirates would have worn, as seen below. Common pirate costumes of this era included bandanas or bicorn hats as headgear, striped or polka-dot shirts, earrings, and leg coverings to simulate high-top boots. (Both, THCPL.)

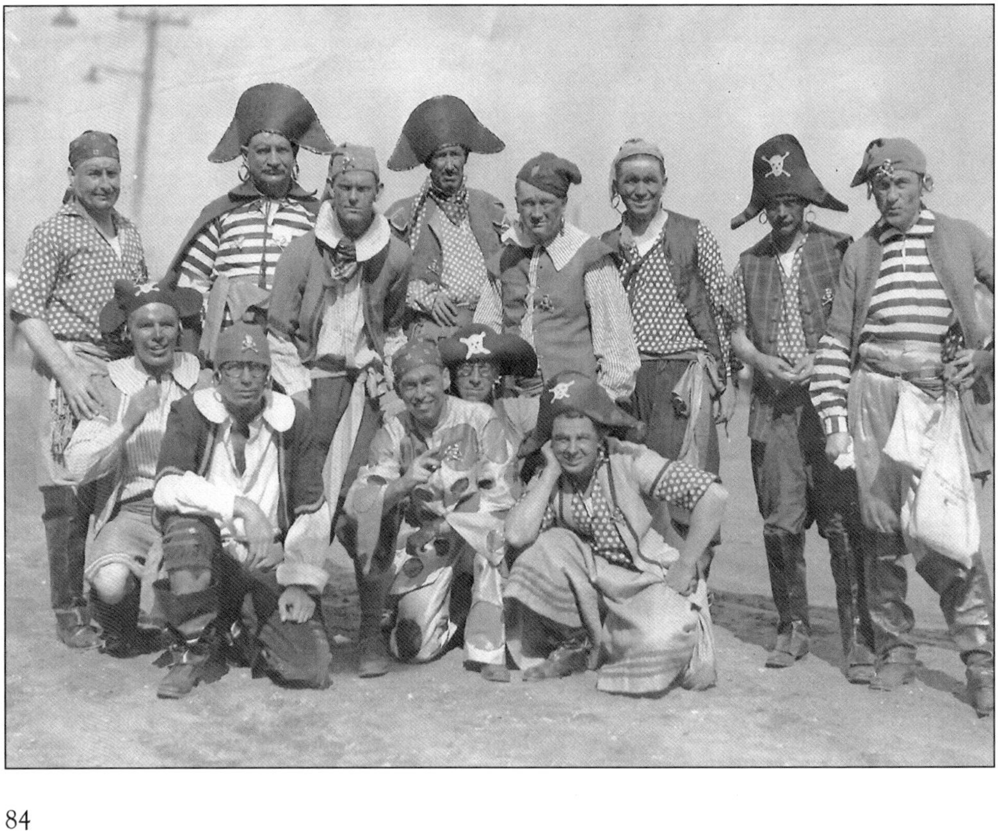

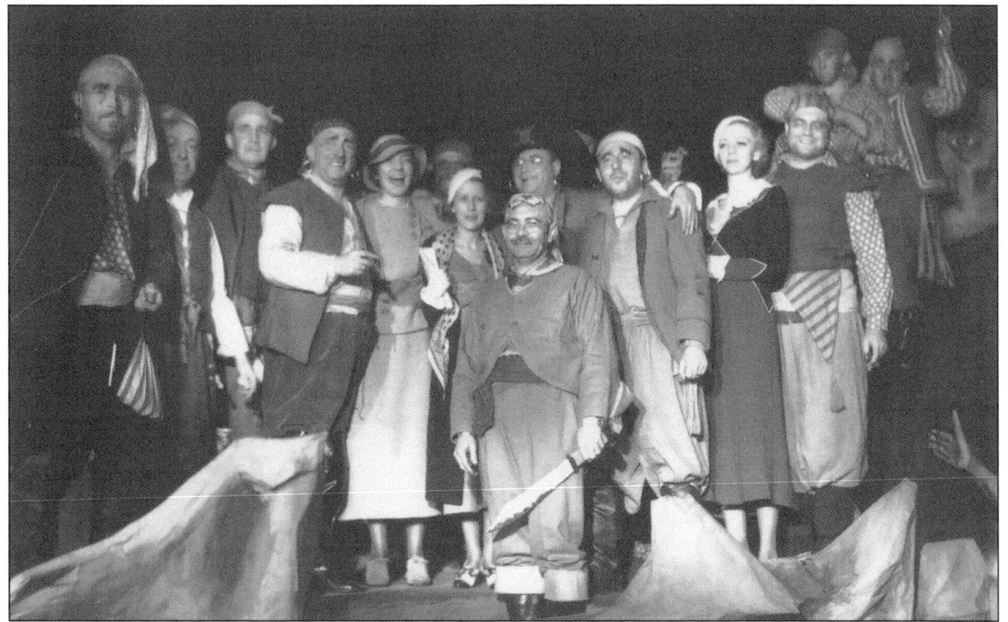

Despite the Great Depression, Ye Mystic Krewe of Gasparilla pirates and guests in this 1933 photograph continued to participate in the Gasparilla celebration but with less colorful costumes. Also in 1933, Tampa Junior College was renamed the University of Tampa and moved its headquarters to the Tampa Bay Hotel, now known as Plant Hall. (THCPL.)

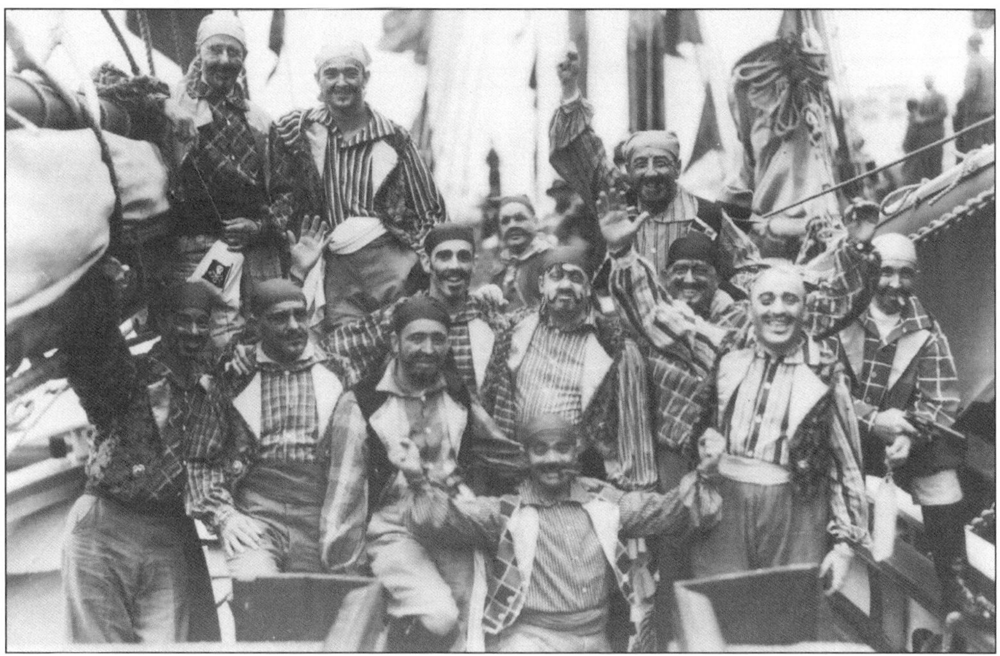

Ye Mystic Krewe of Gasparilla costumes during the 1930s were simpler than today, and many pirates did not wear the heavy stage makeup that they do now. Pirate makeup was not elaborate and primarily consisted of applying facial hair with a black grease pencil. Standing aboard one of the many borrowed ships used for Gasparilla, this group of 1936 pirates prepares to invade the city of Tampa. (THCPL.)

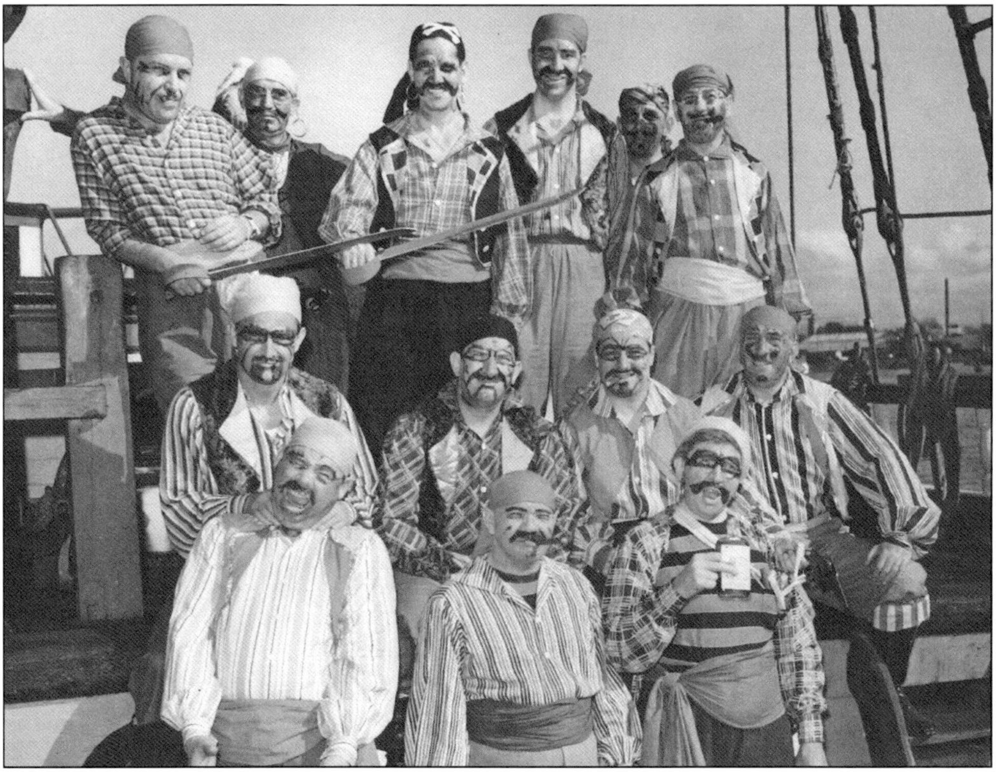

With the Great Depression more firmly in the rearview mirror, pirates started wearing more colorful costumes, and many began wearing more elaborate makeup on invasion day. Several pirate-themed movies produced in the 1930s also inspired the costumes worn by members of Ye Mystic Krewe of Gasparilla. Above, 1939 pirates assemble in preparation to board *José Gaspar*, the first vessel owned by the krewe. Previous ships used for the invasion were borrowed and transformed into a pirate ship for the day. Below, a group of pirates prepares to fire a cannon on board the ship. (Both, THCPL.)

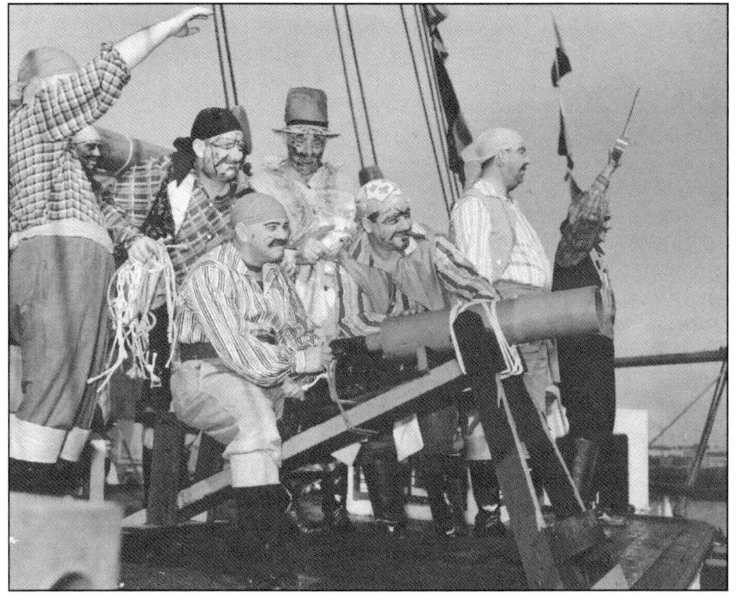

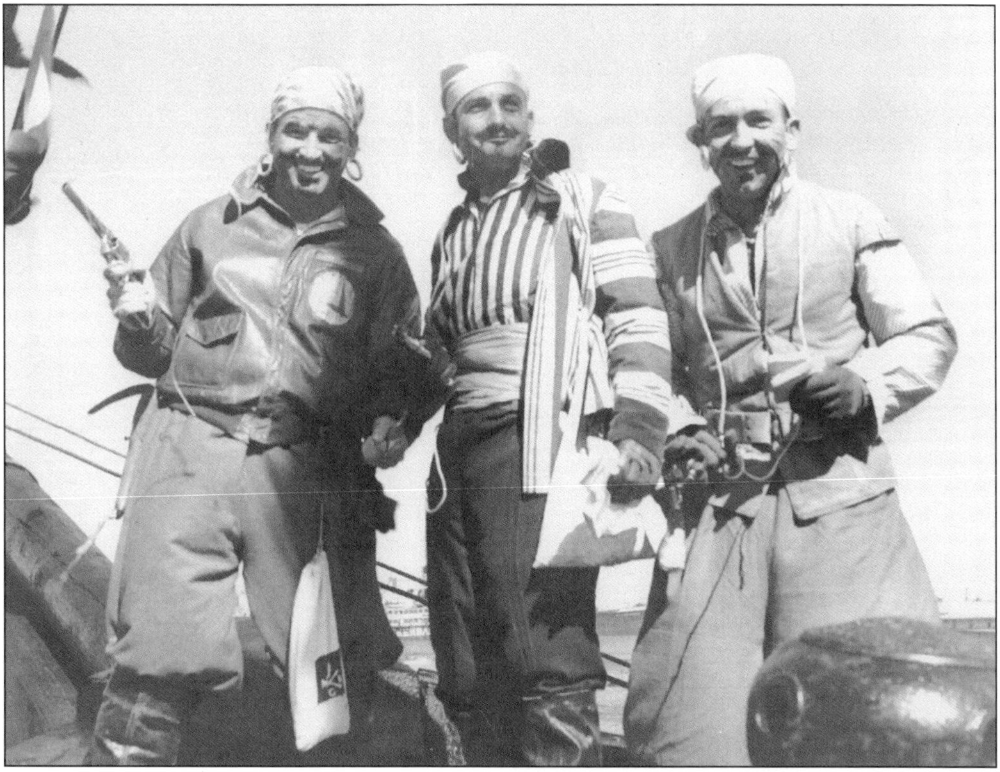

Following a six-year pause in festivities during World War II, Gasparilla revelry resumed with much enthusiasm in 1947. MacDill Field became MacDill Air Force Base in 1947, and Drew Field was renamed Tampa International Airport. The bomber jacket worn by the pirate on the left above reflects a national sentiment of patriotism and victory following World War II. Also notice the bag hanging from the pirate's belt. These bags were used by members of Ye Mystic Krewe of Gasparilla to carry .38 Special blanks or souvenir coins. These vintage bags have become collector's items, as have the thick doubloon coins given out during the parade. (Above, THCPL; right, YMKG.)

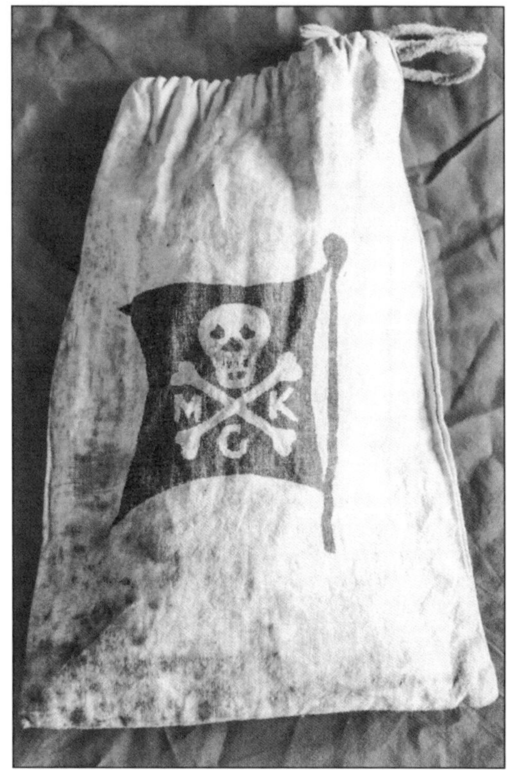

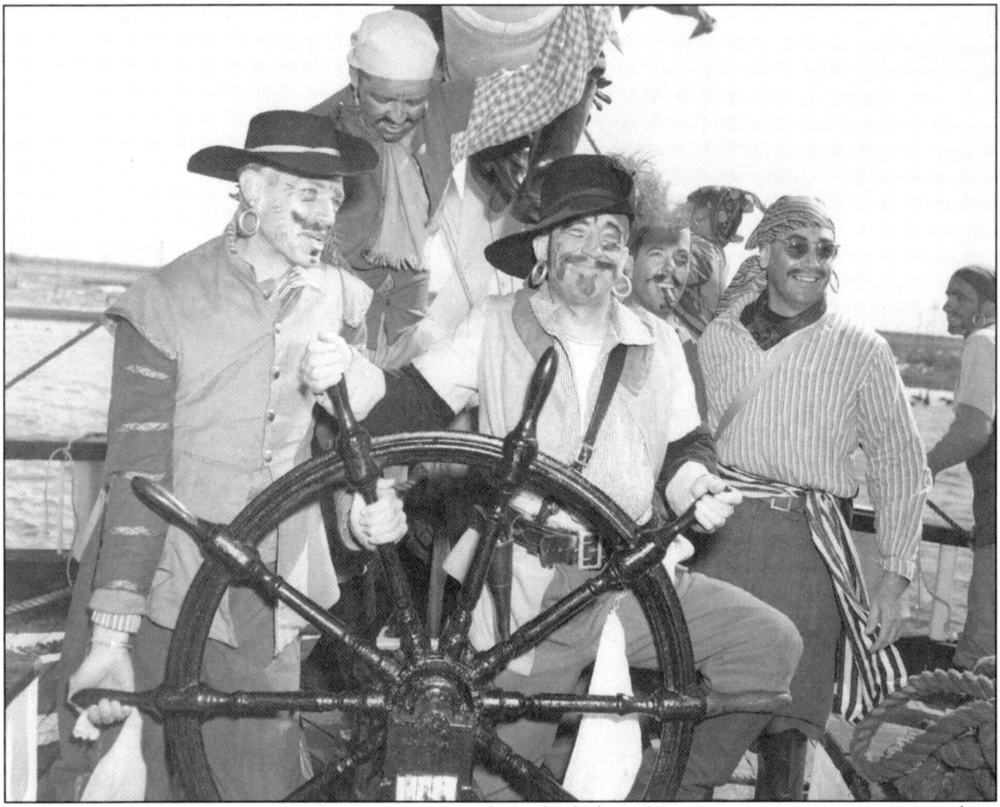

In this photograph, a group of 1947 pirates stands at the helm of *José Gaspar* preparing to set sail on the first Gasparilla invasion following World War II. With stronger prosperity in the United States and Tampa, membership in Ye Mystic Krewe of Gasparilla began to grow during this period, and the City of Tampa began investing in infrastructure projects to support the significant population growth in the area since the end of World War II. (THCPL.)

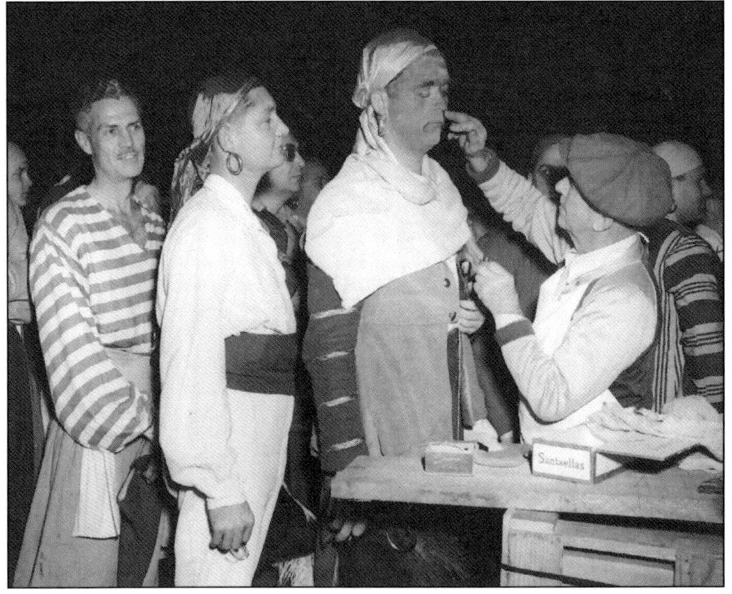

In the early years of the festival, Ye Mystic Krewe of Gasparilla pirates would apply their own makeup, and many would wear homemade costumes. Eventually, a more formal method of getting ready for the invasion was adopted, including the use of makeup artists. This photograph is a snapshot of the early-morning makeup line at the Tampa Yacht and Country Club in 1948. (THCPL.)

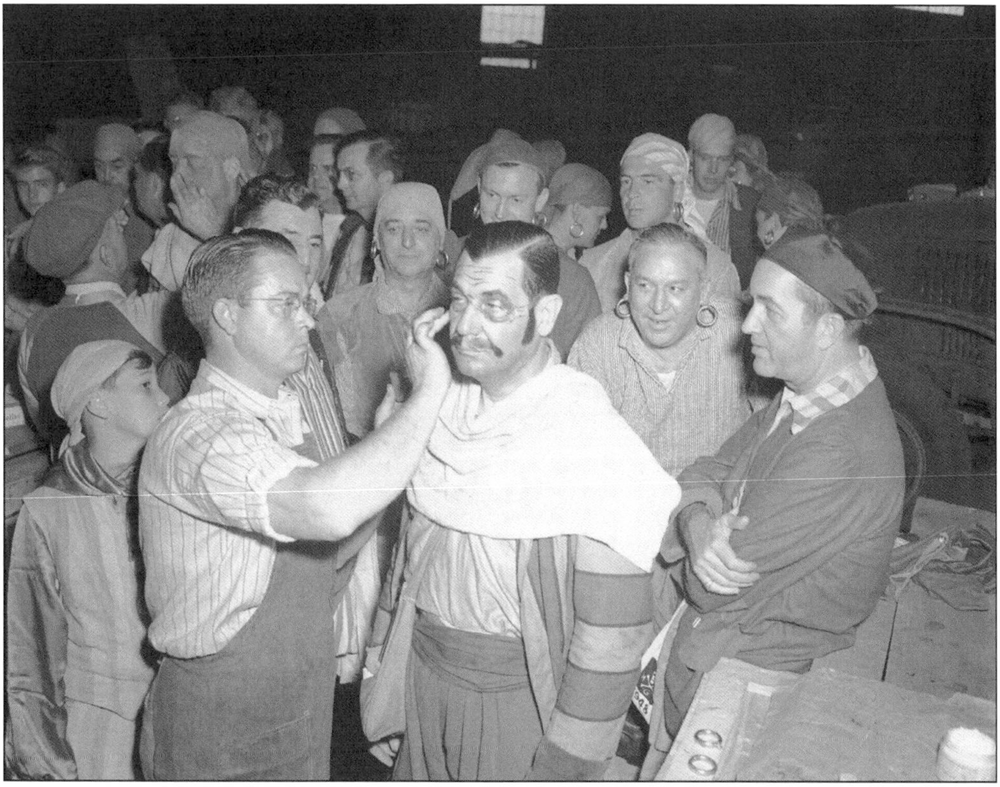

Costumes became more festive following World War II, with pirates wearing more makeup, colorful shirts, Jolly Roger hats, bandanas, and boots. In addition, many pirates of Ye Mystic Krewe of Gasparilla carried pistols that fired .38 Special blanks. The sound of gun and cannon fire has always been synonymous with Gasparilla and can be heard for miles around Tampa on invasion day. Before beads became popular, the empty shell casings and doubloons were the only souvenirs handed out to parade spectators by Ye Mystic Krewe of Gasparilla. Above, 1948 makeup artists apply various scars, beards, and black eyes. The photograph at right shows the look of the day for a 1950s Gasparilla invasion. (Above, THCPL; right, YMKG.)

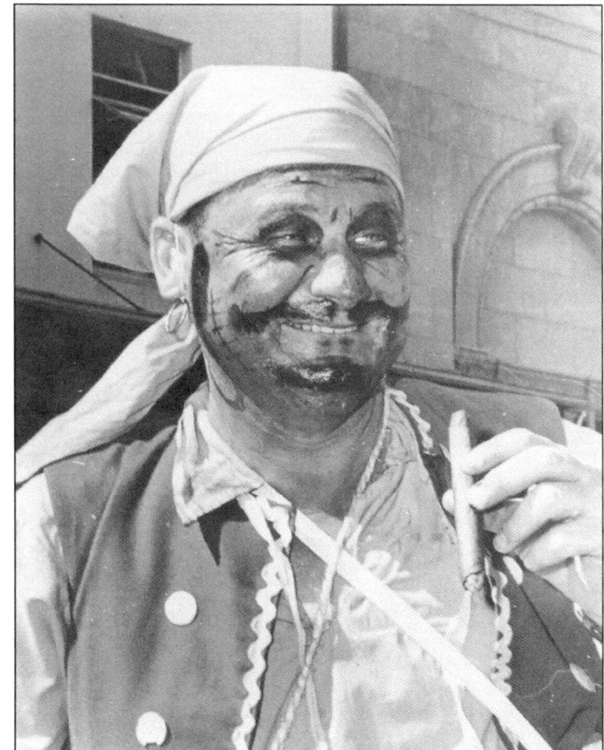

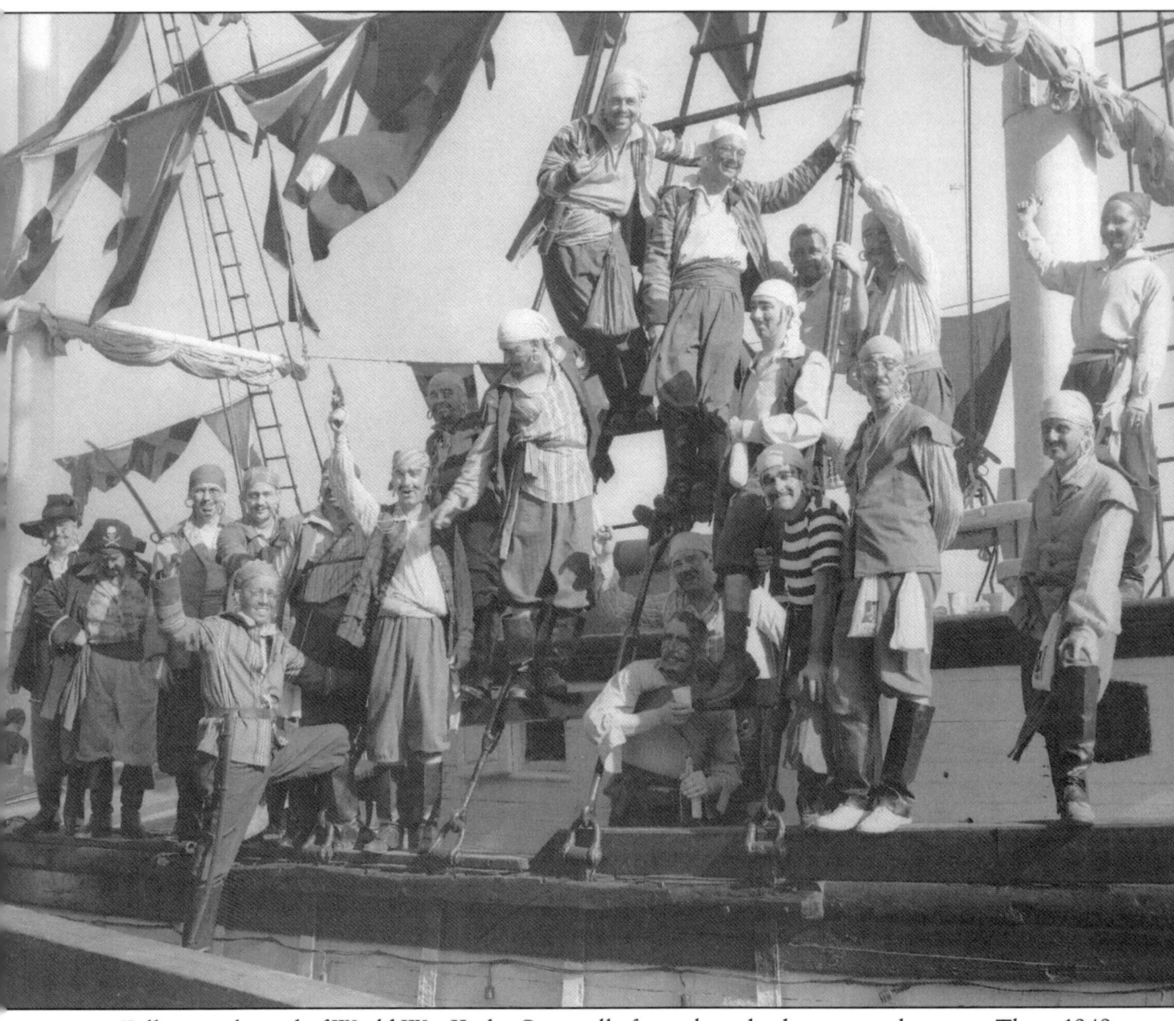

Following the end of World War II, the Gasparilla festival was back stronger than ever. These 1949 Ye Mystic Krewe of Gasparilla pirates are all smiles on board *José Gaspar*, the first vessel owned by the krewe. In 1954, a new ship built for Ye Mystic Krewe of Gasparilla was named *José Gasparilla*. As seen in this photograph, the costumes worn by the pirates were still very basic, with most wearing bandanas, sashes, and fake knee-length boots. The makeup was still mostly black facial hair or scars applied with a black grease pencil. (THCPL.)

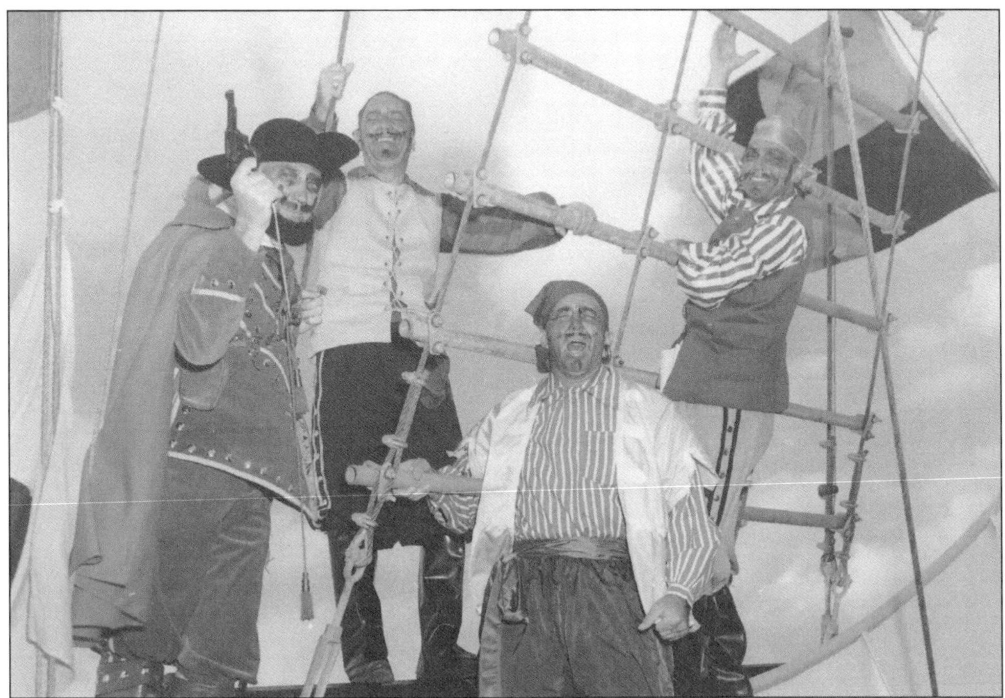

The year 1954 was an important one for Ye Mystic Krewe of Gasparilla. The krewe's new ship, *José Gasparilla*, was christened right before an overcast, windy invasion day. The ship had been built in 1953 for a total cost of $100,000. The Tampa Bay area also celebrated the opening of the Sunshine Skyway Bridge in 1954. Pirates like those in the rigging above adopted a swashbuckling buccaneer style of dress at this time with oversized, blousy shirts and bandanas. In these two photographs, members of Ye Mystic Krewe of Gasparilla are carrying .38 Special guns that shoot blanks, which, along with 10-gauge salute cannons, are a foundation of the revelry on invasion day. (Both, THCPL.)

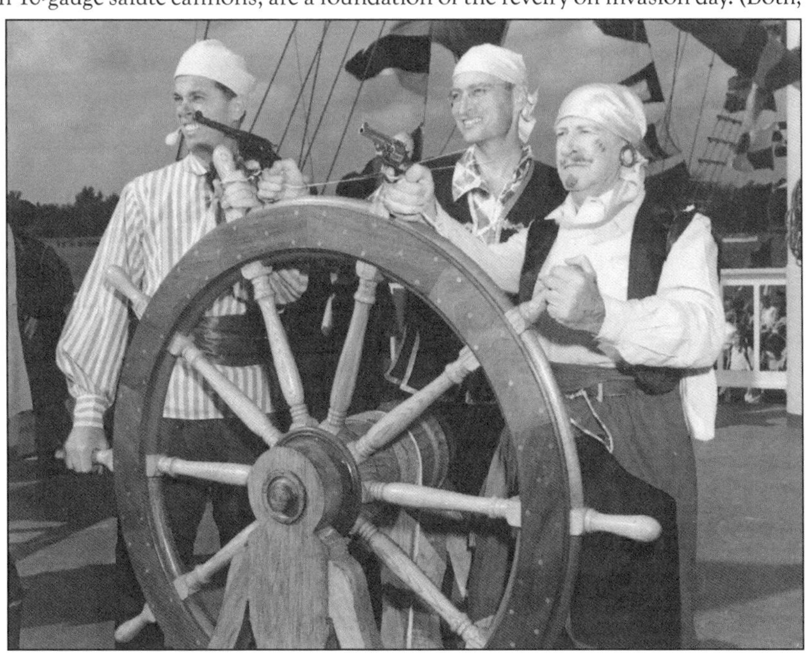

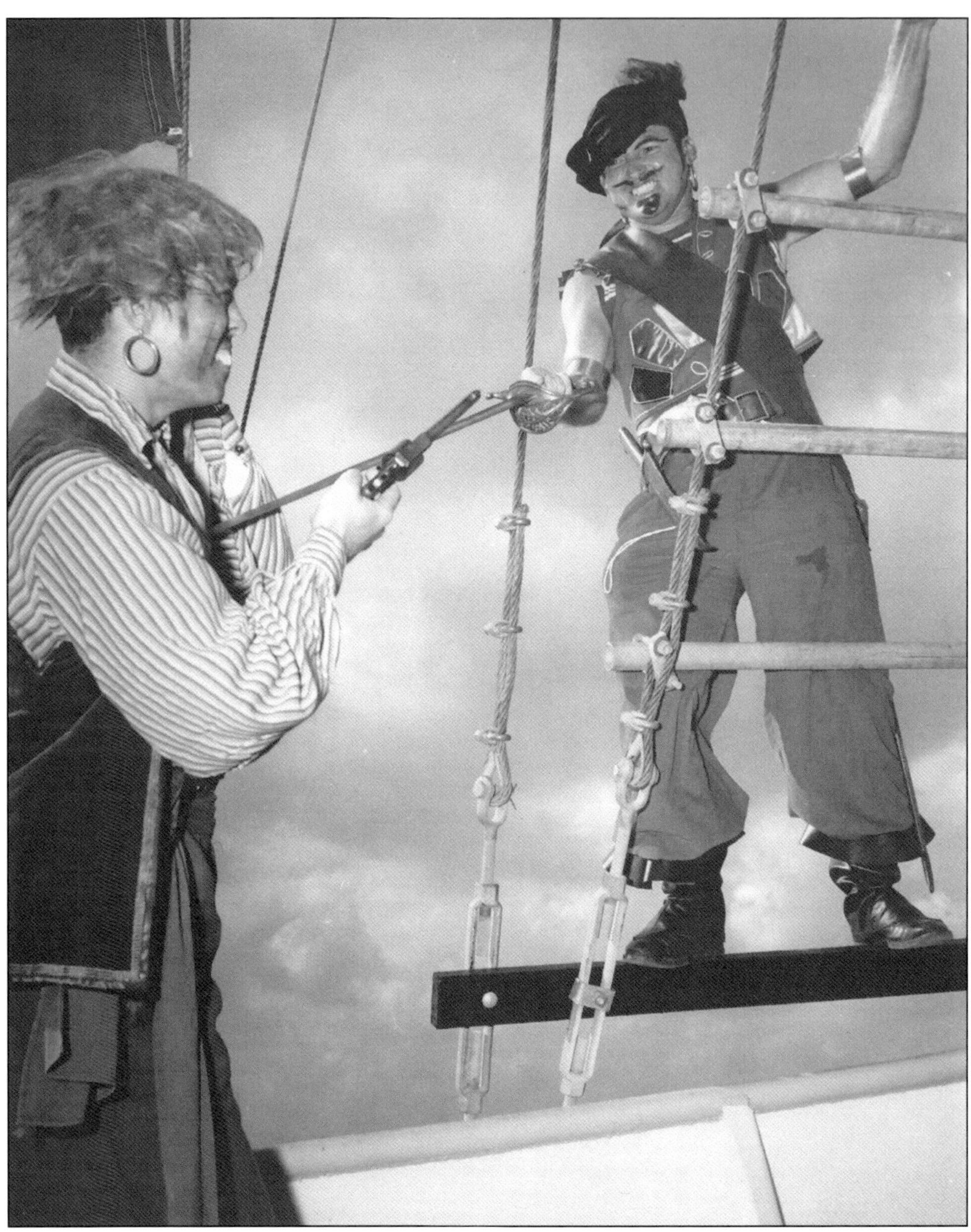

This 1954 photograph shows two pirates of Ye Mystic Krewe of Gasparilla posing for a promotional picture in the rigging of the new *José Gasparilla*. Costumes at this point included accessories such as earrings and wigs. (Notice the crooked wig on the pirate on the left.) This ship was built specifically for use as a "pirate" ship and was much larger and safer than prior vessels used for the invasion. From earlier experiences with previous ships running aground in Hillsborough Bay and the Hillsborough River, *José Gasparilla* was designed as a steel flat-bottomed barge. The ship is 137 feet in length with a beam of 36 feet and has much more room than previous vessels. Some Ye Mystic Krewe of Gasparilla members prefer to make the voyage into Tampa sitting or standing in the rigging, while others prefer to climb all the way up to the crow's nest, which provides a spectacular view of the invasion. (THCPL.)

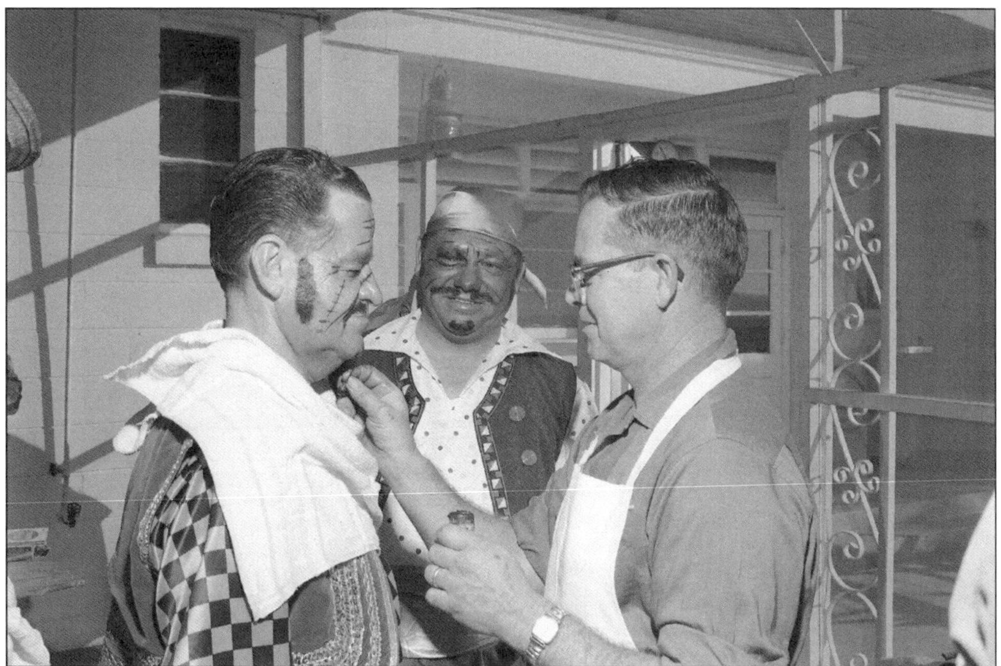

Above, the makeup used by Ye Mystic Krewe of Gasparilla pirates in the late 1950s and 1960s was still fairly basic, with scars and facial hair applied with the use of black grease pencils. Eventually, a more structured approach for transformation into the look of a pirate was adopted, as seen below. Makeup artists and stylists are now used for the process, which begins early on invasion day. Although several private clubs in Tampa now have makeup breakfasts and parties, the Tampa Yacht and Country Club, established the same year as Gasparilla in 1904, remains the standard for pre-invasion activities. (Above, THCPL; below, YMKG.)

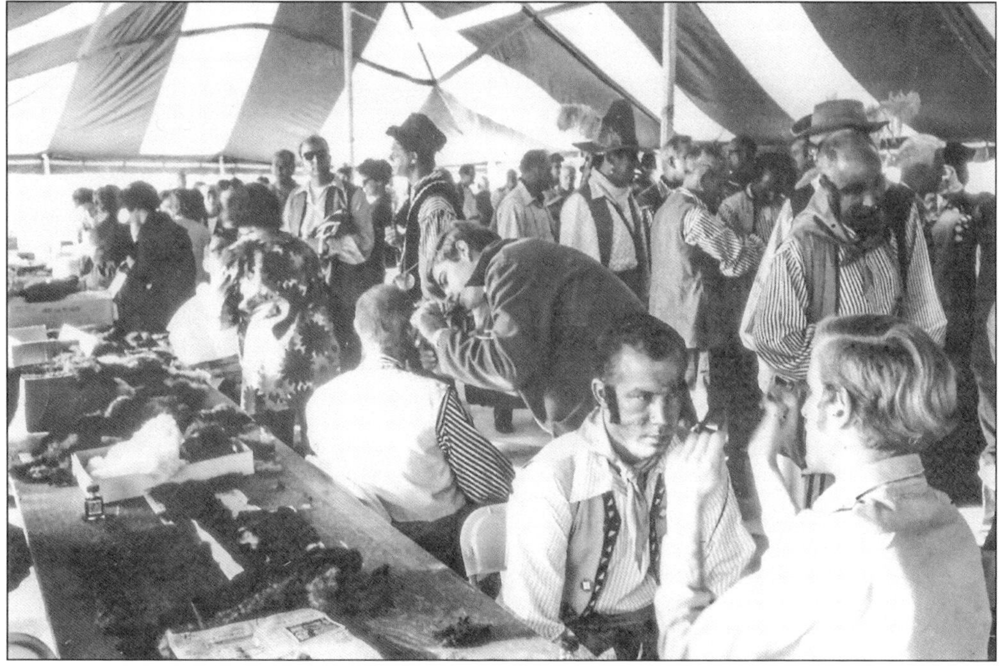

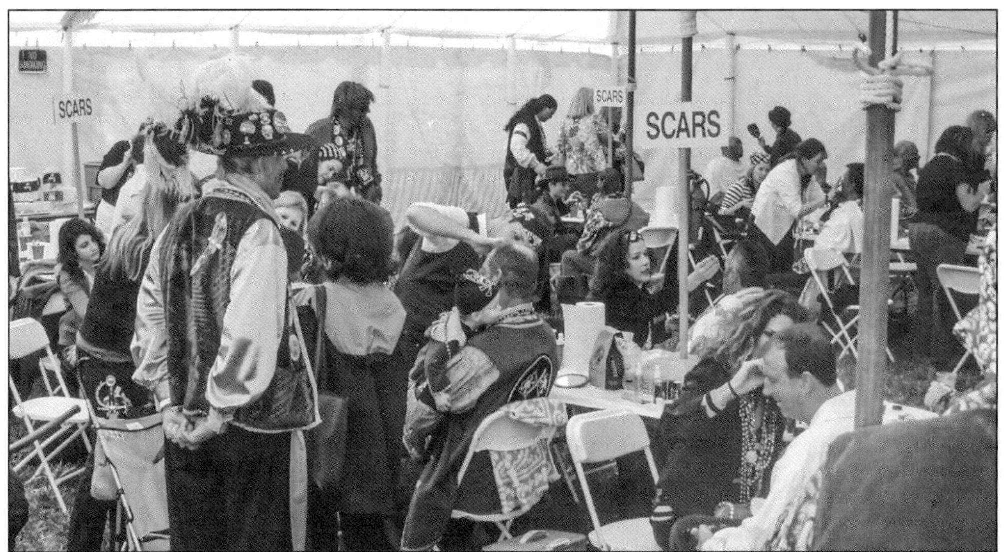

Although some pirates prefer to apply their own disguises, most members of Ye Mystic Krewe of Gasparilla prefer to use professional makeup artists and stylists. At the Tampa Yacht and Country Club, the most popular location for pre-invasion readiness, there are specific stations for base makeup, scars, hair, and facial hair, as seen above. The costumes now worn by most krewes participating in Gasparilla are custom-made themed outfits that represent the culture of their krewe. Members of Ye Mystic Krewe of Gasparilla wear costumes with either "YMKG" or the older "MKG" insignia and wear feathered hats. Below, a member of Ye Mystic Krewe of Gasparilla's Gunners Guild prepares to shoot a cannon as *José Gasparilla* leaves the Ballast Point Pier. (Above, YMKG; below, William Carson, MD.)

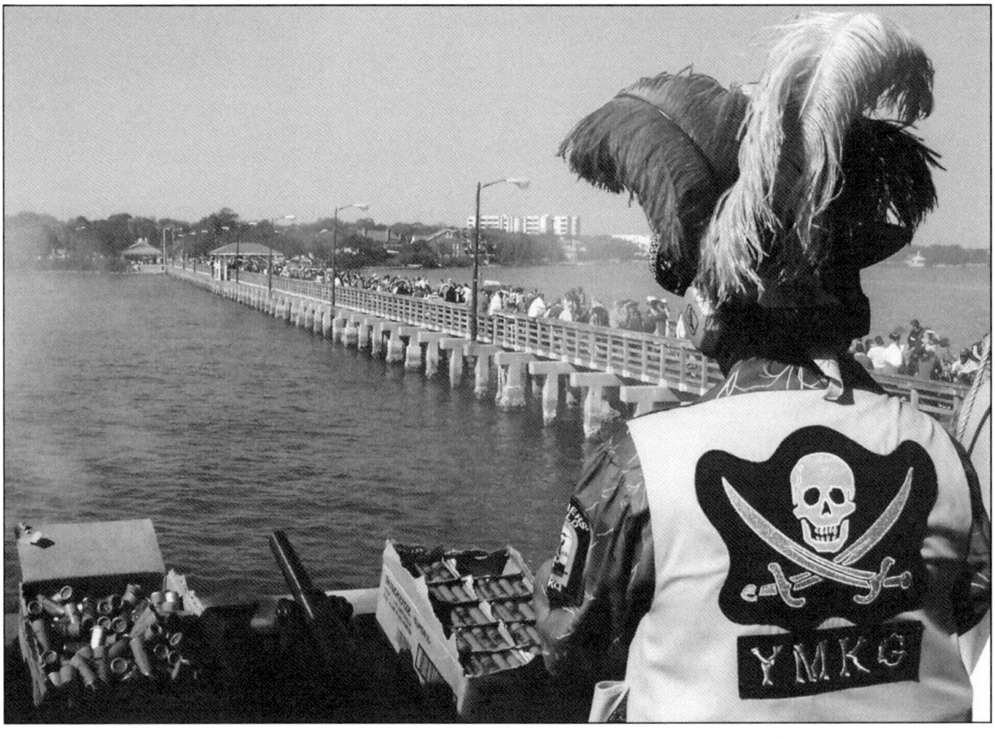

Eight

More Krewes Join Gasparilla

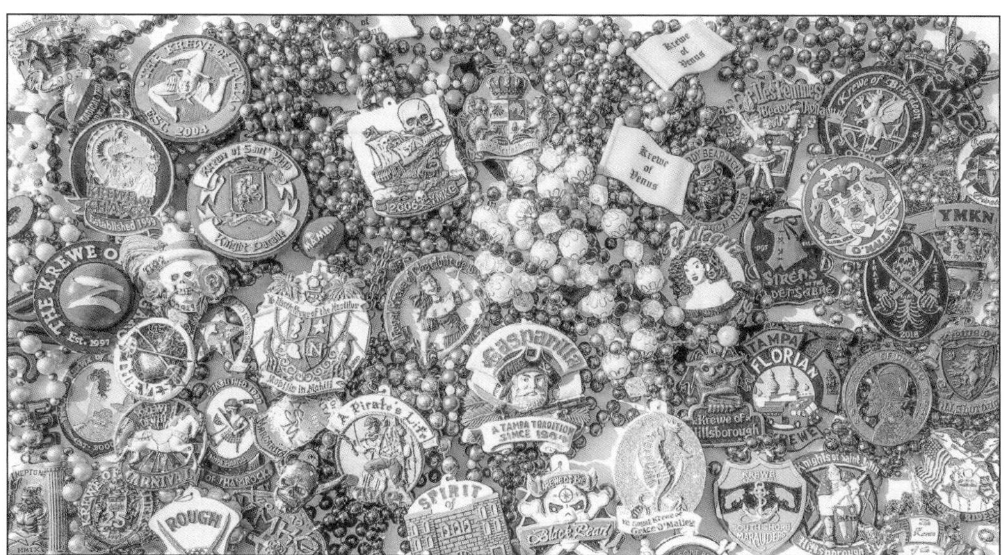

From 1904 to 1965, Ye Mystic Krewe of Gasparilla was the only krewe in the Gasparilla invasion and parade. There are now 68 krewe members of the Inter-Krewe Council of Tampa, whose community contributions have helped thousands in the Tampa Bay area. The krewes listed in this chapter are just a few of the oldest and most popular organizations that have helped contribute to the success of Gasparilla. (Inter-Krewe Council of Tampa.)

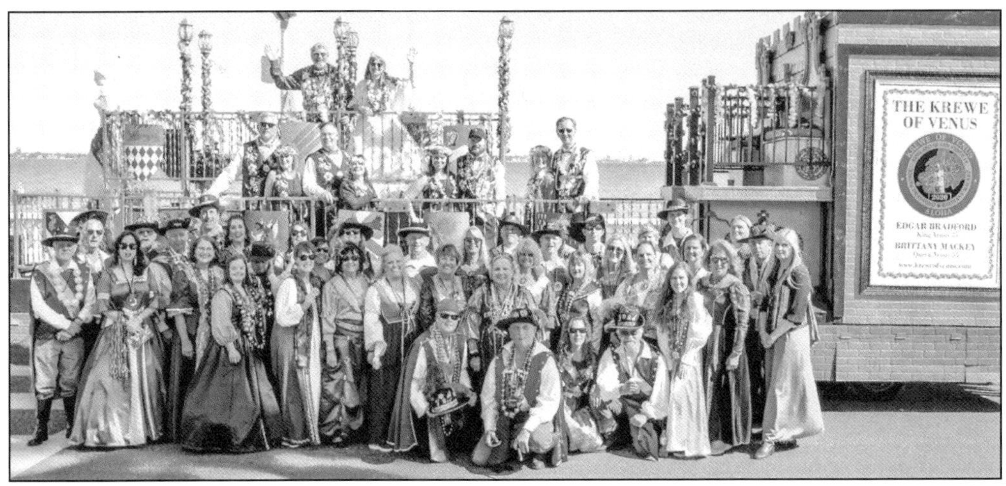

Founded in 1965, the Krewe of Venus became the second-oldest krewe to participate in Gasparilla. The organization is a coed social club with an emphasis on friendship and community. During the Gasparilla parade, members wear Renaissance costumes and throw accompanying beads. The Krewe of Venus is credited with starting the tradition of throwing beads at Gasparilla. This photograph shows Krewe of Venus members at the 2020 Gasparilla. (Krewe of Venus.)

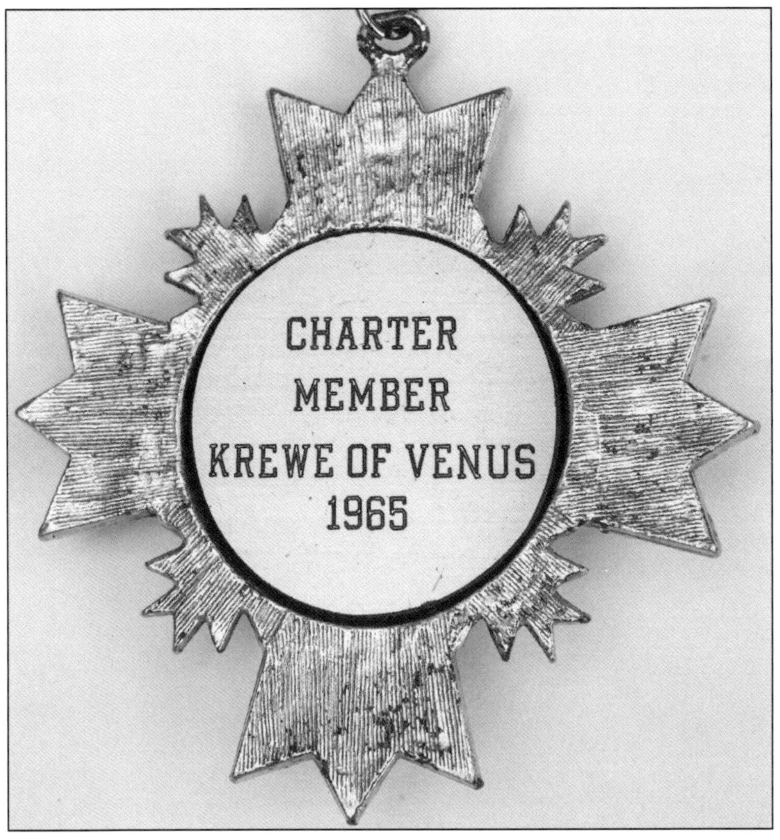

The Krewe of Venus was founded on December 8, 1965. On this date, 275 charter members met at the Tampa Woman's Club on Bayshore Boulevard and were provided with a medallion to commemorate the occasion. Tampa's new krewe was named in honor of New Orlean's Krewe of Venus, which had played such a vital role in its birth. (William Carson, MD.)

With support and representation from the Krewe of Venus of New Orleans, the inaugural event of Tampa's Krewe of Venus was a Mardi Gras–style coronation ball at the old Curtis Hixon Hall (Convention Center) on November 13, 1965. Custom-made costumes, spectacular stages, sets, and scenery were flown in from New Orleans for the well-attended event. Pictured here is the cover of the event's program. (William Carson, MD.)

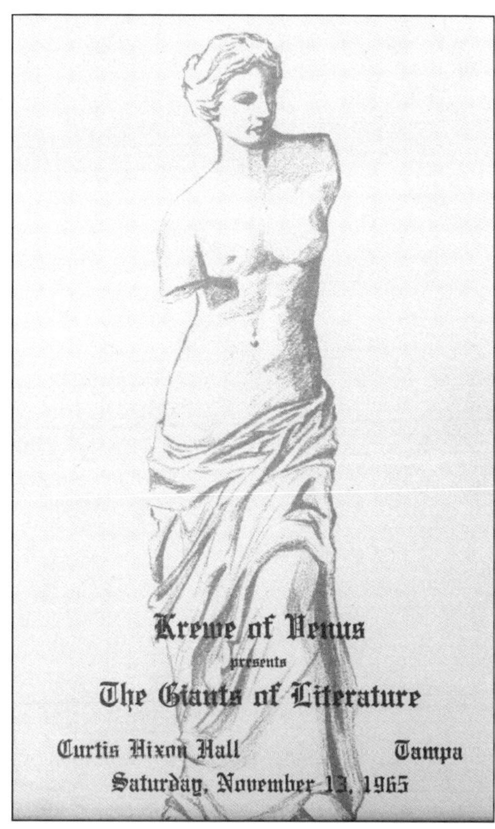

When participating in the Gasparilla parade, Krewe of Venus members either ride their float or walk beside it. If one of the krewes participating in the Gasparilla parade selects a king and queen of the organization for the year, they usually ride a royal float, along with other members of their court. Seen here is one of the royal floats of the Krewe of Venus. Notice the statue of Venus on the front of the float and the Renaissance costumes. (Lori Ballard Photography–Tampa.)

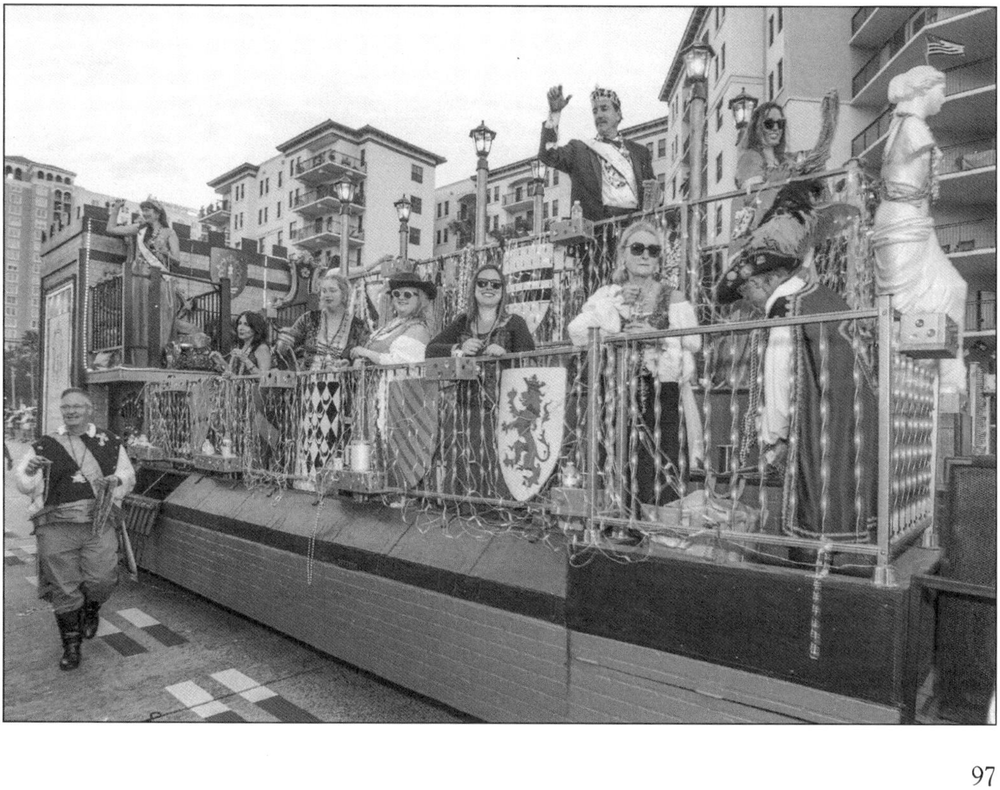

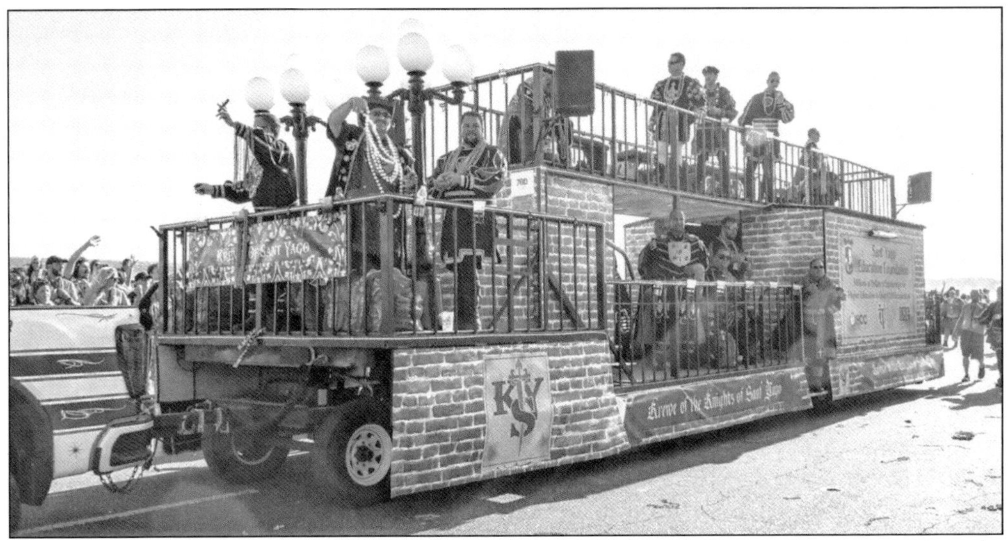

Established in September 1972, the Krewe of the Knights of Sant' Yago is dedicated to the perpetuation and enhancement of Tampa's proud Latin heritage, culture, and mores. The krewe dedicates itself to the continued improvement of life and cultural progress in the city of Tampa and its surroundings. Pictured here are several of the 300 members on their float at the Gasparilla parade on Bayshore Boulevard. (Ocasio Images.)

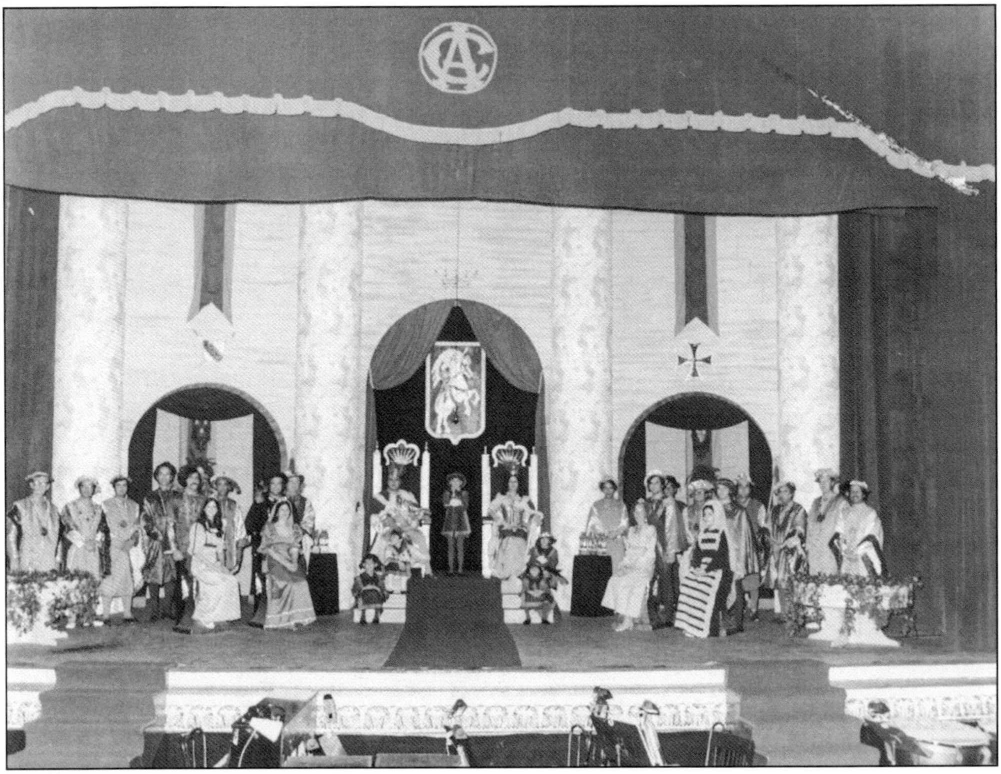

The Krewe of the Knights of Sant' Yago held their first coronation in January 1973 at Centro Asturiano de Tampa in Ybor City. Since then, Sant' Yago has held over 50 coronations, debutante balls, and Knight parades and has grown to 300 members. (Krewe of the Knights of Sant' Yago.)

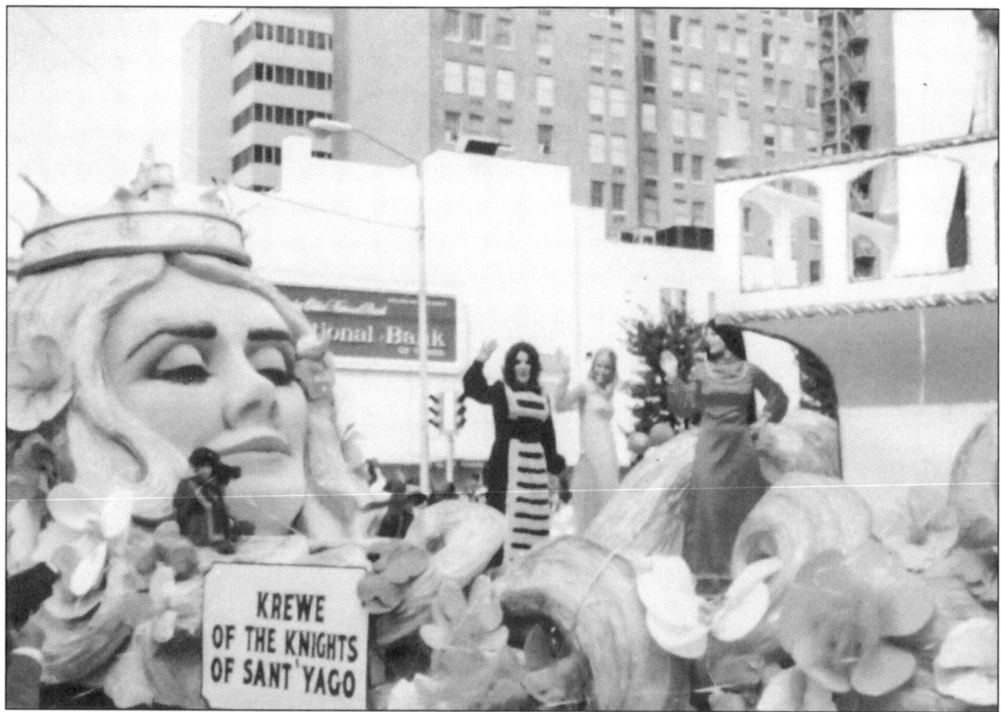

The Krewe of the Knights of Sant' Yago's first appearance in the Gasparilla parade was in 1973. Its float was decorated in the image of Sleeping Beauty with the theme "Like a Sleeping Beauty Tampa's Latin Culture Awakens." Sant' Yago was the third krewe to participate in Gasparilla and has participated in every parade held since 1973. (Krewe of the Knights of Sant' Yago.)

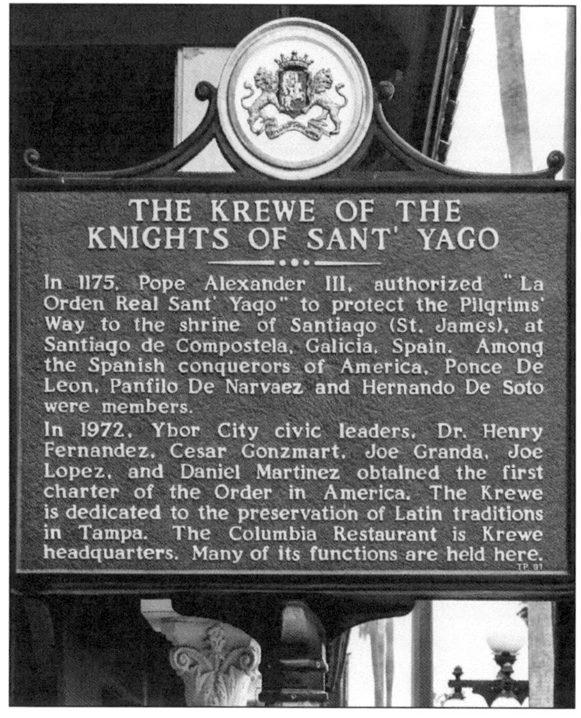

A plaque honoring the Krewe of the Knights of Sant' Yago is located in front of the world-famous Columbia Restaurant on Seventh Avenue in historic Ybor City. The inscription pays homage to La Orden Real Sant' Yago, the knights who protected those traveling to the shrine of Santiago (St. James). Ybor City is also the site of the popular and well-attended Illuminated Knight Parade, hosted by the Krewe of the Knights of Sant' Yago since 1974. (William Carson, MD.)

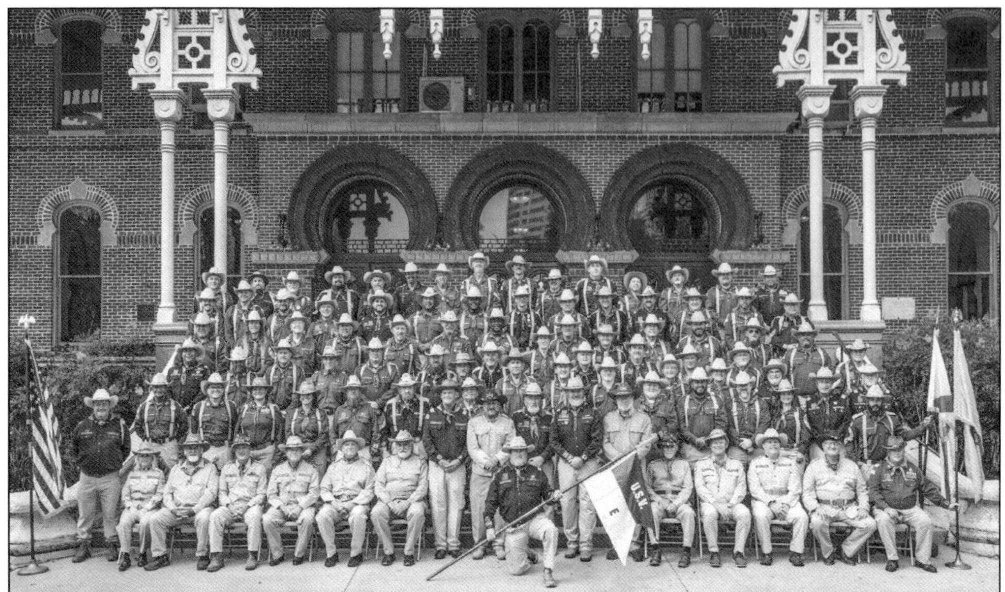

The Krewe of the 1st US Volunteer Cavalry Regiment Rough Riders was founded in 1978 to create a living memorial to the unique accomplishments of Pres. Theodore Roosevelt and the members of the 1st US Volunteer Cavalry Regiment, known as the Rough Riders. Pictured here are krewe members at Plant Hall at the University of Tampa, formerly known as the Tampa Bay Hotel, where Teddy Roosevelt stayed prior to the Spanish-American War in 1898. (Rough Riders.)

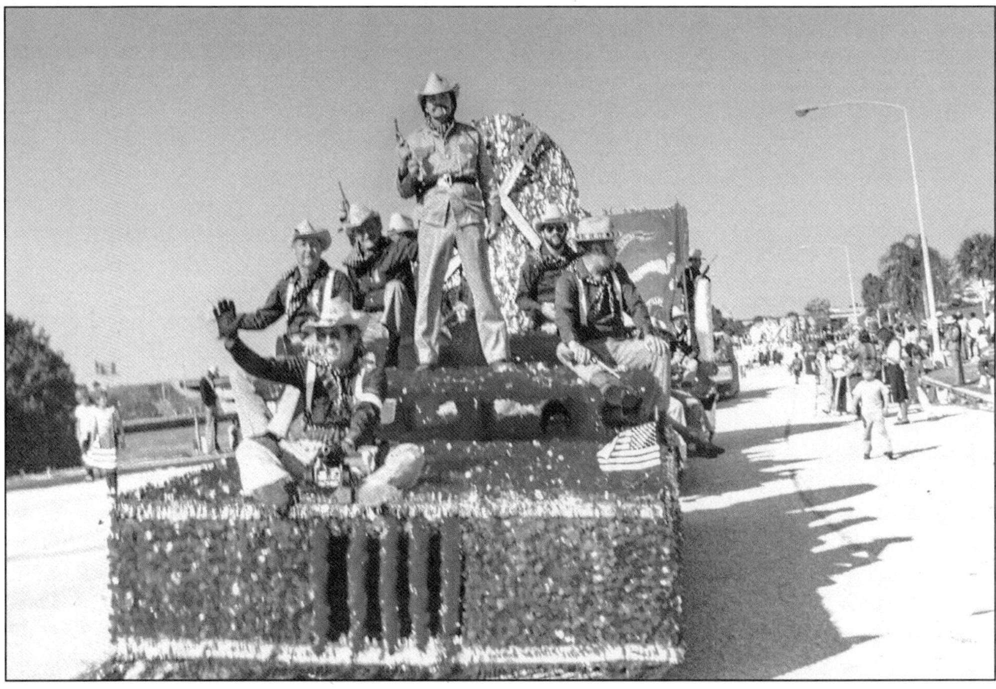

Pictured here is one of the earliest floats used by the Rough Riders in the Gasparilla parade. The krewe uniforms pay homage to the Rough Riders of the late 1800s, who wore a distinctive uniform to stand out from other troops. They wore a slouch hat, blue flannel shirt, brown trousers, leggings, and boots, along with handkerchiefs knotted loosely around their necks. (Rough Riders.)

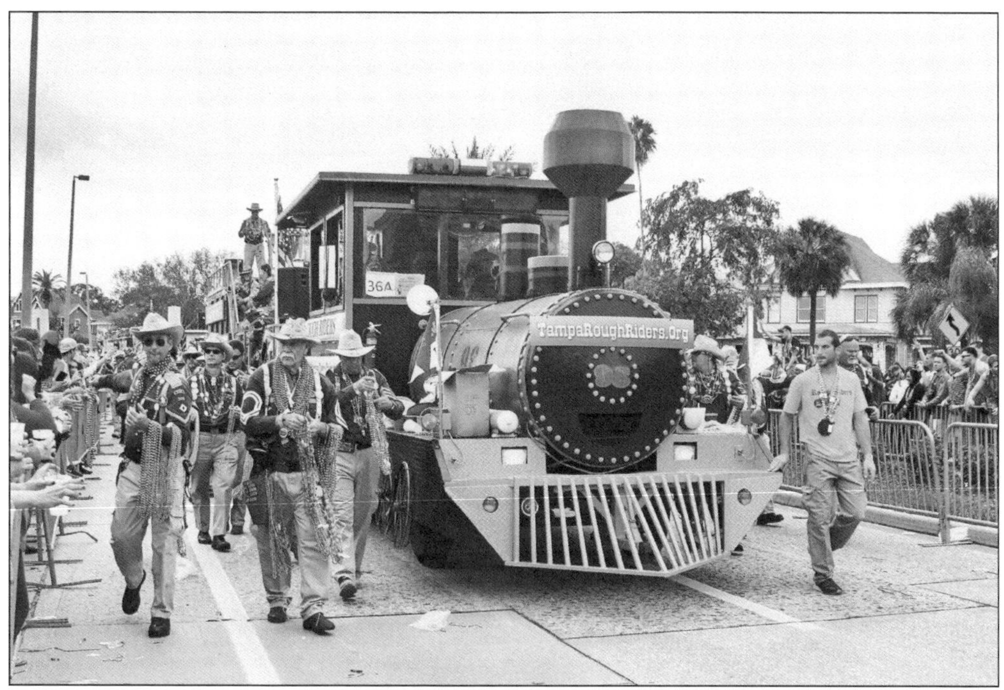

Members of the Rough Riders walk beside their Old No. 98, a turn-of-the-century train float. In addition to Gasparilla, the krewe also supports several local charities. Every year, the Rough Riders organize an annual "Teddy Bear Run" and distribute thousands of teddy bears to hospital patients, cancer survivors and their families, centers for abused women and children, community health centers, special needs day care centers, and foster children. (Brian Brantley)

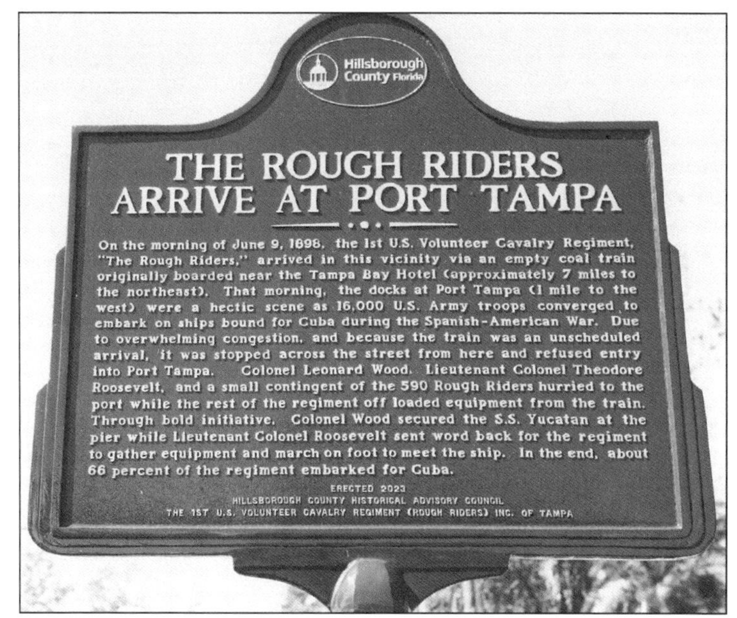

Teddy Roosevelt and the Rough Riders spent time in Tampa preparing for the United States' involvement in the Spanish-American War of 1898. There are several monuments in the city that honor their presence here. One of the tributes is in Port Tampa near the intersection of Westshore Boulevard and Interbay Boulevard. It was near this location that the Rough Riders embarked for the conflict in Cuba. (William Carson, MD.)

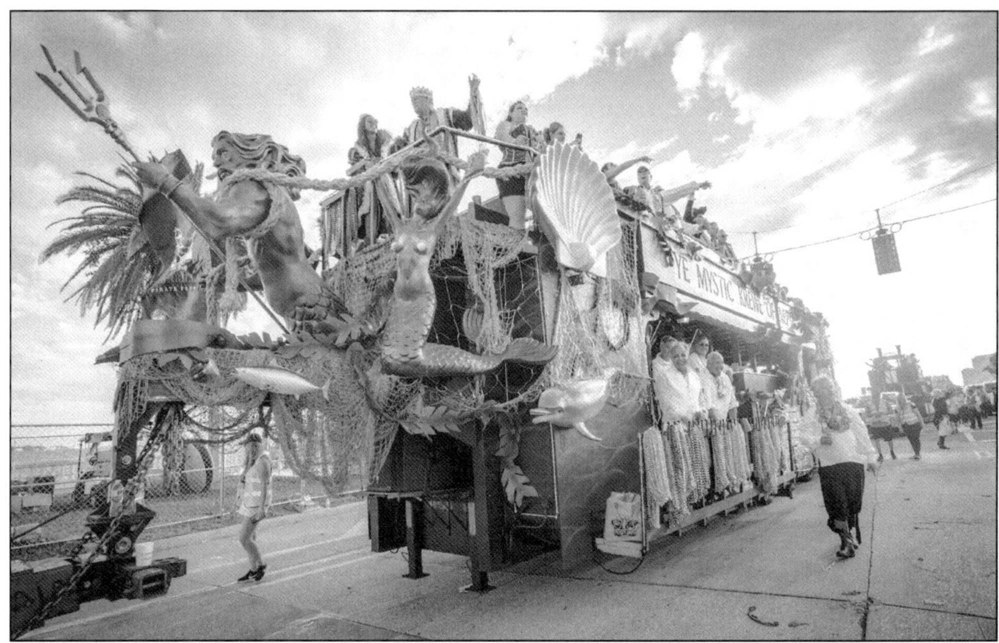

Founded in 1980 in St. Petersburg, Florida, Ye Mystic Krewe of Neptune was established by local businessmen in search of friendship and fun. Today, it thrives as a dynamic social group of 100 members, celebrated for hosting memorable events and fostering lasting connections. The krewe is also a proud founding member of the Inter-Krewe Council of Tampa, an organization that unites and supports krewes across the local community. (Lori Ballard Photography–Tampa.)

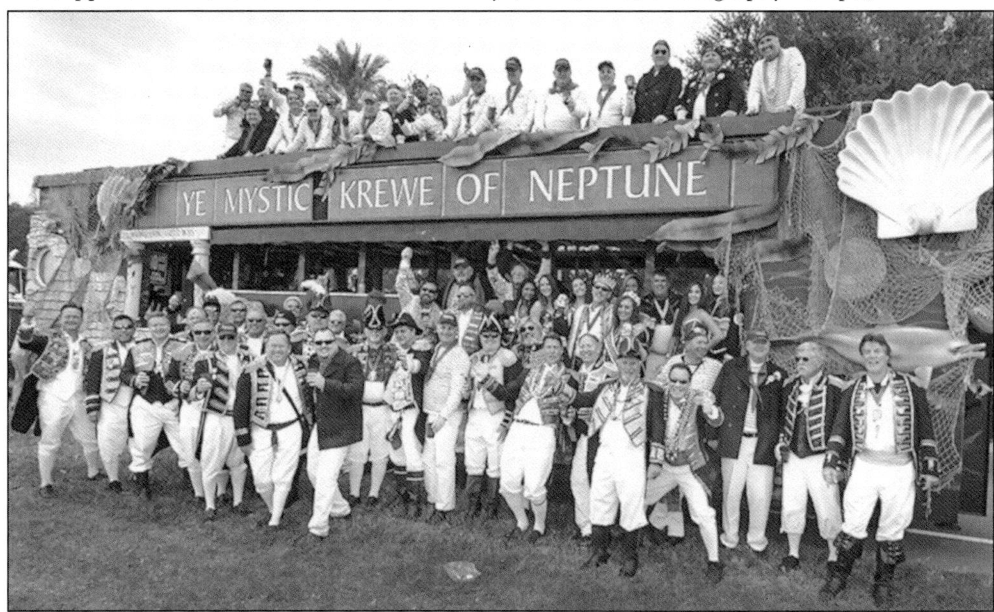

Inspired by the legendary krewes of New Orleans, Ye Mystic Krewe of Neptune brings tradition and celebration to Tampa Bay. During the Gasparilla parade, members—officers, midshipmen, and seamen—wear authentic 1800s British naval uniforms, adding historic flair. While camaraderie and fun are central, the krewe is also dedicated to community service, supporting a variety of civic and charitable causes throughout the year. (Ye Mystic Krewe of Neptune.)

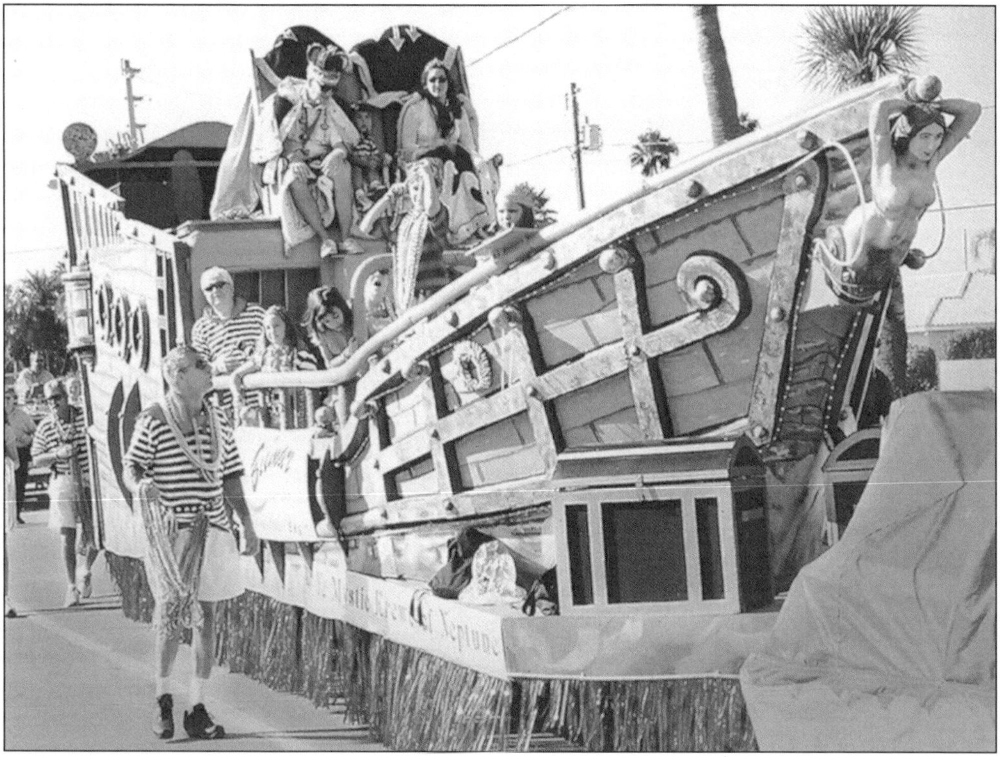

Ye Mystic Krewe of Neptune's first float, towed by a Ford Explorer, flipped when a passing semitruck caused it to fishtail. Though the float, vehicle, and drinks were lost, injuries were minor. Undaunted, the krewe marched on—without a float, drinks, or king. It nicknamed the float "Flipper," proudly used it for years, and proved that even in chaos, the krewe's spirit remained unshaken. (Ye Mystic Krewe of Neptune.)

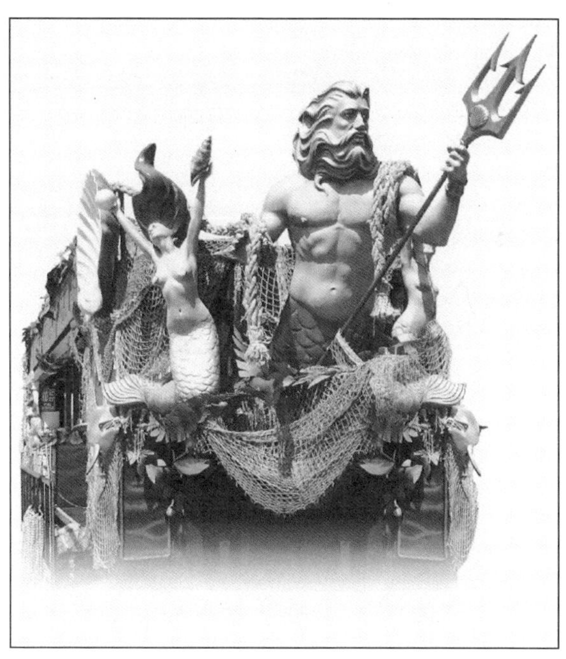

Inspired by King Neptune, the krewe reflects the sea god's strength and unity. Its current float, a dramatic upgrade from the original, is a stunning two-story creation crowned with a towering Neptune statue. It commands attention each year at the Gasparilla parade, serving as a bold emblem of the krewe's legacy. This iconic float leaves a lasting impression, capturing admiration and symbolizing the krewe's enduring spirit and vibrant tradition. (Ye Mystic Krewe of Neptune.)

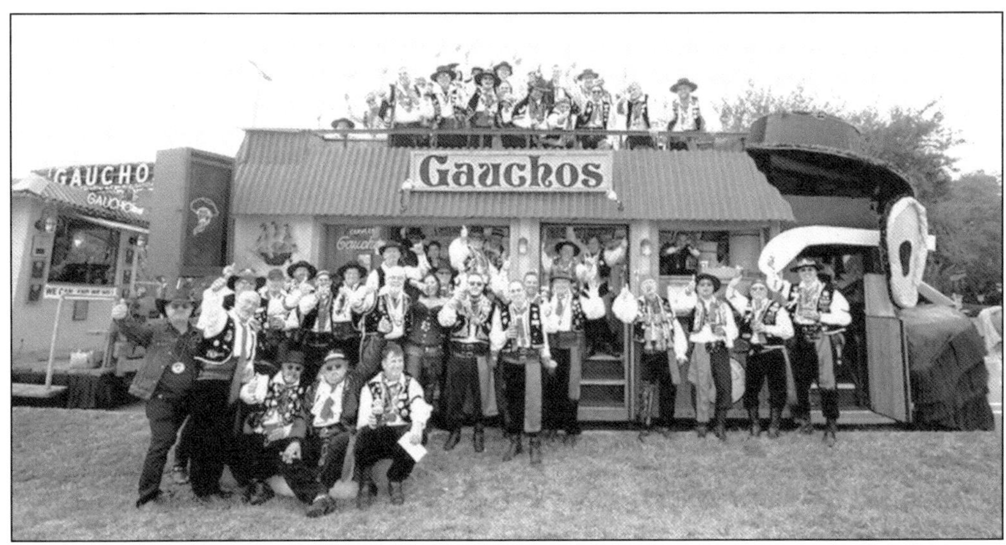

The Gaucho Association was formed in the 1950s to serve as escorts to the Queen and Court of the Latin American Fiesta Association. The group was then incorporated as the Gauchos of the Latin Fiesta in 1960. In 1987, the Gauchos reorganized as a krewe to increase the size of the organization and visibility in the Tampa Bay area. Each year, the group participates in the Krewe of the Knights of Sant' Yago's Illuminated Knight Parade, Dunedin Mardi Gras Parade, Rough Riders' St. Patrick's Parade, New Port Richey's Chasco Fest Parade, and the Tampa Bay Veterans Day Parade. The photograph above shows the Gauchos prior to the Gasparilla parade. The photograph below from January 1950 shows four of the original Gauchos in front of the Tampa City Hall at the corner of Florida Avenue and Lafayette Street, now Kennedy Boulevard. (Above, Gauchos; below, USF.)

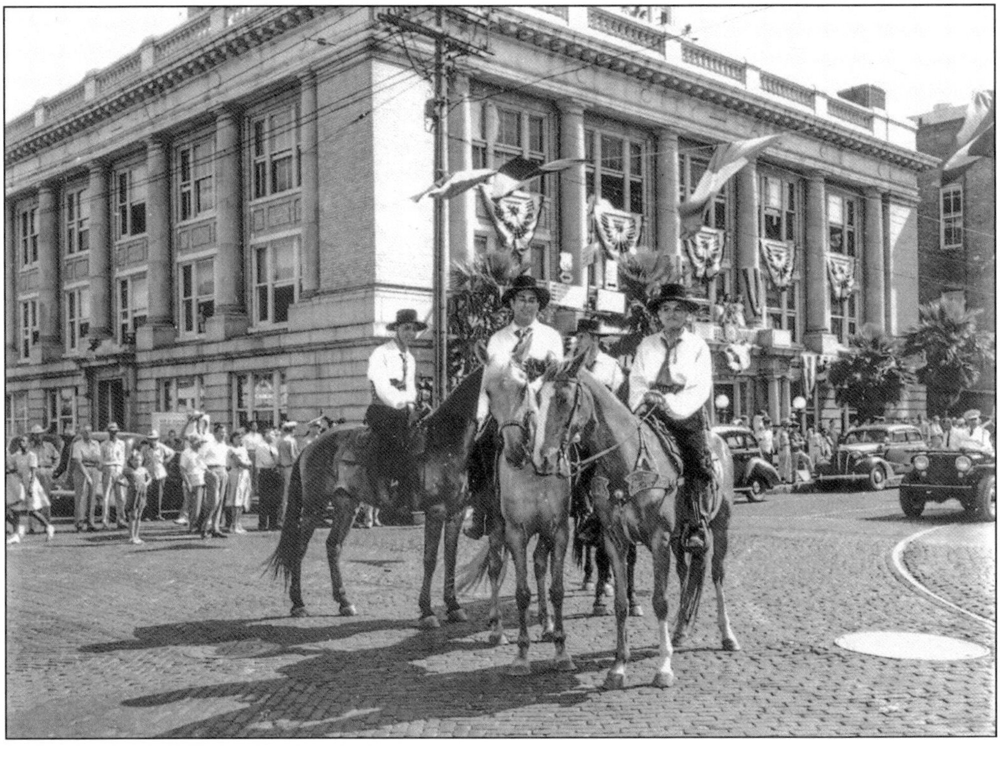

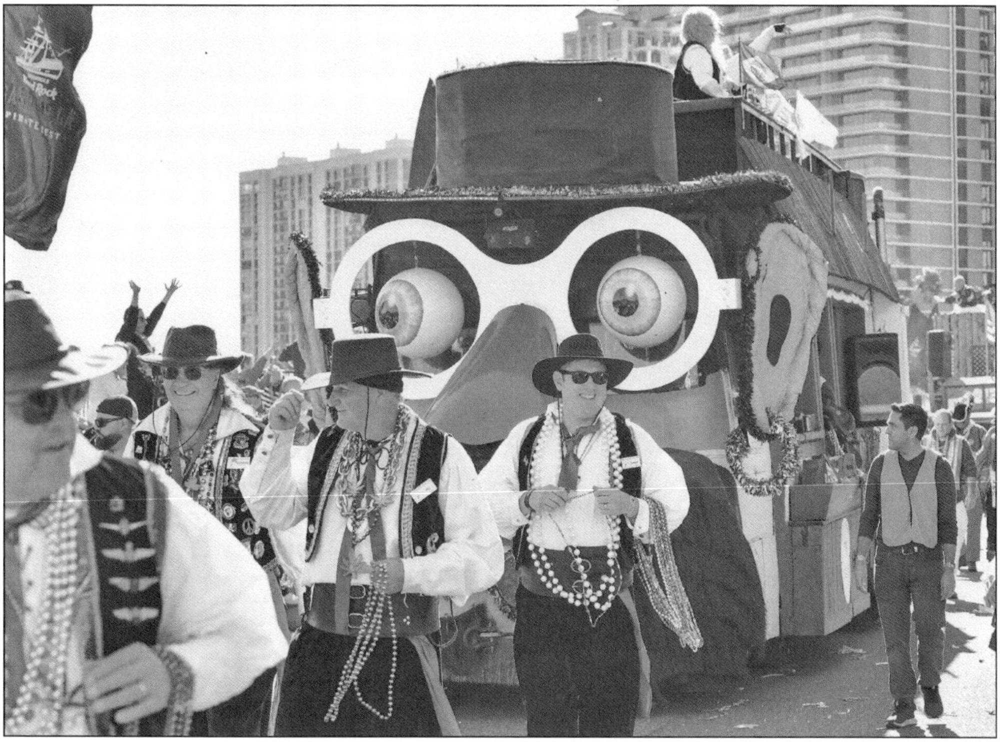

The original 1991 Gaucho float won first place awards in all the major parade events in the Tampa Bay area and was always a crowd favorite. The original float was retired, and in mid-2009, the Gauchos purchased a city bus and created La Casa del Sol Naciente. The handicap features of the original bus were modified so that the Gaucho hat could be raised and lowered when the unit came to a stop. Like the old unit, the float is adorned with moving eyes, eyebrows, and a large smoking cigar jutting out from under the large black mustache. The face sports a gold earring in the left ear and wears the latest in designer sunglasses. The floats are pictured at the Gasparilla parade on Bayshore Boulevard. The photograph below shows the crowd-pleasing smoke coming out of the cigar. (Above, Lori Ballard Photography–Tampa; below, Steven Watts.)

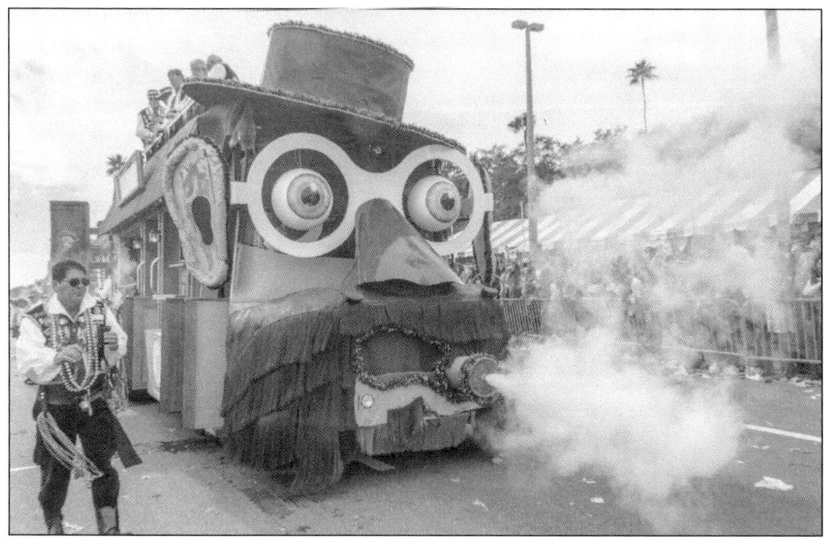

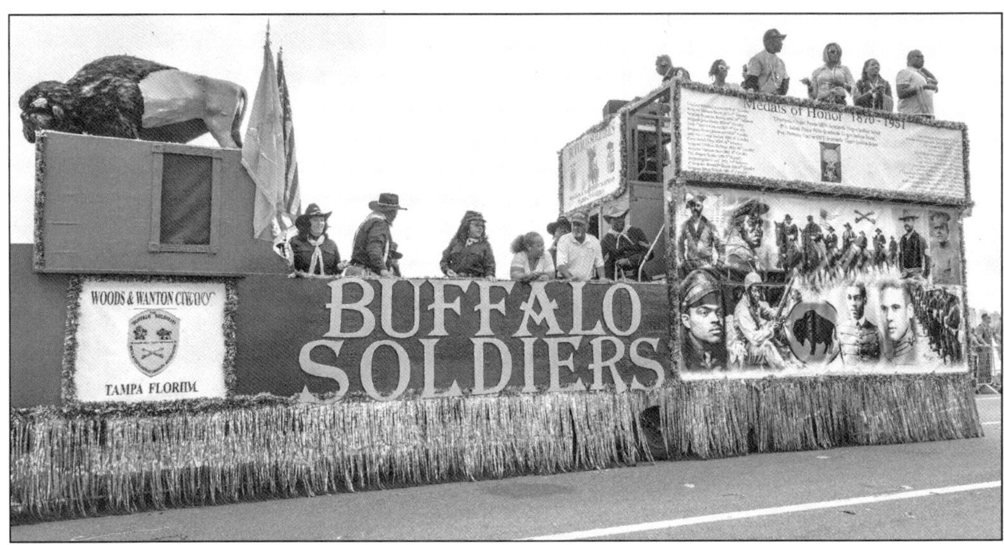

The Krewe of the Buffalo Soldiers, Woods and Wanton Chapter, was organized to pay tribute to African American cavalry descendants with prior military service. Members participated in their first Gasparilla parade in 1998, and the krewe's float now features historical information about Congressional Medal of Honor awardees and photographs of actual Buffalo Soldiers. The crowning jewel of the float is *Lakota*, a cast aluminum buffalo that stands stoically on the front. (Steven Watts.)

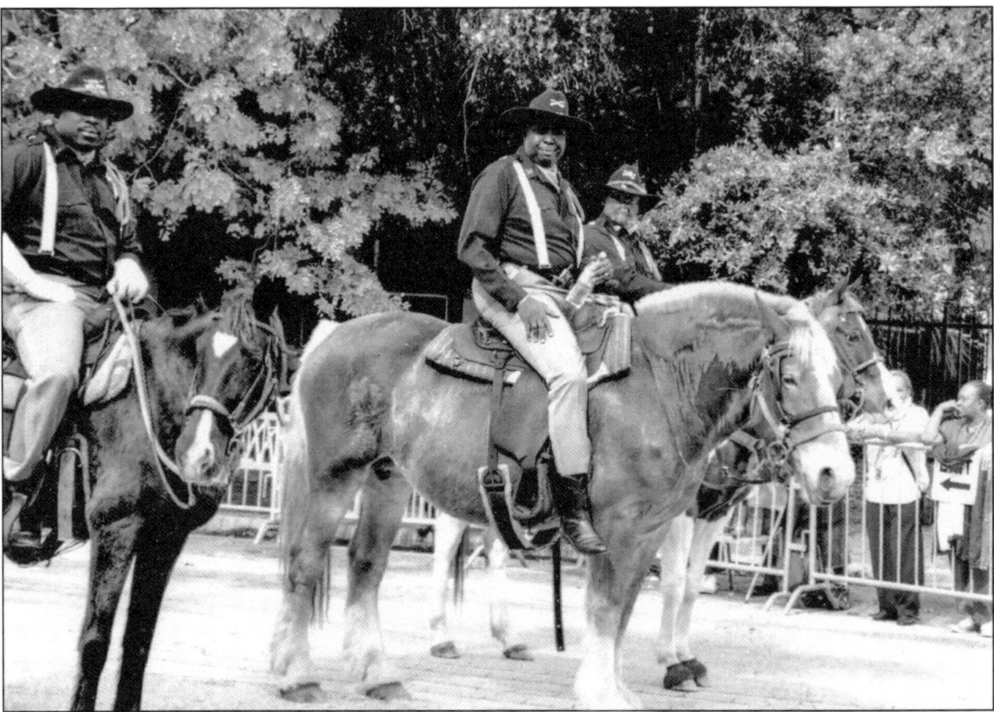

Although the chapter's membership is small, as of 2025, it has awarded over $300,000 in scholarships to high school students in the Tampa Bay area. Members wear a representation of the military utility uniform of the Buffalo Soldiers from 1885 to 1886. By rule, Buffalo Soldier members are not allowed to wear beads or buttons on their uniforms; their gear is not considered or referred to as costumes. (Krewe of the Buffalo Soldiers.)

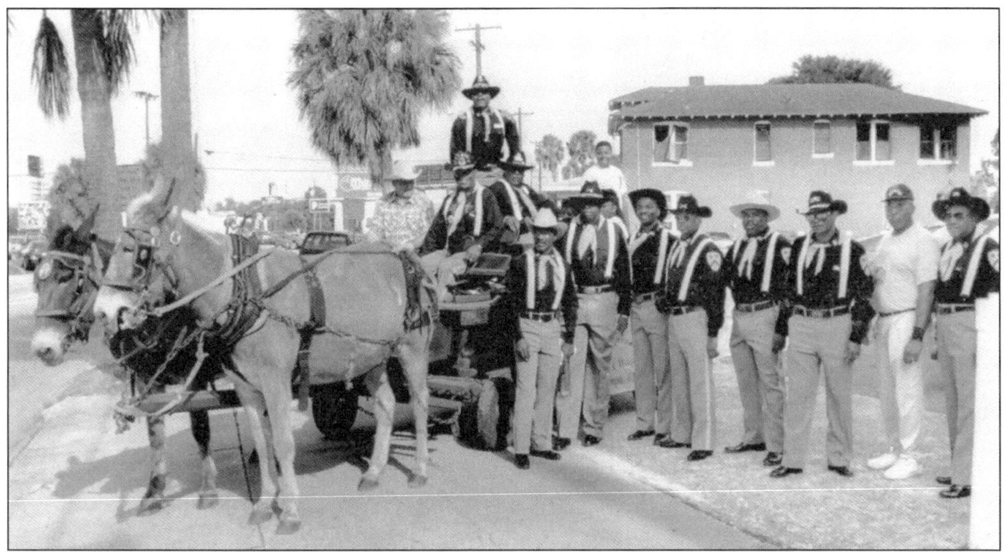

The Buffalo Soldiers chapter is named in recognition of Congressional Medal of Honor recipients Sgt. Brent Woods, Troop B, 9th Cavalry (Indian Wars, 1881) and Pvt. George W. Wanton, Troop M, 10th Cavalry (Spanish-American War). The chapter perpetuates the memory of comrades who have passed on and the history of the many accomplishments of the Buffalo Soldier regiments in the defense of the United States. (Krewe of the Buffalo Soldiers.)

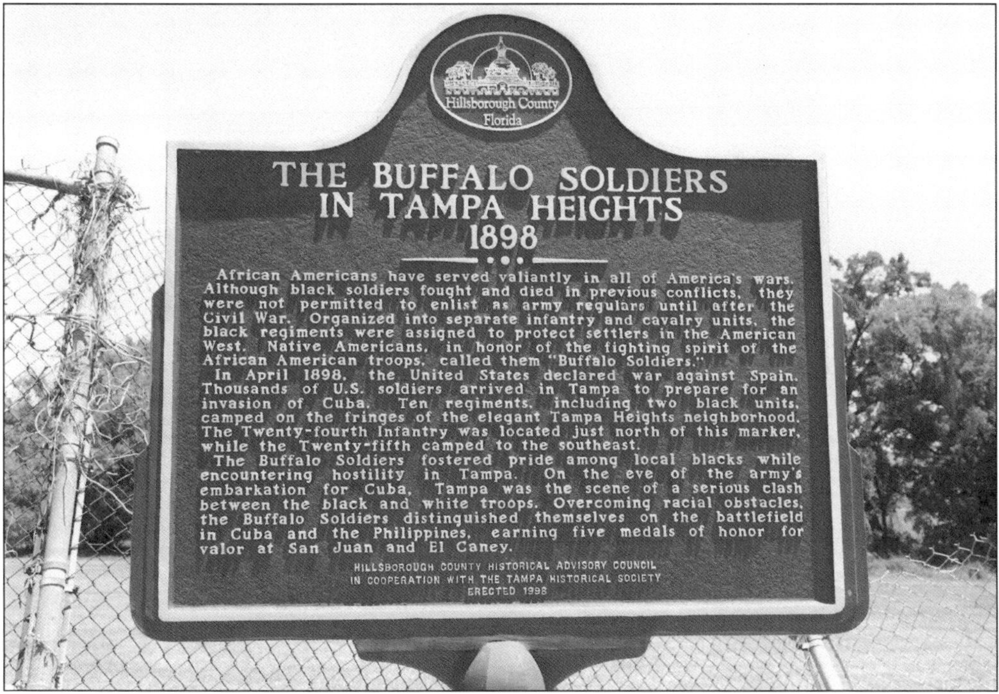

A monument honoring the Buffalo Soldiers is in Tampa Heights at the intersection of East Columbus Drive and North Central Avenue. The marker is beside a grassy field in which the 24th Infantry made camp in 1898 in preparation for the Spanish-American War. Overcoming racial obstacles, the Buffalo Soldiers distinguished themselves on the battlefield in Cuba and the Philippines, earning five Medals of Honor for valor at San Juan and El Caney. (William Carson, MD.)

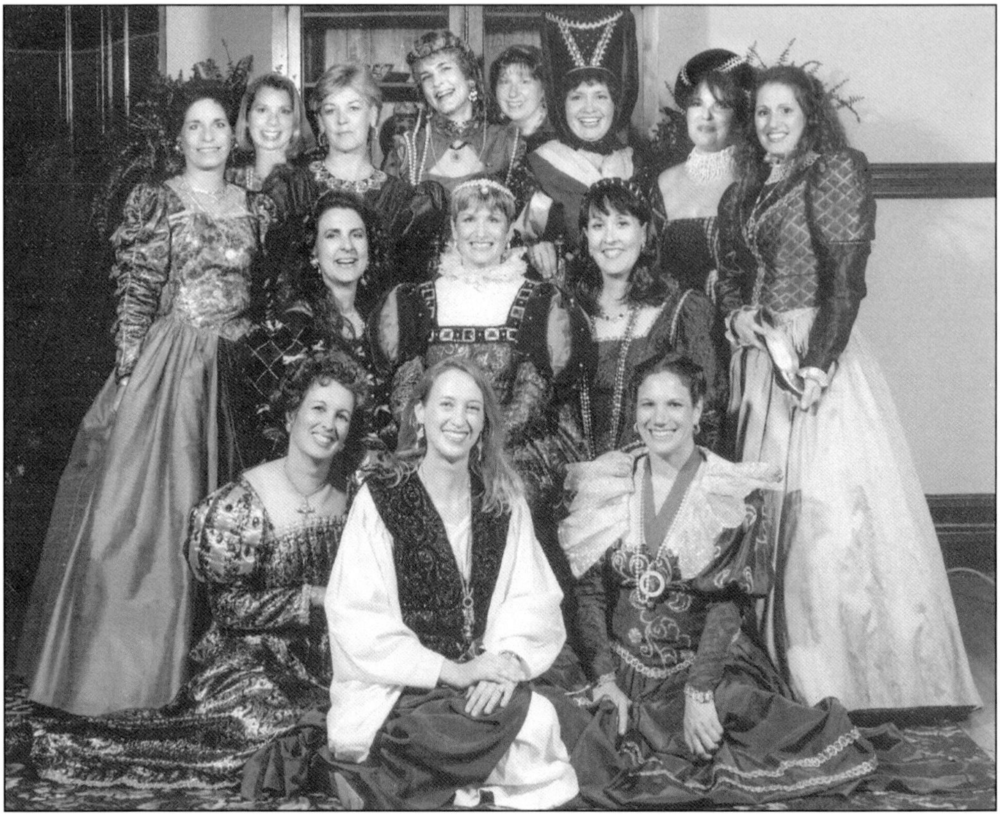

In 1992, fourteen women in Tampa cast their net into the sea of friendship with a vision of forming an all-female krewe, the first such krewe to be invited to participate in the Gasparilla parade. Grace O'Malley, a real female Irish pirate from the 16th century, was the inspiration. Community service is the cornerstone of Ye Loyal Krewe of Grace O'Malley (YLKGOM). All 400-plus members are expected to volunteer throughout the Tampa Bay area. The Krewe annually participates in Making Strides Against Breast Cancer, the nation's largest breast cancer movement. YLKGOM is the only krewe that is officially authorized to participate in costume with their float. Above are the 14 founders of YLKGOM. Below, members walk in the Gasparilla parade. (Above, YLKGOM; below, Ocasio Images.)

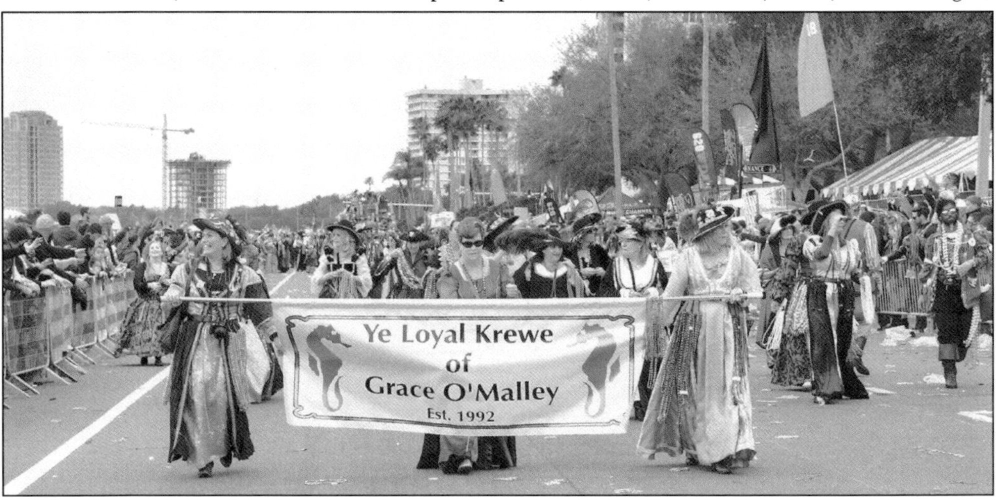

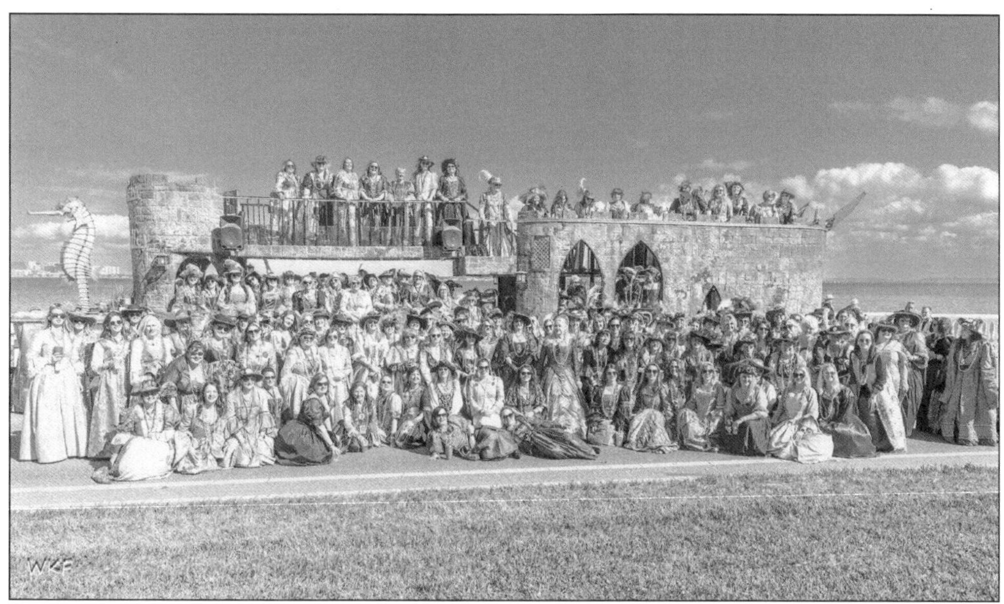

Ye Loyal Krewe of Grace O'Malley has three floats in the Gasparilla Parade: *Rockfleet*, *Grace–Queen of the Seas*, and *The Carrick*. Above are krewe members on Bayshore Boulevard aboard *Rockfleet* prior to the parade. Elaborate gowns are worn as a nod to the significance of a key meeting Grace O'Malley had with Queen Elizabeth. It was at this meeting that Grace wore her finest Elizabethan attire to request that her inheritances be returned to her and for her son and her brother-in-law to be released from prison. Below, members aboard a float hand out beads during the parade. (Above, YLKGOM; below, Brian Brantley.)

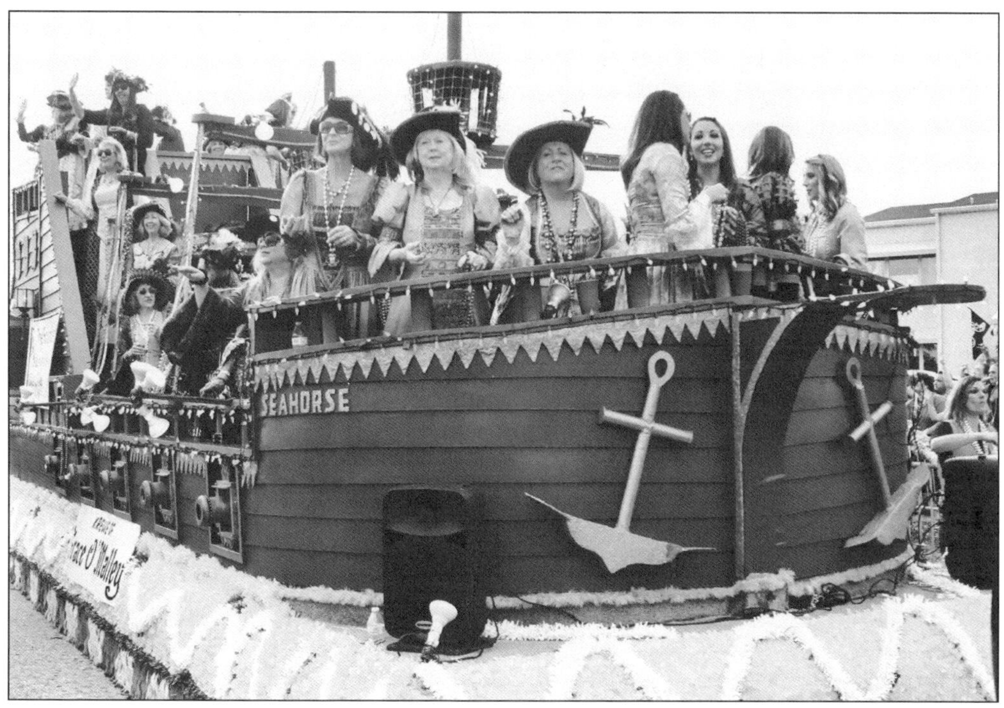

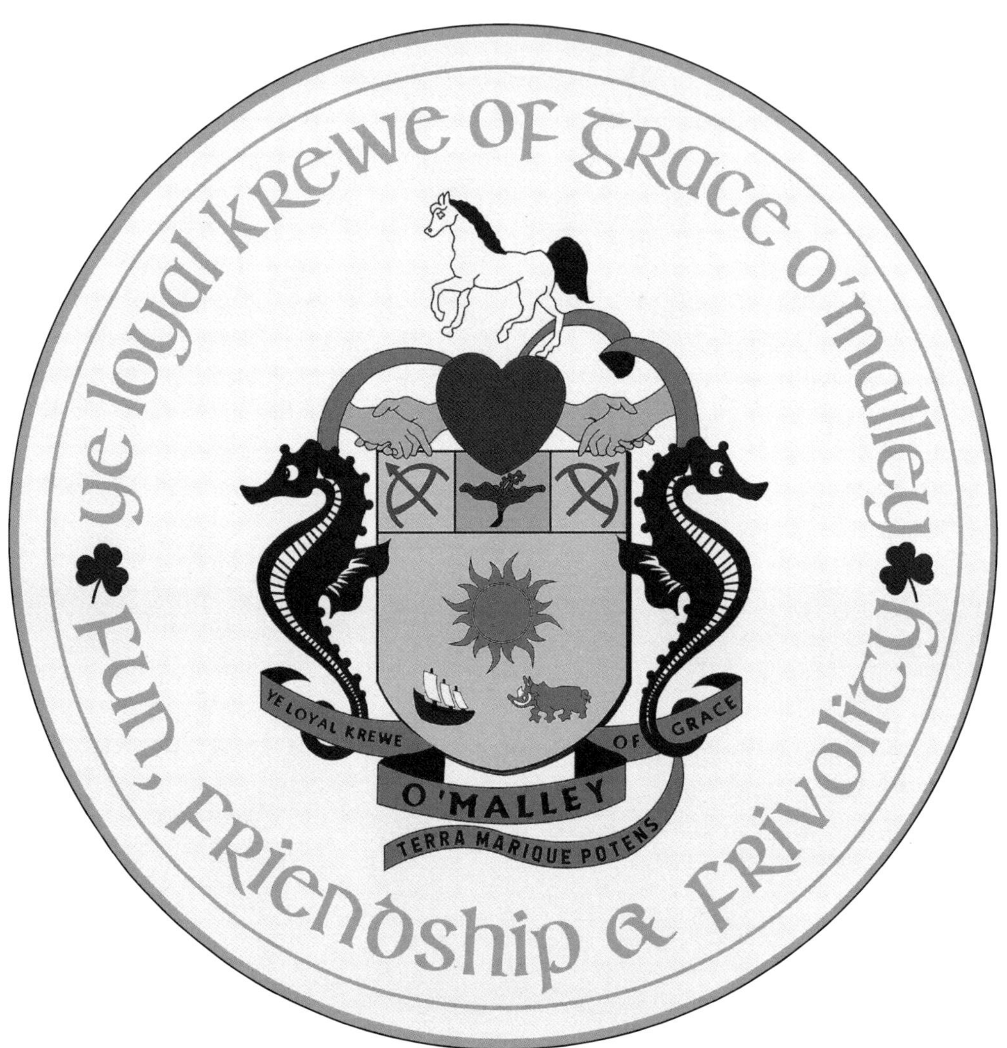

YLKGOM's mascot is a seahorse, a symbol of inner strength, resilience, and balance. Grace O'Malley commanded the *White Seahorse*. The founders felt the seahorse was a perfect fit tying in with her ship and the fact that the male seahorse carries the babies, representing the independence of the all-female krewe. The coat of arms of Ye Loyal Krewe of Grace O'Malley captures the beauty of Ireland. The clasped hands represent friendship, and the heart represents caring and loving. The sun symbolizes enlightenment and the horse loyalty and independence. The hibiscus represents the Florida community and the crossbow and ship power on land and sea. Bravery is shown as the boar and fun and frivolity as the seahorse. The ship, crossbows, and wild boar were borrowed symbols used by Grace O'Malley herself signifying the O'Malley Clan motto of *Terra marique potens*, "All-Powerful on Land and Sea." YLKGOM's motto is "Fun, Friendship, and Frivolity." (YLKGOM.)

Nine

Gasparilla Then and Now

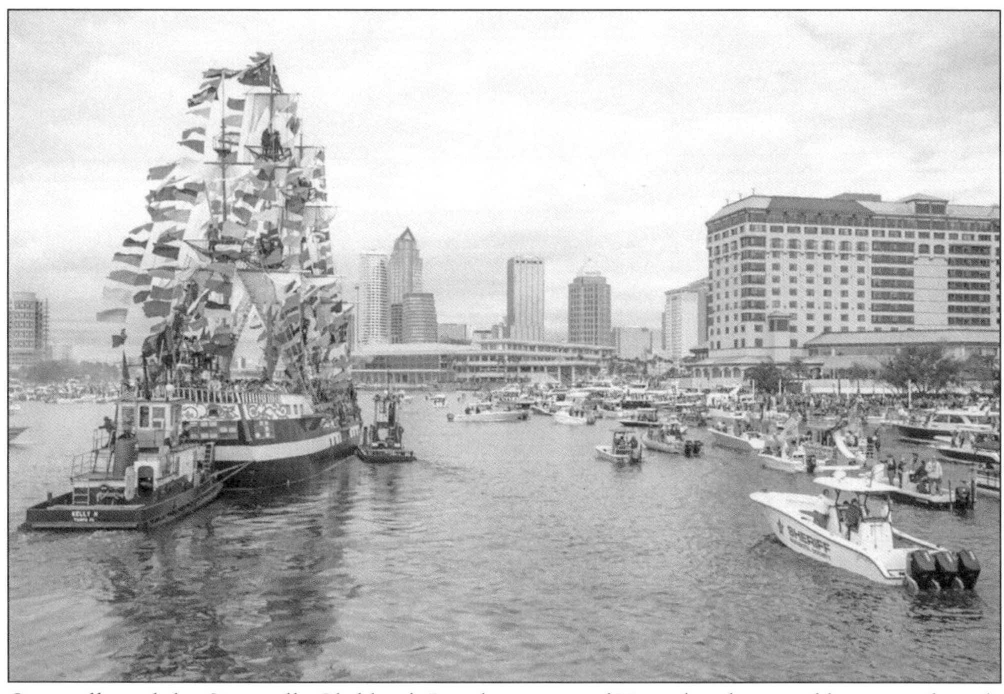

Gasparilla and the Gasparilla Children's Parade are part of Tampa's culture and have significantly contributed to the growth and prosperity of the city. In 1993, Ye Mystic Krewe of Gasparilla contracted with EventMakers Inc. to develop a comprehensive logistics program for the Gasparilla Parade of Pirates. As YMKG's largest strategic partner, EventMakers, followed by its successor EventFest Inc., produces the Gasparilla Parade of Pirates, Gasparilla Children's Parade, and Gasparilla Outbound Voyage. Here, *José Gasparilla* approaches the Tampa Convention Center. (Lori Ballard Photography-Tampa.)

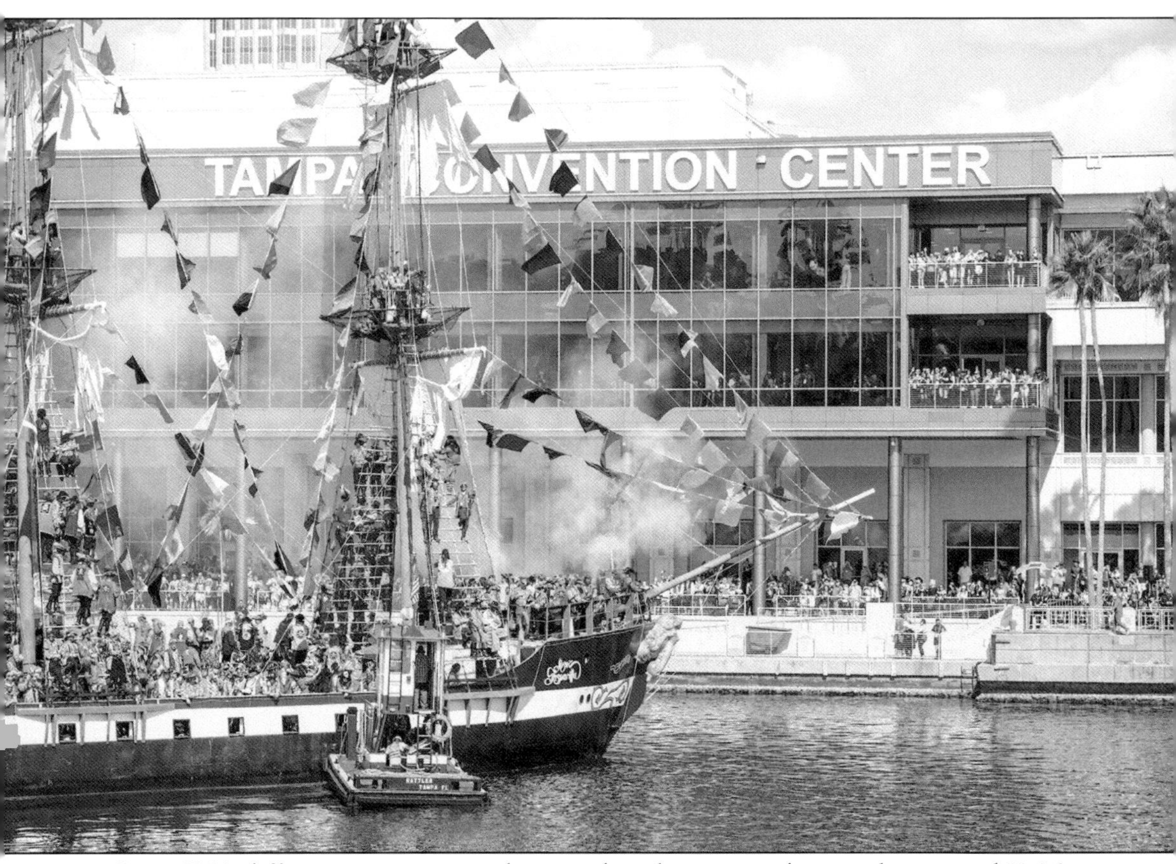

Since 1904, different civic, private, educational, and commercial groups have joined Ye Mystic Krewe of Gasparilla in the parade on foot, horses, motor vehicles, or on floats. It was not until 1965 that other krewes began to form and participate in Gasparilla. As of 2025, there were 67 krewes in the parade with over 2,000 participants. This photograph shows today's YMKG members aboard *José Gasparilla* preparing to land at the Tampa Bay Convention Center, less than a half mile from where Gasparilla began in 1904. (Lori Ballard Photography–Tampa.)

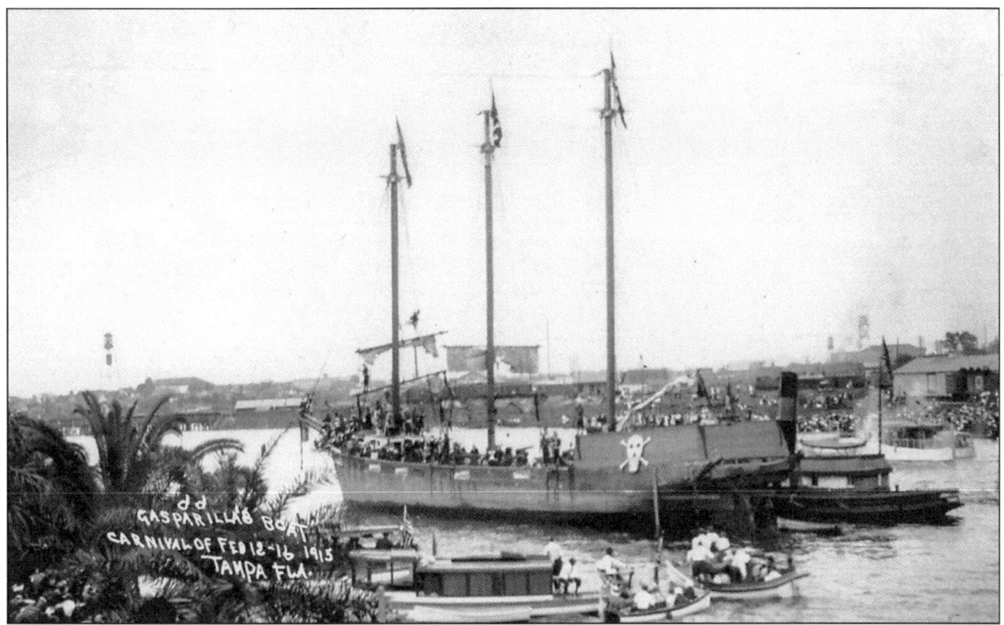

Although Gasparilla was founded in 1904, it was not until 1911 that Ye Mystic Krewe of Gasparilla began using a ship as part of the invasion of Tampa. Often the krewe did not know whether a ship would be available until shortly before the event. Usually a schooner was borrowed for the day and transformed into a pirate ship complete with decorations, skull-and-crossbones flags, and fake cannons. Pictured here is the vessel used for the 1915 invasion. (William P. Curtis collection.)

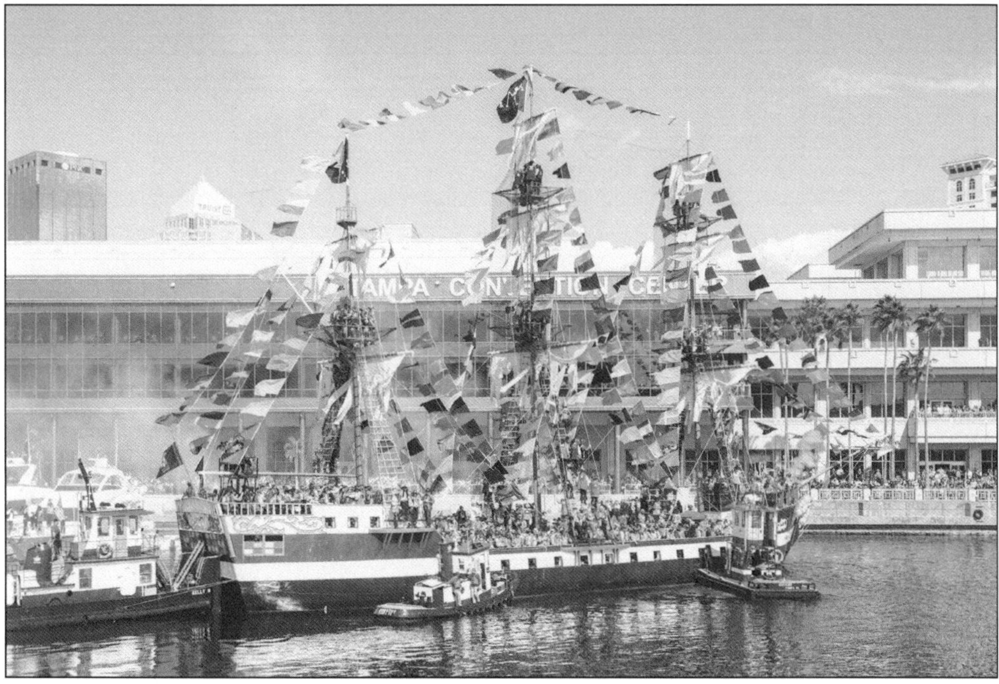

José Gasparilla was built specifically for use by Ye Mystic Krewe of Gasparilla in 1953 and was first used for the invasion in 1954. The ship was built as a flat-bottomed barge to navigate the shallow waters of Hillsborough Bay and the Hillsborough River. (Lori Ballard Photography–Tampa.)

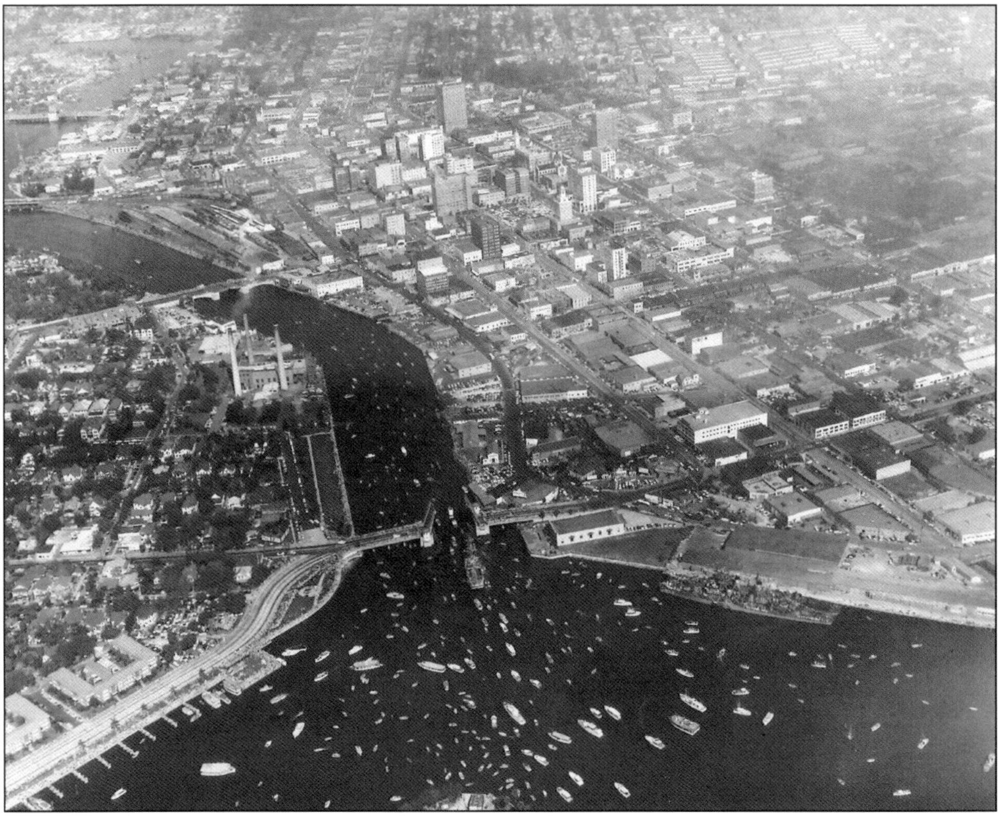

Ye Mystic Krewe of Gasparilla pirate ships have never sailed alone when invading Tampa. Boats of all makes and models have accompanied the ship as it makes its way across Hillsborough Bay to the Tampa Convention Center. On the morning of the invasion, boats arrive early at the Ballast Point Pier to secure a prime spot close to the pirate ship before the journey begins. More boats join the flotilla as the ship crosses the bay and approaches downtown Tampa. The 1956 photograph above shows *José Gasparilla* surrounded by boats as it prepares to pass under the Platt Street Bridge. The 1963 photograph below shows Seddon Island (Harbour Island) on the left as the ship makes its way up Seddon Channel. The Gasparilla flotilla is one of the largest boat parades in the United States. (Both, THCPL.)

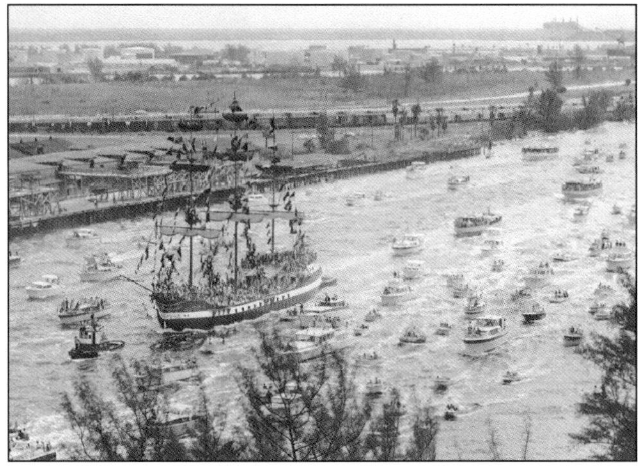

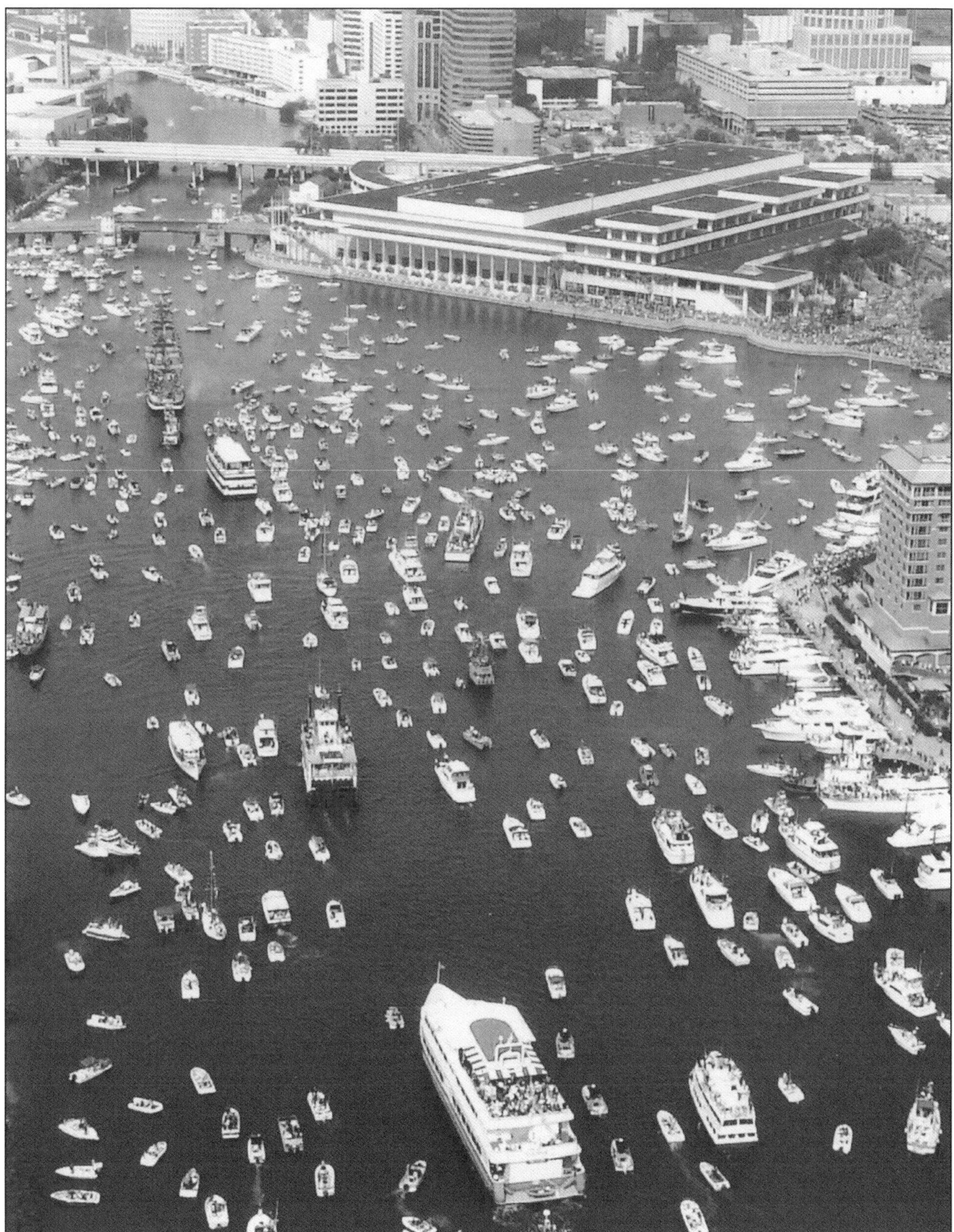

Through the years, the number of boats participating in Ye Mystic Krewe of Gasparilla's invasion of Tampa has increased exponentially to become one of the largest flotillas in the United States, with hundreds of private boats participating each year. On its way to the Tampa Convention Center, *José Gasparilla* (upper left) makes its way up Seddon Channel between Davis Islands on the left and Harbour Island on the right. Prior to 1976, the ship was required to navigate up to five bridges to continue the invasion up the Hillsborough River, seen at the top left. Construction of the stationary Crosstown Expressway, now the Lee Roy Selmon Expressway, precluded the tall masts of *José Gasparilla* from entry into the Hillsborough River. Watching the ship and flotilla arrive is one of the highlights of Gasparilla, viewed by thousands along the waterways. (*Tampa Tribune*.)

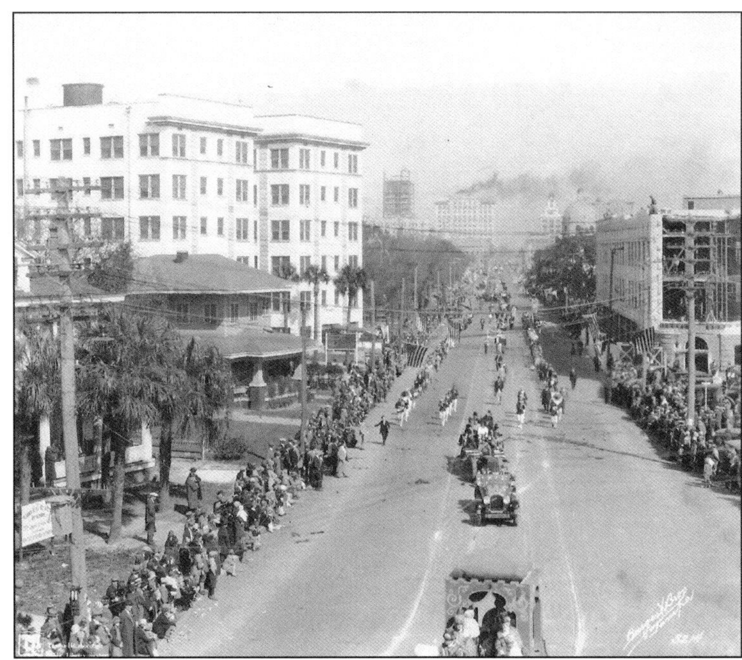

The Gasparilla parade route has changed significantly through the years and initially did not include Bayshore Boulevard, the site of the current event. In this 1926 photograph, the parade is heading west on Lafayette Street, now Kennedy Boulevard, away from downtown Tampa. City hall is seen at the right in the distance. (THCPL.)

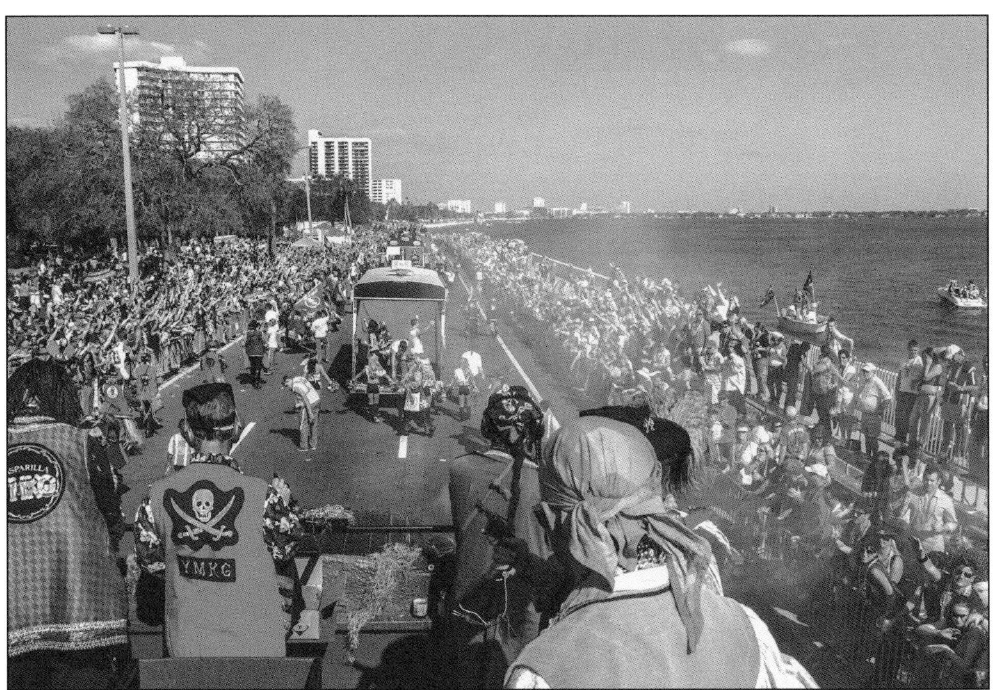

Today, the Gasparilla parade begins on Bayshore Boulevard and ends in downtown Tampa. Because both the crowds and parade have become so large, safety barricades are now required. This photograph was taken from the top of a Ye Mystic Krewe of Gasparilla float where salute cannons are fired. (Lori Ballard Photography–Tampa.)

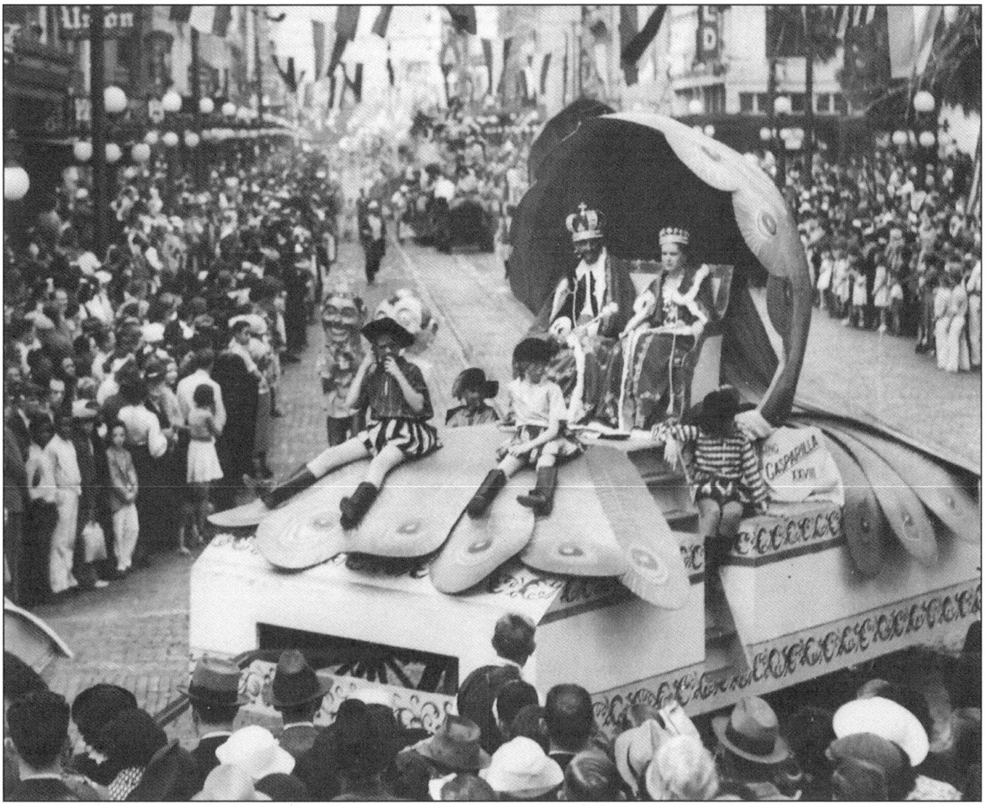

This 1936 photograph shows the float carrying the King and Queen of Ye Mystic Krewe of Gasparilla through the crowded streets of downtown Tampa. The float appears to be quite close to some of the well-dressed and orderly crowd. Notice also the streetcar rails running down the middle of the street. (THCPL.)

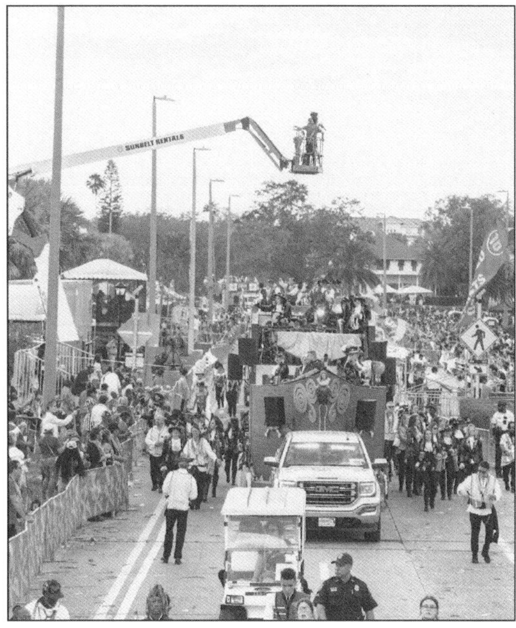

In recent years, attendance at Gasparilla has reached several hundred thousand on the parade route along Bayshore Boulevard and into downtown Tampa. For those unable to attend the nation's third-largest one-day parade in person, the event can be viewed on local television. This photograph shows a television camera hovering above the passing floats. (Lori Ballard Photography–Tampa.)

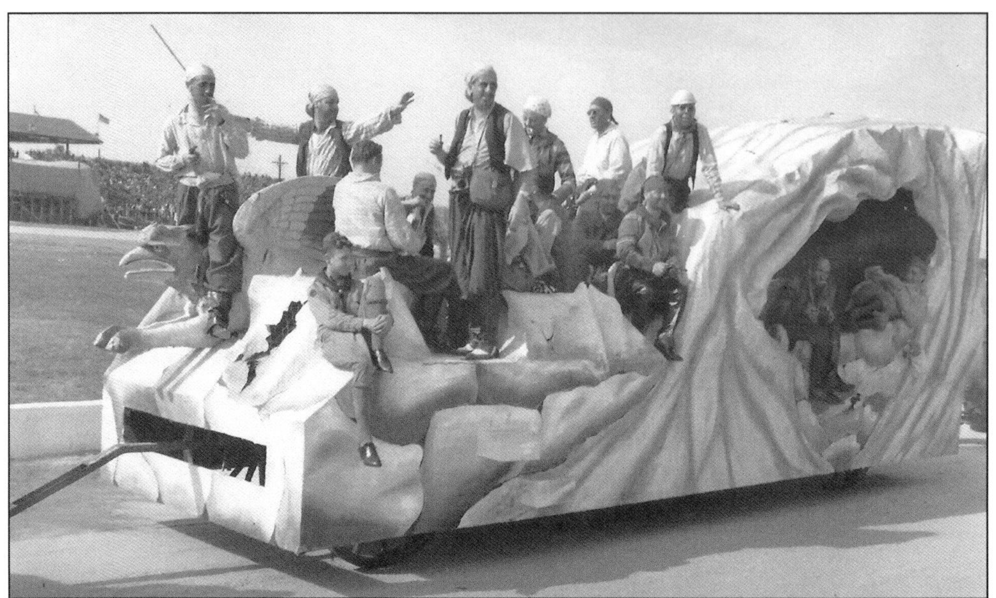

The appearance of the floats used by Ye Mystic Krewe of Gasparilla has dramatically changed through the years. At times, some floats were designed to be self-propelled and motorized, but horses, jeeps, tractors, and trucks have pulled most of them. Here is an example of a very simple float used in the parade in the 1950s. (THCPL.)

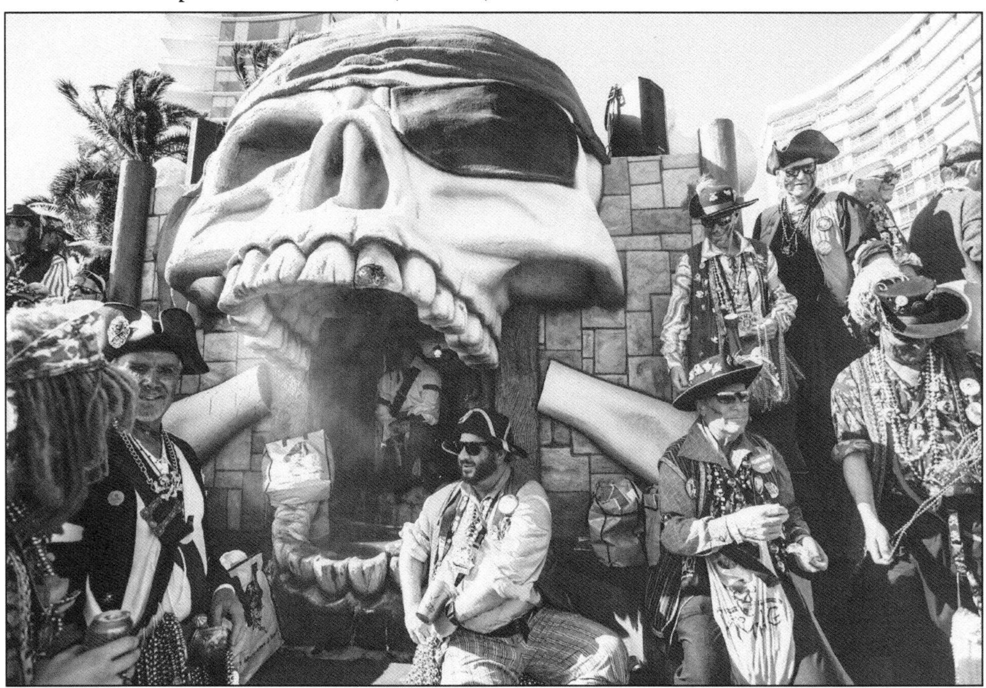

To accommodate the growing membership of Ye Mystic Krewe of Gasparilla, the floats today are much larger than in prior years. Some floats are equipped with elaborate sound systems, moving parts, and theatrical special effects. Here is one of the newer floats used in the parade. When not in use, floats are stored in a 40,000-square-foot warehouse on Cass Street. (Lori Ballard Photography–Tampa.)

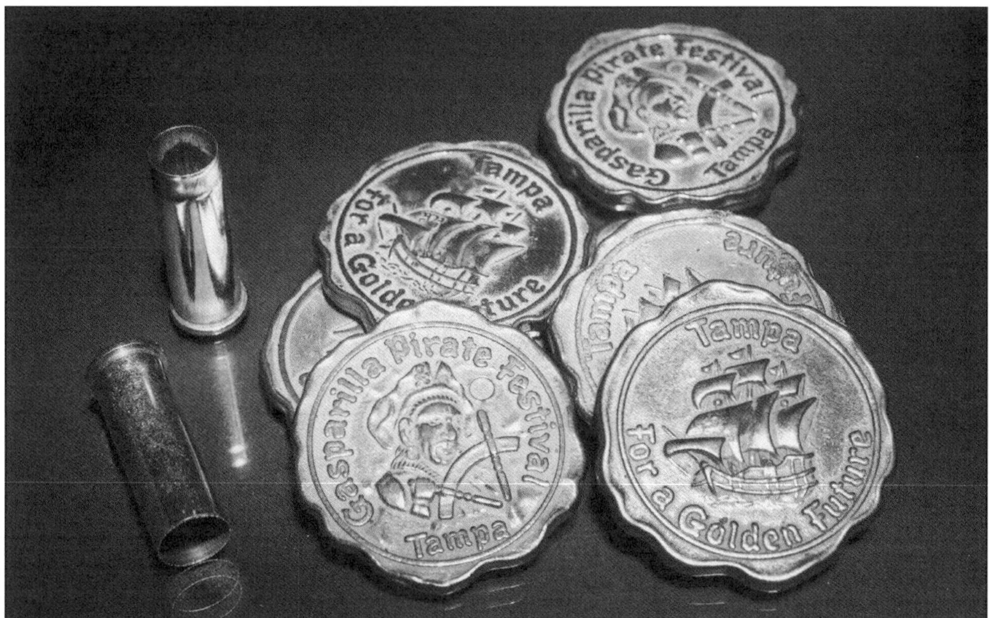

When Ye Mystic Krewe of Gasparilla was the only krewe participating in the parade, the most sought-after souvenirs were thick, gold pirate coins and the empty shells from the gun blanks. The coins were engraved "For a Golden Future" on one side and "Gasparilla Pirate Festival" on the other side. These old doubloon coins are now collector's items. (William Carson, MD.)

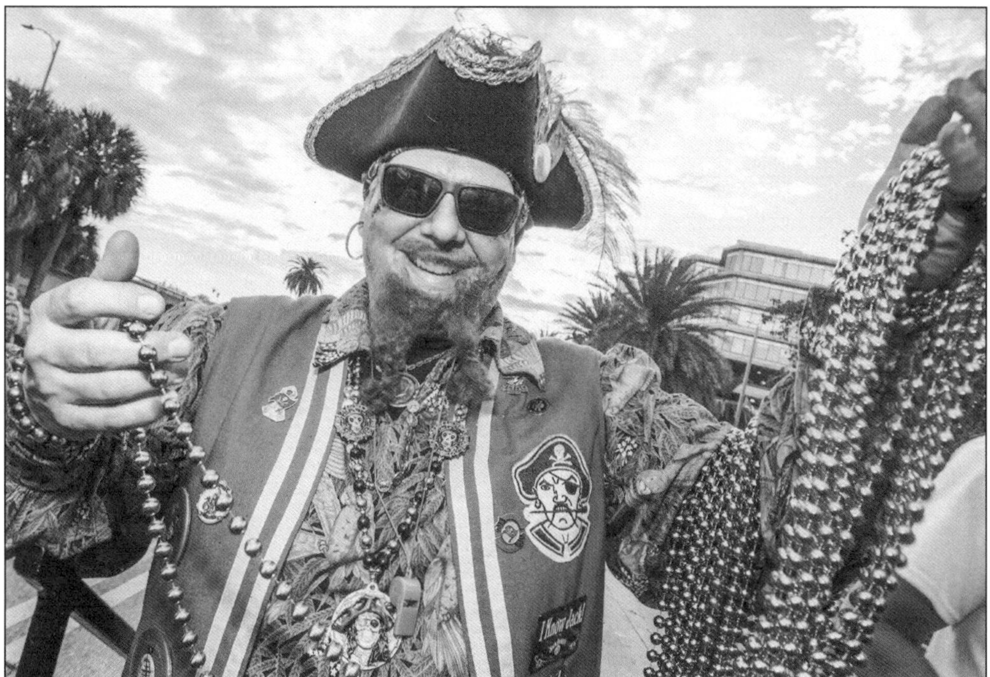

In the mid-1980s, Gasparilla parade participants began the practice of throwing beads to spectators. While many types of generic beads are thrown, most of the krewes throw specific themed beads representative of their krewe. Here, a Ye Mystic Krewe of Gasparilla member prepares to distribute beads during the parade. (Lori Ballard Photography–Tampa.)

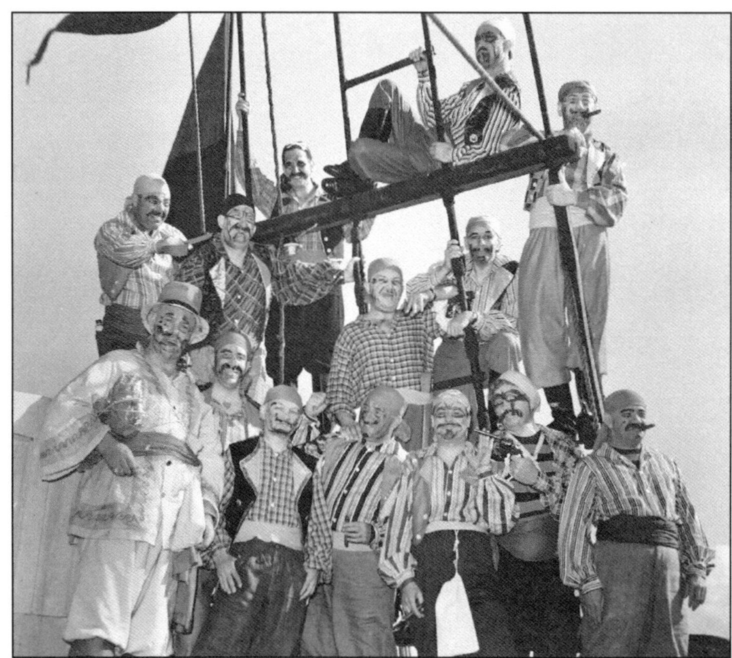

The costumes worn by Ye Mystic Krewe of Gasparilla members have changed significantly through the years. In the earlier parades, pirate outfits consisted of very basic homemade shirts and pants with bandanas used as headgear. The makeup was also fairly simple, with scars and facial hair drawn with a black grease pencil. In this undated photograph, notice the pirate on the far left with the top hat who is dressed more like a clown than a pirate. (THCPL.)

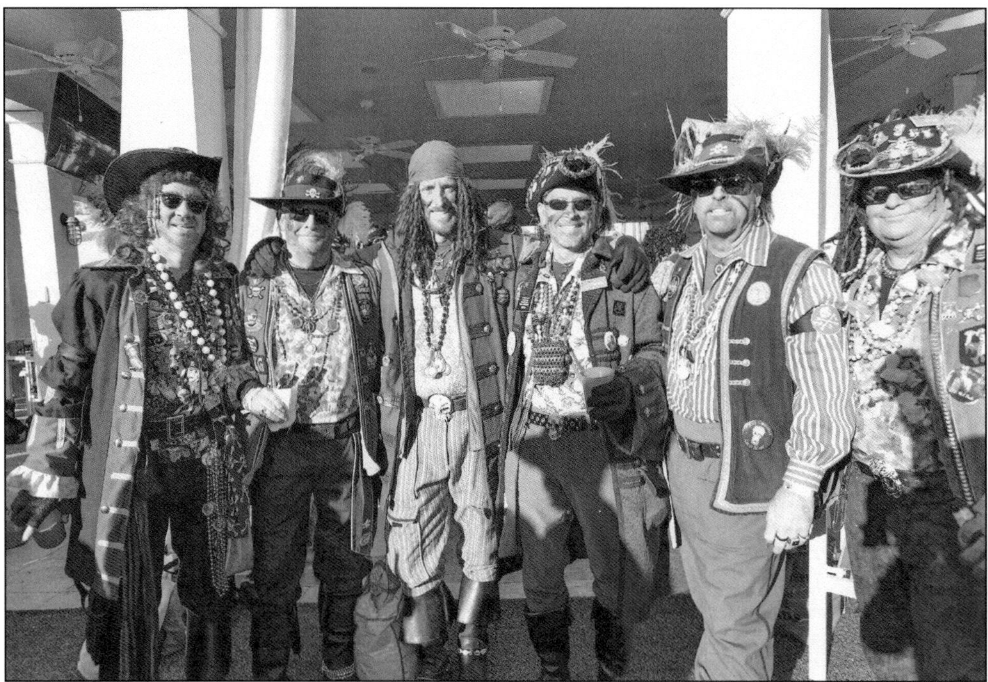

Most current members of Ye Mystic Krewe of Gasparilla wear custom-made pirate costumes, some of which are personalized with jewelry, badges, hats, and other accessories. This group of pirates at the Tampa Yacht and Country Club prepares for the invasion. (Lori Ballard Photography–Tampa.)

In the early years of the festival, Ye Mystic Krewe of Gasparilla members wore very basic makeup, usually applied with a black grease pencil. Pictured here aboard *José Gaspar*, a member of the krewe shows the classic look of a 1940s and 1950s pirate. (SAF.)

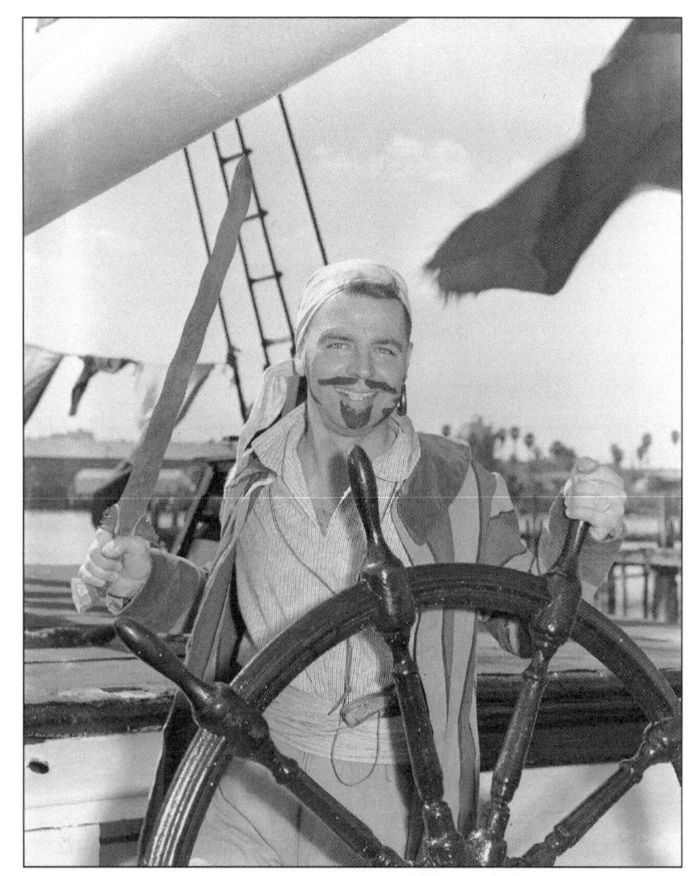

Most Ye Mystic Krewe of Gasparilla members today wear professionally applied theatrical makeup. The process of preparing for the invasion can take several hours, beginning early on invasion day morning. Pictured here are two pirates who are unrecognizable to even their closest friends. (Lori Ballard Photography–Tampa.)

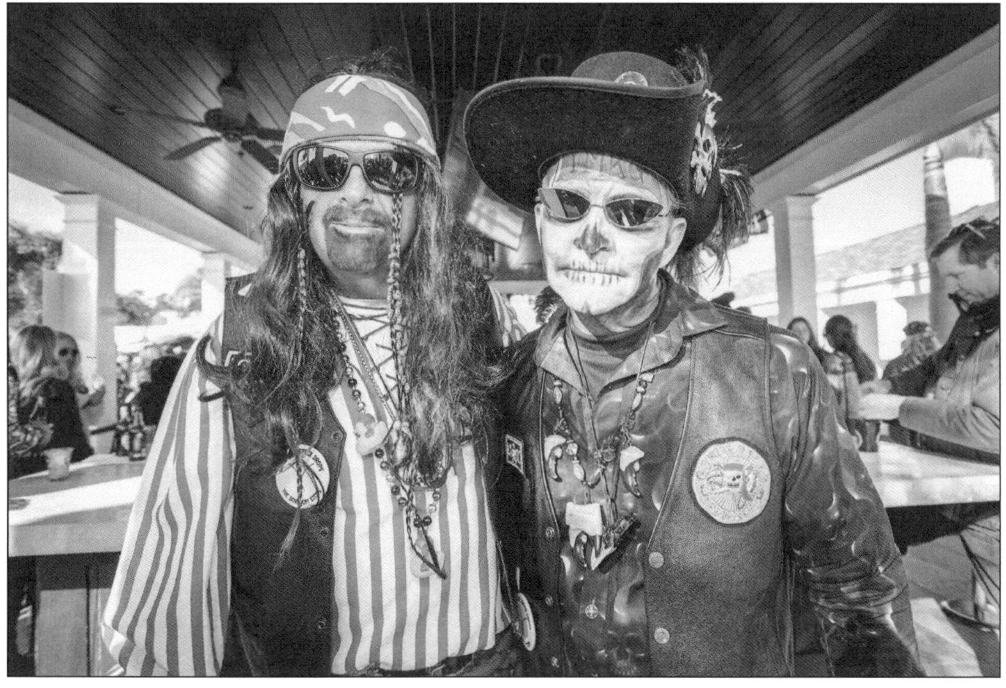

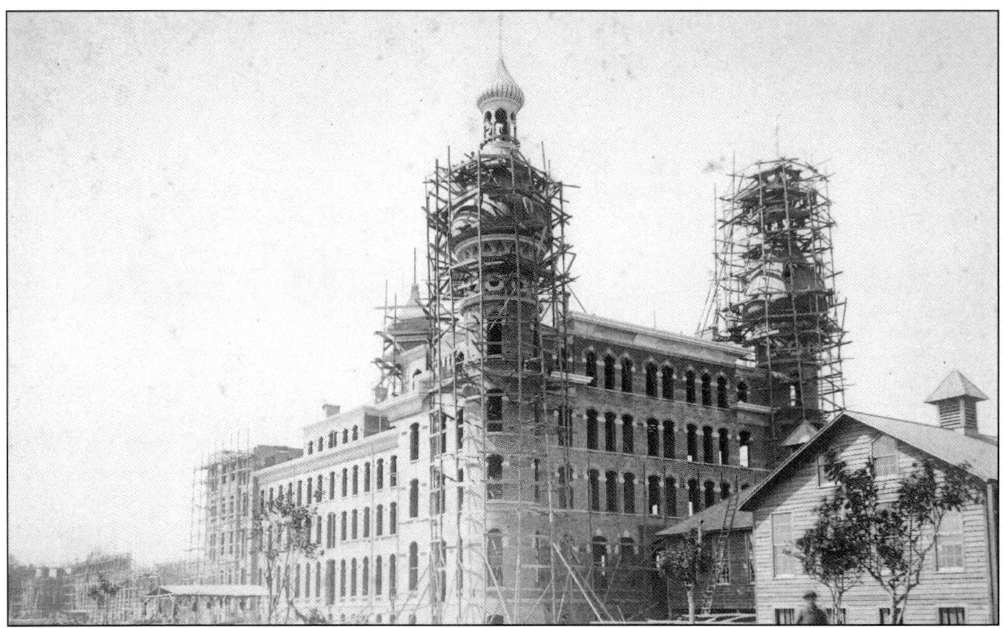

Completed in 1891, the Tampa Bay Hotel, now Plant Hall at the University of Tampa, has enjoyed a long relationship with Ye Mystic Krewe of Gasparilla. The krewe's pirate ship docked here for many years, and several coronation balls and other events were held at the hotel. The hotel is pictured under construction in March 1889. (Henry B. Plant Museum Collection.)

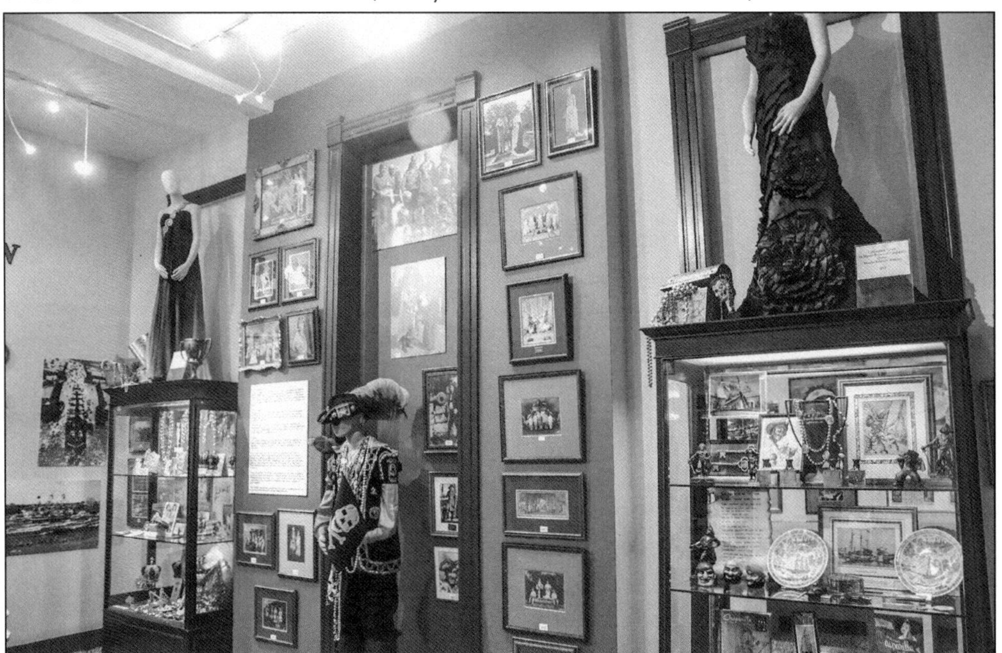

Ye Mystic Krewe of Gasparilla's relationship with the original Tampa Bay Hotel continues today through the Henry B. Plant Museum, located in Plant Hall at the University of Tampa. In 1980, a year-round Gasparilla exhibit was established, and it was replaced with a rotating exhibit in 1991. This photograph shows some of the Gasparilla memorabilia displayed in one of the exhibits. (William Carson, MD.)

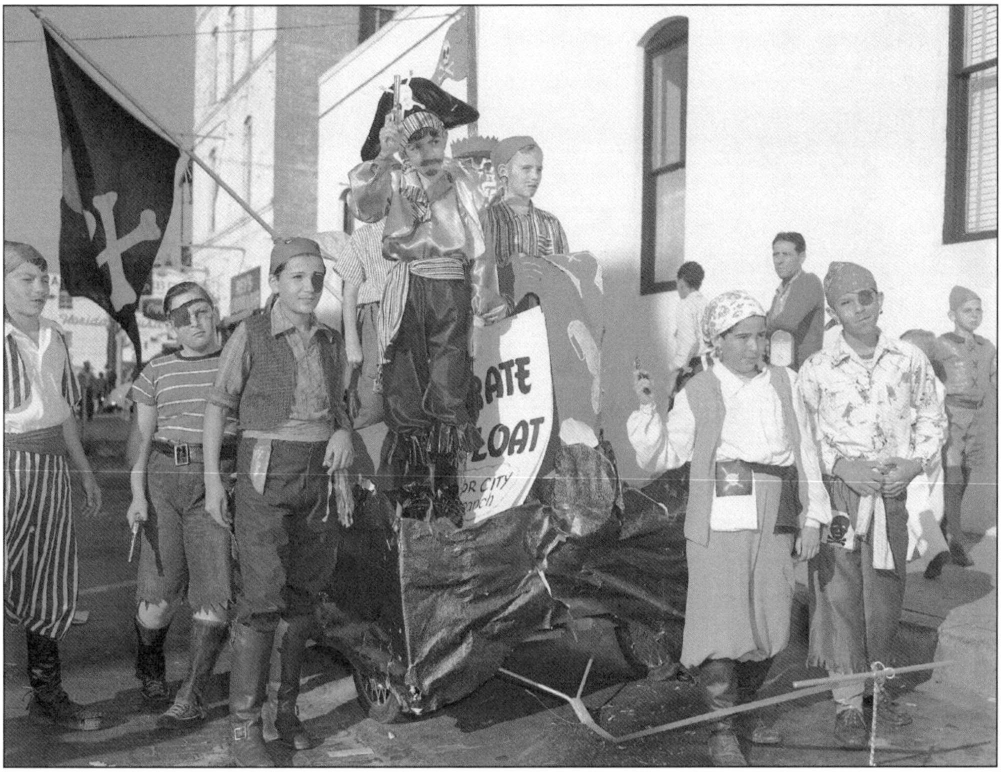

In 1947, Gasparilla began lending its name to the children's parade, and what began as a small event in downtown Tampa has grown to one of the premier children's parades in the country. This February 12, 1949, photograph shows several children in costume and ready for the parade. Today's Gasparilla Children's Parade routinely attracts crowds of several hundred thousand in an alcohol-free and family-oriented celebration of children. (SAF.)

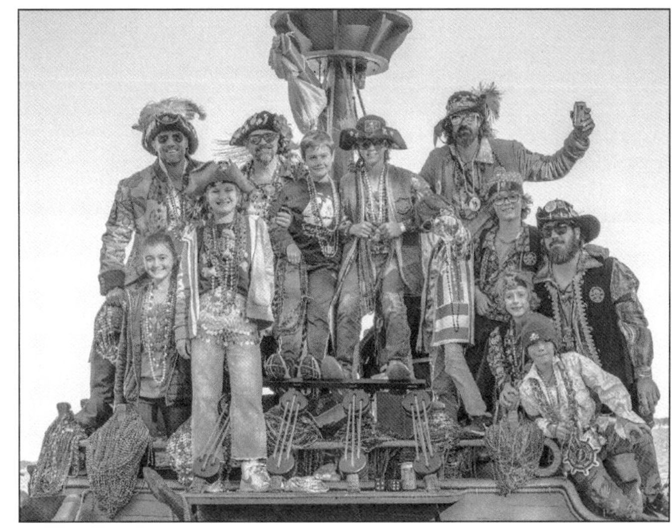

The Gasparilla Children's Parade is an all-inclusive event that features more than 100 units of various krewes, bands, and other participants. Ye Mystic Krewe of Gasparilla members have always enjoyed riding a float with their children or grandchildren. With cannons firing, *José Gasparilla* sails into the bay as the parade reaches its peak, and as night falls, an extravagant Piratechnic fireworks show is staged. (Lori Ballard Photography–Tampa.)

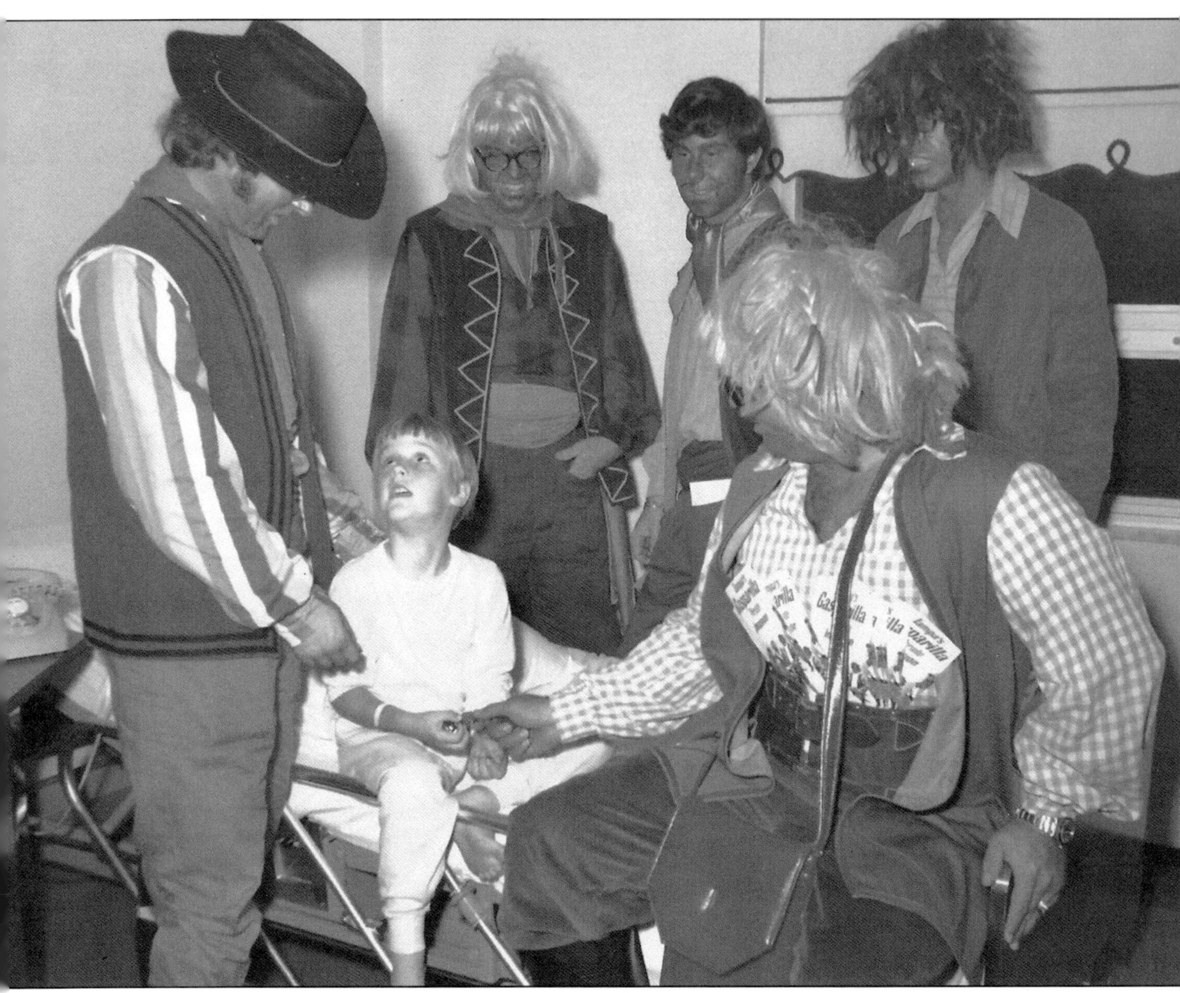

In 1969, Ye Mystic Krewe of Gasparilla began visiting local hospitals at Gasparilla time in full makeup and costume, delivering souvenirs to hospitalized children and other patients. Year after year, these visits expanded to nursing homes, schools, community centers, sports stadiums, and local events. Today, these YMKG pirates (known as "Gaspar's Grenadiers") make appearances, on average, at 60 such public venues annually. This photograph shows one of the first hospital visits. (YMKG.)

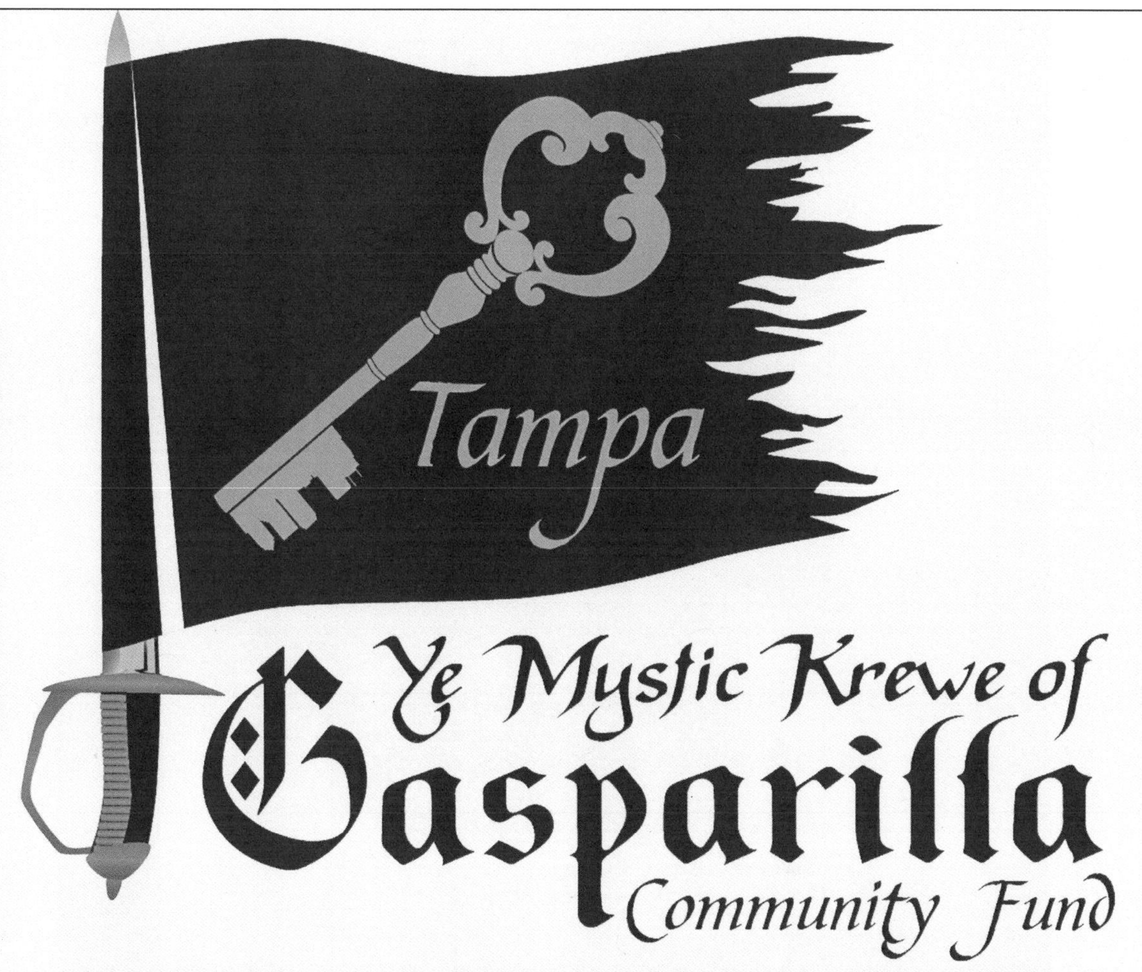

King Gasparilla XXCIII George Steinbrenner, with initial funding provided by the New York Yankees, founded the Ye Mystic Krewe of Gasparilla Community Fund, a qualified 501(c)(3) nonprofit organization that provides scholarships to graduating high school students who need financial help attending a college or university. Each year, this charitable organization reaches out to all public, private, and parochial high schools in Tampa and asks the principals to nominate graduating seniors who excel in academics, athletics, and extracurricular activities. Over the past 28 years, the Ye Mystic Krewe of Gasparilla Community Fund and its preceding organization, the Ye Mystic Krewe of Gasparilla Scholarship Foundation, have awarded over $1.75 million in scholarships, helping students from 34 separate high schools attend 33 diverse colleges and universities across the country. (YMKG.)

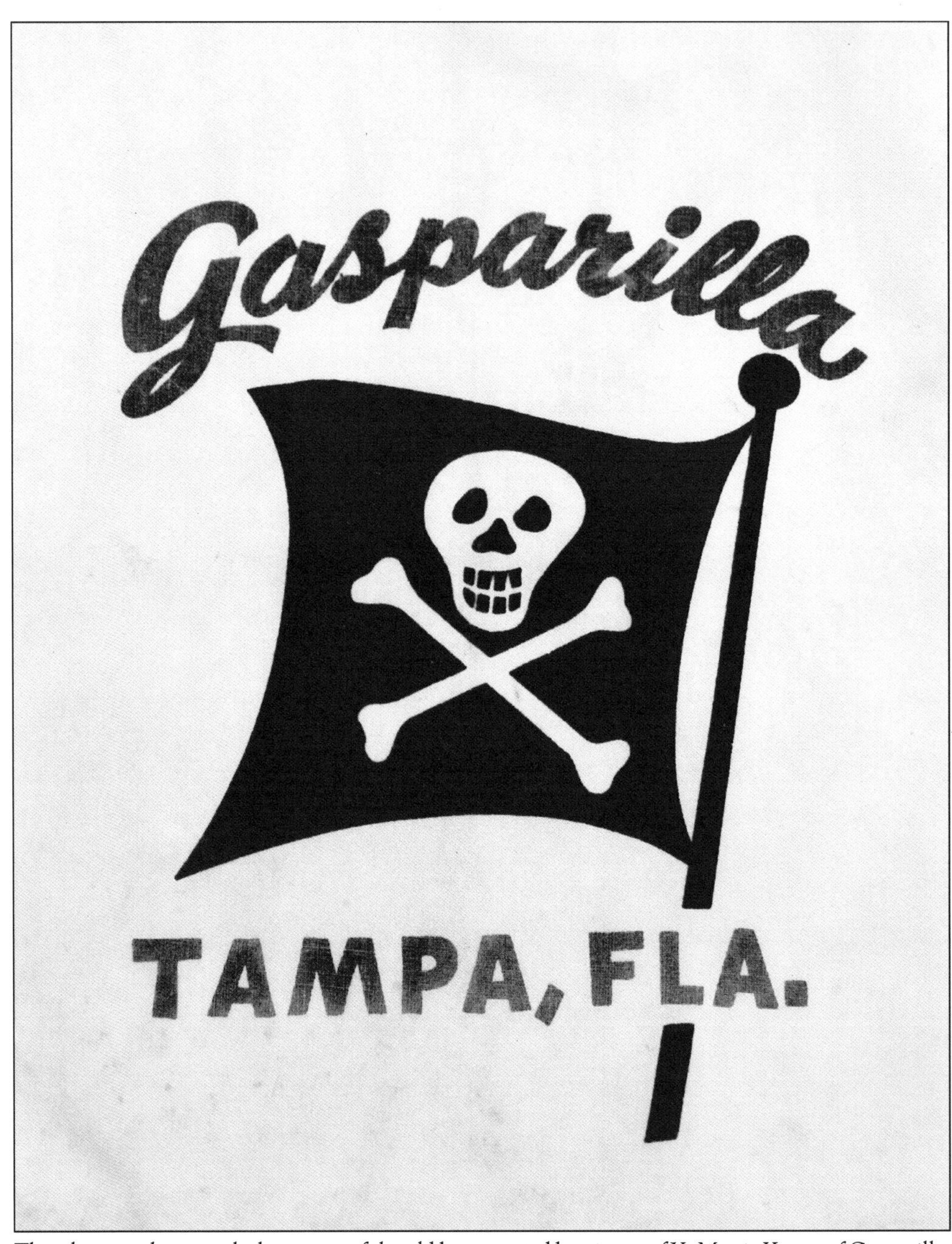

This close-up photograph shows one of the old bags carried by pirates of Ye Mystic Krewe of Gasparilla. For many years, members handed out thick doubloon coins or empty blank shell casings along the parade route. The coins were especially cherished items for thousands of spectators who collected them for years (see page 87). Although similar coins are still handed out as souvenirs during today's Gasparilla parade, beads have become the most sought-after items to take home. The verbiage on the bag is quite fitting as the final image for *Tampa's Gasparilla Pirate Festival*, simply "Gasparilla" and "Tampa, FLA." Since 1904, the city of Tampa has maintained an enduring relationship with Gasparilla, and both have grown and matured together through the years. Tampa without Gasparilla would just not be the same. (YMKG.)

Bibliography

Gary, James-Heath. *The Story of Gasparilla*. Boca Grande, FL: Charlotte Harbor & Northern Railway, 1916. Reprint, Chicago: Tribune Publishing Company, 1980.

Grismer, Karl H. *Tampa: A History of the City of Tampa and the Tampa Bay Region*. St. Petersburg, FL: St. Petersburg Printing Company, 1950.

Groff, Dana M. *The Pirate Gasparilla: His Life & Times*. Tampa, FL: Palmetto Publications, 1988.

Lambright, Edwin D. *The Life and Exploits of Gasparilla, Last of the Buccaneers, with the History of Ye Mystic Krewe of Gasparilla*. Tampa, FL: Hillsboro Printing, 1936.

Savage, Arthur R., and Rodney Kite-Powell. *Tampa Bay's Waterfront: Its History & Development*. Sarasota, FL: Coastal Printing, 2016.

Turner, Gregg M., and Seth H. Bramson. *The Plant System of Railroads, Steamships, and Hotels*. Laury's Station, PA: Garrigues House Publishers, 2004.

Turner, Nancy. *The History of Ye Mystic Krewe of Gasparilla, 1904–1975*. Tampa, FL: Cider Press Inc., 1979.

Ye Mystic Krewe of Gasparilla. *Ye Mystic Krewe of Gasparilla: The First One Hundred Years, 1904–2004*. Tampa, FL: Hillsboro Printing Company, 2004.